Palgrave Studies in Classical Liberalism

This series offers a forum to writers concerned that the central presuppositions of the liberal tradition have been severely corroded, neglected, or misappropriated by overly rationalistic and constructivist approaches.

The hardest-won achievement of the liberal tradition has been the wrestling of epistemic independence from overwhelming concentrations of power, monopolies and capricious zealotries. The very precondition of knowledge is the exploitation of the epistemic virtues accorded by society's situated and distributed manifold of spontaneous orders, the DNA of the modern civil condition.

With the confluence of interest in situated and distributed liberalism emanating from the Scottish tradition, Austrian and behavioral economics, non-Cartesian philosophy and moral psychology, the editors are soliciting proposals that speak to this multidisciplinary constituency. Sole or joint authorship submissions are welcome as are edited collections, broadly theoretical or topical in nature.

More information about this series at
http://www.palgrave.com/gp/series/15722

Wanjiru Njoya

Economic Freedom and Social Justice

The Classical Ideal of Equality in Contexts of Racial Diversity

palgrave
macmillan

Wanjiru Njoya
Law School
University of Exeter
Exeter, UK

ISSN 2662-6470 ISSN 2662-6489 (electronic)
Palgrave Studies in Classical Liberalism
ISBN 978-3-030-84851-4 ISBN 978-3-030-84852-1 (eBook)
https://doi.org/10.1007/978-3-030-84852-1

This Palgrave Macmillan imprint is published by the registered company Springer Nature Switzerland AG
The registered company address is: Gewerbestrasse 11, 6330 Cham, Switzerland

For my Maria

Foreword

In our times, classical liberalism is under attack. Contemporary progressives say that individual liberty and the free market do not suffice for genuine justice. Racial minorities face discrimination, and measures aimed at securing their substantive advancement must be enacted, even if doing so requires that freedom of contract be abrogated. And even this is not enough. Minorities must be protected against offensive speech and conduct, and everywhere we are policed lest we commit acts of 'micro-aggression'.

In this indispensable book, Dr. Wanjiru Njoya of the University of Exeter Law School makes a devastating case against what has unfortunately become a new orthodoxy in many academic circles. She sees in the demands to overthrow classical liberalism the baleful influence of John Rawls. Against this giant of contemporary political philosophy, Dr. Njoya contends that the state has no business in promoting social justice and that the much-vaunted appeal to 'public reason' masks an effort to exclude from discussion views that challenge the current consensus of 'respectable' opinion. Minorities in fact do not need to be cossetted by paternalistic protectors; they thrive in the free market.

I hope that *Economic Freedom and Social Justice* attracts wide attention. Dr. Njoya has with great courage brought to our attention ideas that deserve a wide hearing. It only remains to add that the book is written in a clear and forthright style.

David Gordon
Senior Fellow
Ludwig von Mises Institute
Auburn, USA

Preface

This book challenges the egalitarian foundations of equality legislation, in particular the contemporary theories of distributive justice underpinning the concept of substantive equality. The legislative framework displaces market ordering and voluntary exchange by reallocating rights and liabilities towards outcomes that will better satisfy the demands of social justice, thereby diminishing the scope of economic freedom and individual liberty. In seeking insight into these trends, and especially to understand better the importance of individual liberty in the economic foundations of market societies, the book addresses two central questions posed in David Gordon's 'Wrestling Reality from Rawls': does justice ideally demand equality? Are differences in abilities among people in some sense unfair? (*An Austro-Libertarian View Vol. II*. Mises Institute, 2017: 58).

The main challenge in addressing these questions is that egalitarian ideals often seem to be so emotionally and morally compelling that their ethical dimensions, social costs and implications for individual liberty are rarely subjected to critical scrutiny. In explicating the classical ideal of equality in contexts of racial diversity this book questions the ethical status of egalitarian social and moral ideals. The book draws upon the premise established in Murray Rothbard's *Egalitarianism as a Revolt against Nature* (Mises Institute, 1974), that egalitarian ideals, like all subjective value judgements, must be subjected to critical intellectual inquiry rather than treated axiomatically. On that premise the book argues that equality legislation undermines justice by treating substantive equality as an *a priori* axiom, which in turn raises the false presumption that wherever inequality is observed the situation requires some form of legislative intervention. Drawing upon the legal framework in the UK and other common law jurisdictions, the book aims to show some of the ways in which this presumption, in addition to being false, is costly, harmful and ultimately inimical to justice and liberty.

The primary purpose of the study is to advance our understanding of racial inequality. The book shows that legal entitlements constructed around notions of racial equity and racial justice are wrongly constituted as the main prism through which we govern relationships, such as the employment relationship, in contexts of racial diversity. The book highlights the importance of philosophical diversity, economic freedom and individual liberty in sustaining economic progress through market participation. As Chandran Kukathas argues, 'diversity—cultural, religious, linguistic or otherwise—is of no intrinsic importance. Diversity is a fact of life. But in itself it is of no particular value' (*The Liberal Archipelago*. Oxford University Press, 2003). The book shows this argument to be even more powerful in contexts of racial diversity. In that way the book challenges the mantras of identity politics and the antiliberal methods adopted by egalitarians in their bid to justify policy interventions grounded in theories of race and racism.

I acknowledge a great debt of gratitude to colleagues and friends whose support in writing this book was invaluable. The greatest gift one academic can give another is to read their work and share ideas, comments and suggestions. Time is so precious, and I am deeply grateful to colleagues who have shared theirs with me over the past few years, though they of course bear no responsibility for any shortcomings in this book. To David Gordon for his generosity in reading the book in draft, and being a source of wisdom, inspiration and humour. To John Keown for being a steadfast friend and sounding board all these years; his kindness and encouragement have been a great support. To Nicola Bolton and the adorable plushies for much-needed succour along the way.

My gratitude also to the editors of the *Palgrave Series in Classical Liberalism*, David Hardwick and Leslie Marsh, for their enthusiasm in supporting this project; to the anonymous reviewers for their generous comments and suggestions; and to the editorial and marketing teams at Palgrave Macmillan in particular Geetha Chockalingam, Ruth Jenner, Ruth Milewski and Meera Seth, for their helpfulness and professionalism.

And finally, most importantly, to those special people who have been with me in person or in spirit in writing each page. My dear parents in Kenya, whose longing to see this book has kept me going. And my own dearest Maria, whose companionship on this writing journey has been priceless. This book is dedicated to you, Maria, and I hope it will inspire you to find your own path in life and to live free.

Exeter, UK
June 2021

Wanjiru Njoya

Contents

1

Introduction

This book examines the legal framework of equality and non-discrimination in market societies.[1] Readers familiar with the functioning of free markets might immediately observe that legislative interventions which restrict freedom of contract and freedom of association by selecting certain groups for preferential protection are antithetical to voluntary market-based exchange, and therefore constitute an unlikely subject of study from a classical liberal perspective. Thus it may be helpful to clarify at the outset the aim of the study, namely to challenge egalitarian claims that the ideal of justice demands the equalisation of economic opportunities and the construction of equal economic outcomes between races and other diverse identity-based groups. Any claim presented as a demand for justice holds such powerful moral influence in the legal framework of liberal market jurisdictions that it cannot readily be dismissed out of hand. Such claims

[1] 'Market societies are differentiated societies whose economic sphere is characterised by individual property rights, the pursuit of self-interest, highly divided labour, and complex mutual dependencies': Herzog, L. (2013). *Inventing the Market* (p. 1). Oxford University Press.

W. Njoya, *Economic Freedom and Social Justice*, Palgrave Studies in Classical Liberalism,
https://doi.org/10.1007/978-3-030-84852-1_1

must instead be met by engaging squarely with the underlying theories of justice from which they derive their moral authority.

This need not, and this book does not, entail an exegesis of specific philosophical texts. It does require, however, clear delineation of the specific claims underlying the labels of 'justice' and 'fairness' that are often lobbed back and forth in the equality debates. To that end we explore the symbiotic relationship between economic progress and liberty in contexts of racial diversity, focusing in particular on the pursuit of racial equality. The book defends the ideal of formal equality which is upheld by the classical ideal of justice. Formal equality does not allocate rights and liabilities based on race or other markers of group identity. Instead, under formal equality we are regarded as equal in virtue of our humanity and thus equal in the eyes of the law. This ideal of justice based on formal equality is central to the rule of the law which underpins the essential functioning of market societies. Therefore the aim of the book is not simply to present a general analysis of the role of equality legislation in free markets, to which it might be objected that there is no legitimate role to be played by legislation that restricts freedom of contract and association and other individual liberties. Instead, the aim is to examine the implications of the classical ideal of justice for contemporary racial equality debates with a view to addressing the progressivist egalitarian claims that justice in the classical tradition is inadequate in so far as it excludes a role for promoting racial equality.

Thus the book is not concerned with the facets and parameters of racism, a subject on which much may be said without gaining further insight into the questions of economic progress with which this book is concerned. The aim is instead to address specific questions arising from the interaction between law and markets in situations where it is feared that free markets present inordinate risks and challenges for racial minorities. The debate concerns the need for tailored legal intervention, for example prohibiting discrimination or enforcing a duty to take positive action to promote diversity, which offers special protection to market participants based on their race or ethnicity. As will be detailed later in this chapter, the interaction between law and markets is narrowed down further still to study the employment context in more detail, in particular the interaction between the contract of employment and equality legislation. Our discussion is thus much more tightly focused than might be expected from such wide-ranging topics as economic freedom and social justice. The discussion is primarily concerned with the impact of 'social justice' legislative programmes on the scope of individual liberty, in contexts where such programmes are justified by reference to racial equality and racial justice. The aim is to understand how the surrounding policy debates may be understood from a classical liberal perspective.

For those who value liberty as their highest ideal, legislative interventions designed to equalise the unequal, to redistribute wealth and reallocate opportunities from privileged to marginalised groups, hold no lustre. In every walk of life we take pride in what we achieve through our own effort. Schemes such as affirmative action, favoured protected group status, preferential treatment in hiring, corporate handouts, political favours and state largesse displace market participation as a basis of human interaction. This in turn displaces human agency, human achievement and ultimately undermines the individual sense of self-esteem and self-respect that is earned through skill or merit or through voluntary exchange on an equal basis with others. Clarence Thomas poignantly describes 'the stigmatizing effects of racial preference' in affirmative action policies that forever cast doubt on the integrity of black academic achievements, prompting black candidates to hide their race on application forms not in order to avoid discrimination but to avoid the stigma of special measures which, ostensibly designed to give them extra help, 'appeared to be suggesting, knowingly or not, that blacks could never catch up with whites'.[2] It is a curious paradox that claims to be treated equally are often substantiated by demands for special measures. As Thomas Sowell argues, such equalisation policies may be designed to help those perceived to need the sorts of extra support that free markets do not offer, but they cannot at the same time be regarded as a path to progress and equality. The equality produced through unequal measures is only make-believe equality:

[2] Thomas, C. (2008). *My Grandfather's Son: A Memoir* (pp. 75, 80). Harper Perennial. See also Steele, S. (2015). *Shame: How America's Past Sins Have Polarized Our Country.* Basic Books.

> Many people who advocate what they think of as equality promote what is in fact make-believe 'equality'. In economic terms, taking what others have produced and giving it to those who have not produced as much (or at all, in some cases) is make-believe equality.[3]

There would be nothing wrong with make-believe equality derived through voluntary transactions. A parent racing or play-fighting their toddler and holding back to let the toddler win is a heart-warming picture that can be extrapolated onto many life situations in the natural impetus to share, to let others go first, to help those around us especially those most in need of help. Mutual help, human kindness and charity are essential to social harmony. Thus make-believe equality is not problematic in itself. It only becomes wrong when the schemes designed to implement it are coercive, when we force people to behave in ways that we consider to be kind even though they disagree and have their own different vision of how to express kindness to others, when we transform mutual aid from a moral, social or community mandate into a legal requirement to be enforced through financial or other penalties. The virtue of kindness soon turns sinister when it is backed by the force of the state and used to subject others to our will. It is no less sinister if we can find others who agree with us, not even if we co-opt a majority of citizens to our view and label our coercive scheme 'social justice'.

Coercive schemes, no matter how well intentioned or how illustrious the banners under which they march, are anathema to the liberal tradition. Liberalism, in the classical tradition discussed in this book, is the philosophy of freedom.[4] The book explores the meaning of freedom, especially economic freedom, in contexts where this freedom is depicted in progressive scholarship as an obstacle that prevents society from achieving the substantive equality of all races. The classical liberal ideals of free speech, freedom of contract, freedom of association, freedom of conscience and other components of individual liberty are increasingly under attack from those who would pursue racial equality to whatever end, willing to trade freedom to achieve the equal outcomes demanded

[3] Sowell, T. (2013). *Intellectuals and Race* (p. 138). Basic Books.

[4] Mises, L. v. (2005). *Liberalism: The Classical Tradition* (B. B. Greaves, ed.). Indianapolis: Liberty Fund (Original work published 1927).

by their social justice ideals. In pursuit of the worthy goals forged in the anti-racism civil rights movement they are 'confident in resorting to coercion, indifferent to imposing financial burdens on future generations, and willing to put existing constitutional freedoms at risk in order to secure new ones'.[5] They tolerate no dissent from their progressive agenda, denigrating as 'Uncle Tom' any black scholar who dares to be sceptical of their racial rhetoric.[6] As Jason Riley observes, much of the intolerance of classical liberal perspectives such as that advanced by Sowell 'comes from black [progressive] liberals, in particular, who often respond as if any disagreement with the left-wing consensus view is not merely misguided but also malevolent'.[7] Such intolerance denies the importance of viewpoint diversity and debate in advancing our knowledge and understanding of the demands of justice in modern liberal democracies.

Progressive egalitarians would assert thateighteenth the modern liberal democracy has evolved from century rudimentary moral philosophies into a higher form of liberalism wherein we may disagree about minor logistical or definitional aspects of implementing social justice but we would all agree on the basic premise concerning the priority of equality. From that perspective classical ideals are perceived as an anachronistic overhang from the Enlightenment era, ill at ease with contemporary demands for racial justice. The Enlightenment itself has fallen into disfavour based on the failure of its expositors to pay sufficient tribute to identity politics. Classical liberal ideals are also felt to be incompatible with the dominant culture of psychic safety that requires nothing harmful or offensive to be seen or heard in relation to group identity. Even the last refuge of those who care nothing for politics, the simple but trusty expedient of keeping one's head down and not getting involved in

[5] Caldwell, C. (2020). *The Age of Entitlement: America Since the Sixties* (p. 12). Simon & Schuster, writing in the context of the political framing of civil rights as fundamental human rights.

[6] For example Joseph Epstein remarks in relation to Shelby Steele that 'Speaking out about the false bargain that blacks have made with the new liberalism will doubtless earn him, if it hasn't already done so, the old opprobrious title of Uncle Tom. The irony here is that Shelby Steele might just be a Tom of a different kind—a black Tom Paine, whose 21st-century common sense could go a long way to bringing his people out of their by now historical doldrums': Epstein, J. (2015, March 20). Shelby Steele's Thankless Task. *The Wall Street Journal*. https://www.wsj.com/articles/book-review-shame-by-shelby-steele-1426885452.

[7] Riley, J. L. (2021). *Maverick: A Biography of Thomas Sowell* (p. 12). Hachette Book Group.

ideological disputes, has fallen under siege to the social, moral, and now *legal* duty to engage with other people's lived experiences. In fulfilment of their legal duties to promote equality employers roll out mandatory unconscious bias training schemes to signal that we are all 'actively antiracist'.[8] No longer does it suffice simply to 'live honestly, to injure no one, to assign to each his own', to live and let live.[9] The mantra that 'silence is violence' transforms the presumption of innocence and the right to remain silent, both of which are essential to individual liberty, from a defensive principle into a putative declaration of war against those who regard the silence of others as a source of oppression.

We all hold varying philosophical ideas on the issues arising in these debates, and different views on the appropriate content of justice and morality. That philosophical diversity is central to the purpose of this book. The debate surrounding racial equality requires robust scrutiny of the claims advanced under the ideal of equality, and such scrutiny would be impossible if we were to be compelled to accept the premise that only egalitarian perspectives are worthy of respect in a liberal democracy. The attempt simply to shut down those who hold a conception of the good that dissents from the dominant view is an unlikely path to social harmony, as evidenced by the increasingly confrontational language in the political debates. The contemporary 'culture war' is often depicted as an existential battle between mutually exclusive ideals.[10] Racial equality is symbolised as a 'war on racism' and by implication a war on those with the misfortune to be denounced as racists. Free speech and the desire to defend individual liberty are in turn championed as a defensive 'war on cancel culture' by 'angry citizens who sense that their most fundamental rights to freedom and formal equality have been illegitimately taken

---

[8] Under the Equality Act 2010 public bodies in the UK have a duty to 'foster good relations' between different races (s. 149). A public body, as will be discussed later in the book, includes anybody with a public-facing role even if they are not supported by state funding.

[9] 'Honeste vivere, neminem laedere, suum cuique tribuere': Flew, A. (1986). Enforced Equality—Or Justice? *Journal of Libertarian Studies, 8*(1), 31–41, p. 34.

[10] See discussion of 'Liberal accretion and the warlike quality of contemporary liberalism' in Corey, D. D. (2020). Liberalism and the Modern Quest for Freedom. In D. F. Hardwick & L. Marsh (Eds.), *Reclaiming Liberalism* (pp. 125–162), p. 151 et seq. Palgrave Macmillan Studies in Classical Liberalism.

away'.[11] The profound sense of grievance on both sides is exacerbated by a deeper lack of clarity surrounding the meaning and implications of demands for racial equality, the connection between equality and fundamental human rights, and the interaction between individual liberty and social justice. For example, it is easy to say that the law upholds free speech and does not recognise a right not to be offended, but when the perception of feeling offended is linked to charges of racism the legal rights and liabilities at stake assume a wholly different character. Suddenly social infractions engage equality and antidiscrimination law as well as a raft of civil and criminal offences defined as 'hate-speech'. This trend poses a threat to freedom by linking group identity to legal rights and liabilities, heightening the sense of grievance and injustice arising from what might otherwise be merely unpleasant or unfriendly interactions and elevating interpersonal disputes to existential demands for justice. Individual liberties are then depicted as mere selfish indulgences, which are derided as rather trivial in light of the existential demands of justice. In this way racial identity, like other forms of collectivism, inevitably erodes liberty when it is treated as the primary basis for delineating legal rights and liabilities.

Against that background this book argues that equality legislation, and the egalitarian ideas underpinning that legislation, are inimical to justice. The book analyses various ideas and themes in support of that argument, namely that the legal framework is impractical, ineffective in meeting its stated goals, inadvertently gives rise to a host of perverse incentives, produces unintended effects including hurting those it is designed to help, undermines the self-reliance and resilience of its selected vulnerable groups, and gives rise to inordinate costs. Ultimately, as Sowell argues, make-believe equality aspires to a vision of cosmic justice which is unattainable, costly, and harmful. But the core concern of this book is with liberty. The central purpose of the book is to defend the value of economic freedom as a component of individual liberty, by arguing that any form of 'justice' which imposes one person's concept of moral duty onto others through legal mandates is unethical and unsound.

[11] Corey, Liberalism and the Modern Quest for Freedom. Ibid., p. 154.

Our discussion of individual liberty focuses primarily on the freedoms that underpin productive enterprise. The benefits of economic freedom as a component of individual liberty are self-evident in the general sense that even the most ferocious social justice devotees have private lives wherein they appreciate the freedom to speak their minds, to earn a living and to pursue productive activities that they value. Even totalitarians tend generally to argue that their socialist dreams promise some form of freedom—freedom from inequality, freedom from discrimination, freedom from the indignity of feeling less valued by society than others. But in single-minded pursuit of their vision of equality, egalitarians seek to enforce their moral certainties—the duty to be actively anti-racist, the decolonisation of established institutions, mandatory training on critical race theories, and the like, without acknowledging dissenting views or addressing the implications for liberty. These duties are then enshrined as a form of legal obligation, typically by presenting them in institutional guidelines laid down to comply with legislative equality mandates. The notion that equality is a goal for which we are (or ought to be) happy to sacrifice liberty explains the widespread, almost casual, support for extending the scope of legislative coercion to more and more protected groups. Little is said about the importance of liberty for human flourishing, or the threat posed to justice by undermining formal equality. Resistance to these trends generally takes the form of new groups contending to be included within the protective framework of equality law, criticising the legislation not for offering protection to special groups but for failing to designate them as one of the special groups. For example, in the UK the Equality Act is criticised not for offering special protection on grounds of race, but for failing to extend this protection to disadvantaged white boys whose needs are overlooked as they are not in a minority ethnic category. Such concerns address the operational weaknesses of the law while disregarding the more fundamental principle that legal protection ought to apply equally to all, not to designated special groups. By criticising the basis of such designations the critiques imply that the law is in principle sound, although perhaps misapplied. This book focuses not only on the application of the law, although many shortcomings are highlighted, but also on the cogency of its underlying premises.

Looking ahead to anticipate future trends, progressive social justice is on track further to erode the classic ideal of formal equality. Ins a volte-face that may seem surprising to those who have not followed recent events, equality legislation introduced in the 1960 to protect racial minorities by enshrining formal equality regardless of race is now criticised on social justice grounds for impeding progressive dreams of substantive equality. The formal equality that once protected racial minorities precisely by overlooking race, is now said to impede the welfare of racial minorities by overlooking racial disadvantage and exploitative historical legacies. For example in London the Metropolitan Police Commissioner has pleaded for special dispensation from equality law; she seeks licence to 'favour minority recruits' as a 40% black police force would better reflect the racial demographics of London.[12] In the same vein California's legislature attempted to repeal the principle of equal protection which stands in the way of positive discrimination for disadvantaged groups,[13] while the American Medical Association has devised a programme of 'racial justice' and 'health equity' to prioritise ethnic minority patients with greater health needs.[14] The notion of 'digital equity' requires government funding for broadband to be based on race, while 'vaccine equity' requires public health initiatives targeted at racial minorities.[15] Formal equality is increasingly depicted as potentially harmful to racial minorities because it subjects them to rules and standards which, it is said, are harder for them to meet due to an enduring legacy of historical disadvantage and systemic discrimination. Formal equality impedes governments from implementing positive

---

[12] Hamilton, F. (2021, June 1). Met Chief Cressida Dick Calls for Law to Favour Minority Recruits. *The Times*. https://www.thetimes.co.uk/article/met-chief-cressida-dick-calls-for-law-to-favour-minority-recruits-z0kcxq62l.

[13] California Proposition 16 proposed to amend the California constitution by repealing the principle of non-discrimination, in order to permit affirmative action and other forms of discrimination favouring those thought to need positive discrimination.

[14] American Medical Association. (2021). *Organizational Strategic Plan to Embed Racial Justice and Advance Health Equity, 2021–2023*. Retrieved June 26, 2021, from https://www.ama-assn.org/system/files/2021-05/ama-equity-strategic-plan.pdf.

[15] https://www.theguardian.com/inclusive-sustainable-future/2020/oct/20/digital-equity-financial-inclusion-economic-recovery; https://www.who.int/news-room/commentaries/detail/a-new-commitment-for-vaccine-equity-and-defeating-the-pandemic.

discrimination measures such as affirmative action or hiring by quota and is therefore said to stand in the way of true justice for racial minorities.

1.1 Justice and Public Reason

This vision of substantive equality and racial justice is part of a broader progressive liberal vision of the fair and just society. The progressive argument is that a more 'real' form of substantive equality, often referred to as 'equity', is needed to meet the demands of social justice. In evaluating that argument this book distinguishes between that form of 'social justice' and the classical ideal of justice. The classical ideal of justice which underpins the rule of law in liberal democracies is blind, meaning that it treats everyone the same without fear or favour. Rights and liabilities are determined without regard to race or creed. But blind justice is insufficient for egalitarian progressives as it fails explicitly to recognise racial identity or other personal traits and characteristics protected by equality legislation. Blind justice is also criticised for failing to embrace expectations surrounding the group entitlements which confer special legal protection on the colour, culture, religion, opinions, or even physical attributes of racial minorities.[16] Blind justice is denigrated for showing favour to those said to be undeserving of favour due to their 'white privilege'. Just as the ancient philosopher is simplistically presumed to lament the gross unfairness of the sun shining equally on the righteous and the wicked, blind justice is simplistically presumed to bestow even further unfair advantages on those who are already unfairly advantaged.[17] Free markets are regarded with suspicion by egalitarians

[16] For example the claim that Afro hair should be treated as a 'protected characteristic' under the Equality Act or protected under human rights law: 'An employee at a Zara store in Toronto's east end said she will likely quit her job and file a complaint with the Ontario Human Rights Commission after managers gave her a hard time about her hair': Lee-Shannock, P. (2016, April 8). Zara Employee Accuses Store of Discrimination over Her Hairstyle. *CBC*. https://www.cbc.ca/news/canada/toronto/ballah-zara-discrimination-hairstyle-1.3527977.

[17] Solomon laments that 'All things come alike to all: there is one event to the righteous, and to the wicked; to the good and to the clean, and to the unclean; to him that sacrificeth, and to him that sacrificeth not: as is the good, so is the sinner; and he that sweareth, as he that feareth an oath': Ecclesiastes 9:2 (1819). *The King James Bible* Collins (Original work published 1769).

because markets operate blindly, overturning the precepts of socialised justice. Egalitarians are concerned that Adam Smith's invisible hand seems to allocate even more to those who already have too much, while for those who have precious little, what little they have seems only to be taken away. It is then argued that this inequality is symptomatic of market failures, in that the market has failed to produce equal results. A more racialised or socialised form of justice is then proposed, which would be tailored towards favouring the disadvantaged. This worldview suggests that it is right for the classical ideal of justice to follow the unfortunate statue of Edward Colston into the depths of the nearest harbour, never again to be seen in polite society.[18]

In mounting their attack on the classical notion of justice, progressive egalitarians rally behind John Rawls, the great 'philosophical enemy' of those who wish to live and let live.[19] The progressive political agenda finds succour in Rawls's *Theory of Justice*, a theory which offers a sophisticated, theoretically robust and utterly seductive justification for egalitarian legislative policies.[20] Rawls's theory, as it has come to be understood by his academic acolytes, establishes socialist political ideology as an impartial 'overlapping consensus' with which all scholars, being reasonable people, would be expected to agree. Rawls's theory is generally relied upon to defend overtly socialist policies on grounds that such policies are impartial, 'neutral as between a private, pluralistic economic order and total, state-monopoly socialism'.[21] This implies that the tenets of socialism which underpin the modern welfare state, with principles of equality and non-discrimination treated as central to wealth distribution, may be understood as a 'neutral' position, floating benignly between capitalism and that form of 'total state-monopoly socialism' known as communism. Socialist policies are regarded as 'neutral' by contemporary

[18] 'Protagonists of this Procrustean ideal would, if they were both clear-headed and frank, sacrifice the propaganda advantages of presenting it as a kind of justice. Instead, and taking a leaf from the book of the orthopsychiatrists and other self-styled penal progressives, they would mount a bold and radical onslaught on the very notion of justice – denouncing the whole business as antique, gothic, reactionary, and – what is the truth - irreducibly backward-looking': Flew, A., Enforced Equality—Or Justice? p. 32.

[19] Flew, ibid., p. 35.

[20] Flew, ibid.

[21] Flew, ibid.

Rawlsian liberals because they do not leave markets perfectly free and unregulated in a private property absolutist, dog-eat-dog, survival of the fittest Darwinian dystopia in which there is no welfare state, no public services and the people starve (that would be too extreme to command respect). But neither do socialist governments abolish private property, enforce communal shared ownership of personal items like pens and toothbrushes, and sentence all who dare speak against the state to life in the Gulag (which would also be too extreme to command respect). The Rawlsian consensus which dominates intellectual discourse positions itself between such extremes in order to commend itself as objective, reasonable, measured and balanced.

Within this moral 'consensus' Rawlsian liberalism views its impartial social priorities as tending only ever so mildly towards tyranny, so mildly that nobody need be unduly alarmed.Rawlsian liberals do not believe in slippery slopes, nor do they care to follow the steps in reasoning that link egalitarian visions to totalitarianism.[22] They regard the excesses of cancel culture in which people are banned from social media platforms as rather minor and inconsequential in the wider scheme of things. They view their preferred framework of social justice as defensible because it is on the whole amiable and pleasant, in the words of Peter Hitchens a 'new, sweet and sticky marshmallow totalitarianism' that is readily embraced because at least it is *nothing* like North Korea.[23] After all nobody ever died from being banned from social media platforms or from being no-platformed by a university student society so it seems that there is no credible cause for concern. Free speech is enshrined in the institutional framework and protected in human rights legislation, so within this consensus it should not matter too much if those who cause offence

[22] 'Mises and Hayek demonstrated incontrovertibly that a socialist economy cannot work; to make matters worse, the attempt to establish such an economy makes likely the onset of a totalitarian order ...[but] rationality is not a trait much in evidence among the socialistically inclined. If reason speaks against socialism, is not the solution obvious: out with reason!': Gordon, D. (2017). Finding Meaning. In *An Austro-Libertarian View, Vol. 1*, pp. 361–362.

[23] 'She is not claiming that the modern West is like the thuggish Kim regime. She is saying that we willingly give in to what has to be forced on to Koreans by police terror, sealed borders and labour camps'. Hitchens, P. (2021, June 19). Now Even This North Korean Warns We're Being Brainwashed! *Daily Mail*. https://www.dailymail.co.uk/news/article-9704389/PETER-HITCHENS-North-Korean-warns-brainwashed.html.

are subjected to harsh consequences—in the 'neutral' state people are free to say what they like but the mob is then free to hound them out of their jobs and homes. Social justice takes priority over freedom in the 'neutral' state. We are daily warned to be careful what we say as there are legal limits on free speech. We are regularly reminded that those who speak freely should not be surprised to face opposition. The *New York Times* intones that 'individuals are not entitled to speech that presents a "clear and present danger" to society', a significant drawing of the lines in a political context where danger is feared to be ubiquitous and the state is enjoined to keep us all safe.[24] This worldview holds that those who have no harmful intentions should have no reason to worry about impositions upon their freedoms, meaning that only those who intend to cause offence need be troubled—and why should society care about the troubles of those who have 'struck first' by offending others with their thoughtless remarks and irreverent jokes? These interpretations of contemporary liberalism dominate the social justice discourse which constitutes 'the reigning ideology of the academic elite' and provides the principal philosophical underpinning for social justice defined as distributive justice.[25] It may or may not be what Rawls explicitly wrote or intended, but his theory of justice has settled comfortably into the role of the Socialist Manifesto. As Flew observes:

> Just as Plato in *The Republic* developed a uniting and justifying ideology for the absolute rulers of his supposedly ideal state, so Rawls too has, in his own somnambulistic and pedestrian way, done the same thing for that New Class which sees its own most unequally powerful and most unequally prosperous future in the enforcement, through the ever expanding welfare-state machine, of equality for all others.[26]

[24] Gonchar, M. (2018, September 12). Why Is Freedom of Speech an Important Right? When, if Ever, Can It Be Limited? *New York Times*. https://www.nytimes.com/2018/09/12/learning/why-is-freedom-of-speech-an-important-right-when-if-ever-can-it-be-limited.html.

[25] Described by John Tomasi as 'left liberalism': 'left liberals are sceptical of the moral significance of private economic liberty. They are skeptical also of distributions of goods that result from the exercise of those capitalist freedoms': Tomasi, J. (2012). *Free Market Fairness* (p. xiii). Princeton University Press.

[26] Flew, A. Enforced Equality—Or Justice? p. 35.

The putatively neutral prioritisation of wealth distribution and identity politics is underpinned by a theoretical framework of justice as fairness, based on an overlapping consensus derived through public reason within which people may hold differing, but reasonable, worldviews. But as will be seen in the next chapter, closer inspection of this apparent moral consensus reveals that it admits only those who accept Rawls's premise of public reason as the appropriate starting point in theorising about key philosophical concerns in political theory. David Gordon summarises the influence of public reason in Rawls's theory:

> People in deliberating publicly should not appeal to their conceptions of the good, or at least not do so exclusively. Instead, they should rely on 'public reason.' That is, they should appeal to neutral principles that everyone who shares the desire to reach agreement with others could reasonably accept. If they do, they will wind up endorsing Rawls's own theory of justice. In what he calls an 'overlapping consensus,' each person will find reasons within his own conception of the good to endorse Rawls's theory.[27]

The prominence of the Rawlsian understanding of public reason seems to imply that those who do not meet its gate-keeping preconditions in deliberating about justice are patently unreasonable, and unreasonable concerns should of course be discounted in evaluating the prevailing moral consensus. Rawls's concept of public reason in effect validates only those views it regards as legitimate in arriving at a consensus on the pursuit of justice. The apparent consensus reflected in legislative mandates is said not to be coercive because it is derived through public reason. As David Gordon points out, this notion of public reason is indeed 'respectful and non-coercive — to those who accept its tenets. Those outside the "legitimation pool" of these accepters do not count'.[28] Gordon adds:

---

[27] Gordon, D. (2021, June 4). *Mises on Dealing with Rival World Views*. Mises Institute. Retrieved June 26, 2021, from https://mises.org/library/mises-dealing-rival-world-views.

[28] Gordon, D. (2017). The Problems of Public Reason. In *An Austro-Libertarian View (Vol. I: Economics, Philosophy, Law)*. Mises Institute, p. 391.

> Public reason shows much less respect for people than its advocates claim for it; and the view has consequences that are themselves coercive... defenders of public reason do not in fact show respect for everyone's comprehensive doctrine. It is only those deemed "reasonable" who have to be taken into account. If you hold a comprehensive doctrine that is not "reasonable," then you are excluded: it is not necessary, in public argument, to offer you a reason that you would find acceptable.[29]

Rawls's framework appeals greatly to social justice adherents because it depicts socialist goals as the outcome of public reason, while according only a token respect for economic freedom. It is clear that far from being an overlapping consensus, this has come to be treated as a philosophical justification for socialism. It is very convenient for socialists if the 'impartial' reasoning proposed by Rawls proves that socialism implemented by a left-liberal government is the *only* reasonable, fair and just political agenda.[30] Classical liberalism is excluded from the scope of 'reasonable' views because it lacks the requisite distributive role for the state.[31] But a form of public reason inherently designed to produce the result preferred by socialist political parties can only achieve such form of 'consensus' that excludes conservative and libertarian political thought. As Robert George and Christopher Wolfe have argued, to define public reason in a way that excludes dissenting perspectives 'is not much more than playing a game with loaded dice'.[32] Rawlsian liberals then assert that the burden falls upon a classical liberal who wishes to 'expand' the Rawlsian consensus, in hopes of making a case for inclusion of economic

---

[29] Ibid.

[30] It was certainly welcomed thus by socialists: 'In his Critical Notice in the New York Review of Books, the lifelong British socialist Stuart Hampshire wrote: "I think that this book is ...a noble, coherent, highly abstract picture of the fair society, as social democrats see it. ... This is certainly the model of social justice that has governed the advocacy of R. H. Tawney and Richard Titmuss and that holds the Labour Party together': Flew, Enforced Equality—Or Justice? p. 32.

[31] 'In Knight and Johnson's terminology, Rawls envisages a central "second-order" role for the state in monitoring and correcting the background distributive conditions in which other institutions operate. It is the absence of such mechanisms under classical liberalism that for Rawls disqualifies it from the family of "reasonable" worldviews': Pennington, M. (2017). Robust Political Economy and the Priority of Markets. *Social Philosophy and Policy, 34*(1), 1–24, p. 17.

[32] George, R. P., & Wolfe, C. (Eds.). (2000). Natural Law and Public Reason. In R. P. George & C. Wolfe (Eds.), *Natural Law and Public Reason.* Georgetown University Press.

freedom as a basic liberty, to justify the reasonableness of their position.[33] Thus we have arrived at an impasse: vibrant academic debate about equality unfolds only *within* the framework of Rawlsian reasoning with little attention paid to the classical tradition prioritising economic freedom which falls *outside* that framework. Classical liberalism gains admission to the academic citadel only to the extent that it satisfies Rawlsian demands.

Since Rawls's theory of distributive justice treats equality as an essential component of social justice, his concept of public reason supplies a favourable philosophical foundation for the social and moral 'consensus' surrounding demands for the equality of assorted identity groups. For example equality law in the UK recognises such groups based on nine designated protected characteristics: age, disability, gender reassignment, marriage/civil partnership, pregnancy/maternity, sex, race, religion/belief and sexual orientation. More grounds are proposed, such as geographical location or socio-economic status. The concept of race occupies a central role within that broader framework of identity-based equality. Race is now established as a key avenue through which social justice may be advanced, meaning that the racialisation of law is deemed to be necessary in order to meet the demands of social justice. By 'racialisation' we mean understanding the scope of legal rights and liabilities through the interpretative lens of race. An example of racialised law may be taken from the UK's Equality Act 2010, which declares race to be a protected characteristic encompassing colour, nationality and ethnic or national origins. Race is protected by prohibiting words, conduct, decisions, intentions or even 'unconscious' thoughts that subject people to detriment because of their race. Similarly crimes may be 'aggravated' by the presence of a racial motive, thereby incurring harsher penalties. It then follows, given

[33] Thus Tomasi's defence of a thick concept of economic liberty, has been criticised for failing to justify an 'expansion' of basic liberty to include economic liberty. Tomasi points out 'I note first that "expansion" is not quite the correct (or relevant) term for my proposal for the recognition of thick economic liberty. After all, it is the high liberals who are advocating a contraction of the basic liberties, so as to exclude the thick conception of economic liberty widely affirmed by the (historically) classical liberal thinkers. I call this call for contraction the platform of economic exceptionalism—the thesis that economic liberties should be singled out from the traditional list for "thinning down"—and I challenge high liberals to defend that platform by way of moral argument.' Tomasi, J. (2015). Market Democracy and Meaningful Work: A Reply to Critics. *Res Publica, 443*, 446.

that *social* justice is understood as *distributive* justice, that racial justice is ultimately conceptualised as a demand for equal distribution of wealth and power between races, measured by reference to racial disparities in income and attainment.

Equality legislation and the corpus of policy guidelines to which that legislation gives rise have in this way departed from Ronald Dworkin's argument that the law ought not to treat people unequally in order to produce more equal outcomes.[34] But measuring wealth redistribution along racial lines and taking from the advantaged to give to the disadvantaged, is not viewed by egalitarians as a potential form of injustice. Instead, the Rawlsian interpretation of redistribution is that advantages vesting in 'privileged' people are arbitrary and undeserved, the implication being that if merit is undeserved then it is no injustice to divest those said to be privileged of their material advantages.[35] It could be argued that the fundamental objection advanced by this book concerns the legitimacy of redistributive policies, regardless of the lines along which that redistribution is given effect. As Sowell argues, the term 'redistribution' is in a sense misconceived since wealth is created and produced and does not fall to be 'distributed' through government policies to ends said to be socially justified. Such forms of legalised taking are justified by reference to the worthiness of the ends sought to be promoted, chief among which is the notion of racial equality. Racial equality, understood to be implemented through equal opportunities *and* equal outcomes, is deemed to be so self-evidently moral and just that little attention is paid to the potential unfairness it might entail. It seems churlish to be hesitant about so worthy a vision as that of equalising life experiences and outcomes for all members of society especially the most deprived, which is regarded as simply the right thing to do—like taking bread from an overfed and overindulged adult to feed a starving baby. Thus deviations

[34] 'Government must not only treat people with concern and respect, but with equal concern and respect. It must not distribute goods or opportunities unequally on the ground that some citizens are entitled to more because they are worthy of more concern. It must not constrain liberty on the ground that one citizen's conception of the good life of one group is nobler or superior to another's': Dworkin, R. M. (1977). *Taking Rights Seriously* (pp. 272–273). Duckworth.

[35] See for example debates surrounding Sandel, M. J. (2020). *The Tyranny of Merit: What's Become of the Common Good?* Allen Lane.

from the principle of equal treatment which would in ordinary circumstances be regarded as intolerable in a free society are now enshrined in law and welcomed within the Rawlsian 'overlapping consensus' as a gilded pathway to social justice.

1.2 Philosophical Diversity

This book rejects the Rawlsian theoretical framework as the appropriate starting point of philosophical inquiry in defending liberty. Conformity with Rawlsian redistributive theories has become the standard litmus test for identifying policies that are fair and just. The implication is that any dissent must by definition 'be unfair or not a proper principle of justice'.[36] To suppose that a principle is just and fair *only* if it falls within the parameters of Rawlsian ideals would in effect dismiss as unreasonable any rejection of egalitarian ideals. Yet reasonable people can, and often do, disagree about what it means to be just or fair and whether, or when, to harness legislative and state power in the pursuit of moral ideals. It is not heretical for reasonable people to disagree on the ideals to which we aspire. If reasonable people may disagree on fundamental philosophical concepts such as the meaning of fairness or justice, we need not subscribe to egalitarian or socialist theories of justice in deriving a reasonable conception of the good.

The diversity of opinion on the definitional conceptualisation of justice casts doubt on the contemporary presumptions about distributive justice as a starting point for an inquiry into the appropriate role of legislation in enforcing one or other partisan view of justice. As Chandran Kukathas argues, to assert that justice is important and ought to be implemented by the state, so that all that is left is to decide the appropriate content of justice, would be to presuppose the importance of the

[36] 'I agree that the strange conditions of the [Original Position] do eliminate mere bias and so do guarantee that if a principle were agreed on in the OP it would be fair (at least as between the parties to the agreement). But, since "if" is not equivalent to "only if", it is a mere fallacy to infer from this (as much loose writing in the book invites the reader to infer) that if a principle would not be chosen in the OP it therefore would, in the real world, be unfair or not a proper principle of justice.' Finnis, J. (2011). *Human Rights and the Common Good: Collected Essays, Vol. III* (p. 74). Oxford University Press.

very issue that is the subject of debate, namely the power or authority of the state to intrude upon private relationships in a bid to impose just outcomes (irrespective of how justice is conceptualised or theorised).[37] It is self-evident that everyone wants justice; nobody wants *injustice*. But if there is no consensus on the content of justice the lack of consensus suggests that there ought to be limits on the power of the state to do whatever it deems to be necessary, backed by the force of law, to achieve any goal designated as 'just' without regard to the implications for those who do not subscribe to the popular view of what is 'just' in that context.

In understanding the implications of racial diversity from a classical liberal perspective, Kukathas's theory of diversity offers a more appropriate philosophical starting point than the Rawlsian consensus. Rather than being preoccupied with securing moral or cultural consensus in contexts of diversity, a project which can offer only a most unsatisfactory and unstable consensus, peaceful coexistence is more realistically pursued by asking the questions posed by Kukathas: 'who should have authority to act? What makes authority legitimate, and what are its bounds?' and ultimately 'What is the place of authority in a free society?'[38] These questions invite us to consider the appropriate role of legislation in dictating social interaction in the private sphere, including the sphere of the employment relationship. The focus of attention shifts from the level of courtesy and civility that we should exhibit, to the question of who has authority to make that evaluation. By recognising that decision-making authority in a liberal society operates at different levels and vests in different types of decision-makers, Kukathas sets out to identify 'the principled basis of a free society marked by cultural diversity and group loyalties' suggesting a more fruitful way to address the respective claims of cultural minorities and the appropriate role to be played by the state in regulating such claims.[39]

Our discussion of the role of law in contexts of racial diversity therefore draws inspiration from Kukathas's political theory of diversity. Kukathas argues that the key to peaceful coexistence in contexts of

[37] Kukathas, C. (2003). *The Liberal Archipelago: A Theory of Diversity and Freedom*. Oxford University Press.

[38] Ibid., p. 7.

[39] Ibid., p. 3.

moral and cultural diversity is to ensure that the allocation of political authority is legitimate. Peaceful coexistence in this theory of diversity does not require coercing everyone to 'respect' the cultures or moral codes of others as is advised by multiculturalists who deem all cultures to be equal, nor does it consider the promotion of different cultures to be an appropriate function of legislative policy. Kukathas's theory of freedom in diversity therefore does not aim to encourage, much less defend or promote, cultural or group diversity.[40] On the contrary he defends a broad concept of freedom that enables people peaceably to coexist *despite* living in conditions of diversity, based on mutual toleration and a commitment to live and let live. In a liberal society cultural and moral attachments and affiliations allow us freely to associate with those who share our opinions or disassociate from those with whom we disagree, should we so choose. But such attachments or detachments play no part in the allocation of decision-making authority and power in society.

In focusing on decision-making authority rather than the demands of justice Kukathas departs from Rawlsian liberal theories. Rawls's theory of justice posits a closed order with 'a determinate set of institutions' within which rules and practices conform to an objective consensus on social and political and moral questions. Based on the premise that such a consensus is arrived at through a democratic process of public reason then it is right that all should be bound by it. Legislative mandates within the parameters of that closed order, designed to fulfil the prevailing consensus on social justice, would thus be justified to the extent that they reflect the priorities citizens have agreed to uphold. The resulting legislation designed to meet the demands of social or distributive justice acquires legitimacy from that implicit pact, and there would be no reasonable grounds for objecting to its edicts. Kukathas disagrees. He does not see distributive justice as a prerequisite for determining the legitimacy of the rules and edicts binding upon all people living in contexts of cultural diversity and moral disputation.

40 'Diversity is, in fact, not the value liberalism pursues but the source of the problem to which it offers a solution'. Ibid., p. 29.

Kukathas defines a free society as one in which dissent from the moral, political or social consensus in pursuit of that freedom is tolerated. His solution to 'the problem of coping with diversity' rejects the idea that group rights, preferential policies or political representation based on minority-group identity require to be granted or promoted by the state; group claims cannot acquire legitimacy simply by claiming to reflect a social justice consensus which restricts people's freedoms of association and conscience as a means of promoting special groups. Kukathas rejects group rights not in order simply to quibble about whether or not group rights ought to be central to a theory of social justice, but rather on the prior ground that a theory of social justice is not the appropriate starting point in ascertaining the legitimacy of the social order in a free society. A better starting point would consider the allocation of authority, ensuring that such authority is not vested in the state to determine every aspect of life but is instead vested in a multiplicity of decision-making agents.

Group identity is immaterial in the context of decision-making authority. Kukathas argues that 'diversity – cultural, religious, linguistic or otherwise – is of no intrinsic importance. Diversity is a fact of life. But in itself it is of no particular value'.[41] Thus his theory 'does not see cultural integration, or cultural engineering generally, as part of the purpose of the state'.[42] The state has no role in either promoting diversity through special group rights, or undermining diversity by enforcing a superficial equality through suppressing differences of opinion or worldview. Hence he supports 'a politics of indifference' in which the allocation of political authority is indifferent to personal characteristics or group identity. In a politics of indifference legislation would neither favour particular groups nor erase group identity. This is not to say that group identity is irrelevant to human flourishing, but that group identity is a matter for individual and not state decision-making. Nor is the state concerned with human flourishing, as that is pursued through free association and market exchange.[43]

[41] Ibid., p. 32.

[42] Ibid., p. 15.

[43] The state should not 'be concerned directly to promote human flourishing; it should have no collective projects; it should express no group preferences; and it should promote no particular

Kukathas's theory is political rather than 'comprehensive' in that it presents 'a liberal political order…without appealing to the substantial moral conceptions some liberal thinkers have tried to uphold' such as equality or multiculturalism.[44] Thus liberalism in his theory upholds freedom, rather than a specified set of moral standards; it 'identifies principles by which different moral standards may be allowed to coexist'.[45] He defines the free society as 'a collection of communities (and, so, authorities) associated under laws which recognise the freedom of individuals to associate as, and with whom, they wish'.[46] Kukathas conceptualises a free society as 'one in which politics is given priority over morality' thereby delinking moral ideology from state power.[47] He theorises liberalism as 'an account of how different moral standards may coexist [under a regime of toleration] rather than a set of substantive moral commitments by which all communities should be required to abide'.[48] It is true that moral ideology strongly influences people's politics, but morality influences legislation only indirectly through political processes rather than directly through moral sanctions. Kukathas considers the legitimacy of public authority to be a more meaningful and important consideration in a free society than whether that authority is 'just'. The question of justice is fraught with tension and social strife precisely because there is no meaningful consensus on the content of justice. Thus 'social justice' cannot by itself grant legitimacy to coercive legislation in a free society. Legislation can only derive its legitimacy from consent or free acquiescence. Kukathas's 'theory of the free society is therefore an account of the terms by which different ways *coexist* rather than an account of the terms by which they *cohere*'.[49]

As Kukathas argues, identity-based characteristics such as race are normatively irrelevant in understanding the role of the state, though they

individuals or individual interests. Its only concern ought to be with upholding the framework of law within which individuals and groups can function peacefully.' Ibid., p. 249.

[44] Ibid., p. 17.

[45] Ibid., p. 19.

[46] Ibid., p. 19.

[47] Ibid., p. 19.

[48] Ibid., p. 30.

[49] Ibid., p. 5.

might be relevant to private decision-making such as a workplace preference for inter-group diversity. Thus the issue is not whether diversity is, in itself, a worthwhile goal but whether it should be central to delineating the appropriate scope of justice, and more importantly the content of mandatory law and regulation. Kukathas's answer is that it should not. Kukathas argues that 'the primary question of *politics* is not about justice or rights but about power, who may have it, and what may be done with it' meaning that we do not primarily consider whether people want justice, or demand justice, but also the implications for liberty including factors such as whether they ought to have the power to mandate legal compliance with their justice-based demands reflecting their preferred notion of justice.[50]

It can be seen from Kukathas's analysis that any discussion of the appropriate legal framework in contexts of racial diversity is, at heart, a study in how people with different races, histories, cultures and identities can live together in peaceful cooperation. To argue in favour of a legal framework based on social cooperation and shared prosperity may seem in principle to be uncontroversial—everyone would welcome more cooperation and prosperity and we would expect any steps in that direction to meet with universal approval. But it is not sufficient merely to identify desirable social goals with which we would all in principle agree. Social goals must in themselves be ethical and just, and a realistic and sustainable method of achieving those goals is required. Further, while particular policy goals may be straightforward enough to formulate, implementing social ideals is strongly dependent on the social context including the institutional and legal framework within which those ideals are rooted. As Ludwig von Mises highlights, the conceptual and ideological foundations of social institutions matter.[51] Social institutions are not abstractly constituted, but rooted in the ideals that sustain them. To abandon such constitutive ideals risks destroying the institutional framework itself.

[50] Ibid., p. 7.

[51] Highlighting the link between productivity and property rights: 'the fact that [the total product available for distribution] is not independent of the manner in which it is divided. The fact that that product is as great as it is, is not a natural or technological phenomenon independent of all social conditions, but entirely the result of our social institutions': Mises, *Liberalism*, p. 12.

Applying this insight to understanding the role of legal concepts, we argue here that the demands of social justice cannot be evaluated in the abstract by reference only to the 'moral emotionalism', as Hayek termed it, of their virtuous intentions. It is necessary to question whether the underlying legal framework is in fact founded in true ideals, whether it is likely to advance those ideals effectively and if so at what cost to other social values.

Thus the book proceeds on the premise that for those liberals who favour arms' length market distribution over centralised state distribution, a Rawlsian starting point is not only inappropriate, or differing only in a few peripheral particulars concerning the practical demands of justice, but is ultimately opposed to the classical ideals of justice and equality.

1.3 The Landscape of Classical Liberalism

This part of the discussion offers a brief overview of some of the key classical liberal responses to the foregoing developments, in order to situate the approach taken by this book within the broader landscape of classical liberalism. It will be seen that classical liberal perspectives vary in their treatment of equality and social justice. The approach preferred by this book, Kukathas's 'politics of indifference', rejects a Rawlsian starting point because it does not consider the pursuit of social justice or other forms of social engineering to be a legitimate function of state authority. It is on that premise that this this book rejects the egalitarian ideals that underpin equality law. As will be seen later, the book challenges egalitarian ideals on both ethical and practical grounds. It should be clarified at the outset that within the broader landscape of classical liberalism some strands of thought are developed by drawing upon Rawlsian liberalism, and others, while they may not be explicitly Rawlsian, nevertheless do not challenge the philosophical foundations of Rawlsian liberalism but highlight its costs and other practical shortcomings. In framing our argument this book draws upon these different ideas and principles, and it may be helpful at this stage to explain how the key principles of classical liberalism influence, in different ways, the discussion that follows in the ensuing chapters.

The first principle concerns the importance of philosophical diversity for individual liberty. Classical ideals of equality and justice allow the greatest scope for individual liberty, especially freedom of conscience and the freedom to live as one chooses. Pluralism and diversity imply respect for different conceptualisations of moral ideals, and as wide a scope as possible for a private life in which individuals determine for themselves the ideals and values to which they should aspire. Individual diversity is central to this approach.[52] Liberalism in the classical tradition offers no ideological dogmatism, no moral code which all *must* be compelled to follow, but instead embraces 'a conscious rejection of the belief that politics can or should present citizens with a single vision of the good'.[53] It seeks a political framework in which we need not all agree on the ideal form of justice. Rather than engage in an endless, costly and futile clash of deeply held moral ideals, or seeking to compel others to follow moral ideologies with which they do not agree, the liberal institutional framework promotes principles and standards that allow the greatest scope for individual decision-making. It will be seen later that this also supports wide scope for freedom of contract and freedom of association in the employment context, and defends the common law principle of employment at will in which an employer makes decisions for good reason, bad reason or no reason, meaning that his reasons for making decisions are his own and need not be accounted for to anybody other than those entitled to an account under the usual principles of private law.[54]

52 'If individual diversity were not the universal rule, then the argument for liberty would be weak indeed. For if individuals were as interchangeable as ants, why should anyone worry about maximizing the opportunity for every person to develop his mind and his faculties and his personality to the fullest extent possible?' Rothbard, M. N. (2000). *Egalitarianism as a Revolt Against Nature and Other Essays* (Original work published 1974). Mises Institute, p. xvii.

53 Corey, Liberalism and the Modern Quest for Freedom, p. 155.

54 Epstein, R. A. (1984). In Defense of the Contract at Will. 51 *University of Chicago Law Review*, 947.

Therefore classical liberalism encompasses a wide range of different perspectives and priorities.[55] To this we may add a second key principle, namely the importance of economic freedom. Classical liberals would all, to a greater or lesser degree, hold the conviction that economic freedom is essential to human flourishing and view freedom from state command and control as a fundamental facet of freedom. These freedoms have been overshadowed in recent decades by the growth of the democratic welfare state and the vision of the state as a source of economic largesse offering greater social and financial security to citizens. Progressive policy tends to identify new platforms for state intervention without regard to the implications for individual liberty precisely because it is presumed that the benefits to the individual countermand any encroachment on his liberty. The importance of individual liberty in classical liberal perspectives implies that economic freedom should be defended against overweening legislative encroachment, even in cases where such legislation is said to advance the goals of social justice.

With those principles in mind, classical liberal scholars respond to egalitarian claims of social justice in different ways ranging from caution to outright rejection. Some scholars would argue against equalisation policies on the grounds that such policies overlook the deleterious costs and harmful unintended effects resulting from special interest protection. They may accept that the growing policy focus on 'racial equity' is in theory well-intentioned in its attempts to reverse systemic discrimination by systemically discriminating in the opposite direction, but would argue that in practice trying to correct a historical wrong through a modified and updated version of the same wrong simply creates a new set of victims in place of the previous victims. The efforts to advance equity, understood in terms of substantive equality and equal outcomes, are criticised for feeding the hostility and resentment of favoured groups, who become increasingly sensitive to others disrespecting their most-favoured

---

[55] Corey, D. D. (2018) observing that liberalism is not 'a single political philosophy' or a 'single body of doctrine' but a 'slowly evolving history of diverse political ideas and movement's whose pursuit or prioritisation of different kinds of freedom strongly reflects historical context and the particular freedoms at stake in each context: Against the Deformations of Liberalism. *Journal of American Affairs*. https://americanaffairsjournal.org/2018/02/against-the-deformations-of-liberalism/.

protected status. At the same time equalisation programmes incite new sources of hostility and resentment amongst unfavoured groups who feel increasingly side-lined, excluded or under threat. This is no blueprint for peaceful coexistence, and on that ground egalitarian schemes are opposed by classical liberals who promote peace as the ultimate social and moral ideal. Peaceful coexistence requires that we live each according to our own moral code, our sense of individuality, and desist from banding together with others to impose our subjective view of the good on others through legislative mandates. Within the legal framework this requires a wide band or range of reasonable conduct, a broad zone of discretion within which people may disagree without thereby falling outside the boundaries of reasonable conduct, and as broad a scope as possible for freedom of contract and market ordering.

To the extent that Rawls's framework attempts to achieve consensus and avoid warmongering by different moralistic factions, these classical liberal perspectives find much in common with Rawlsian liberalism even though they may disagree on matters such as the importance of economic freedom, the strength of property rights or the extent to which equality should trump liberty. For example John Tomasi endorses a version of Rawls's difference principle, which suggests that 'institutions be designed so that the benefits they help produce are enjoyed by all citizens, including the least fortunate'.[56] Rawls's original position may also be taken as a starting point to derive classical liberal utilitarian outcomes, as Richard Epstein has illustrated: 'Rawls's framework could easily and sensibly be pressed into service by those who had more utilitarian objectives' and 'Rawls's [original] position could be of enormous use even to individuals who thought in terms of incentives and consequences, instead of simply in terms of just outcomes'.[57] In that way, even though it is firmly associated with liberal-left egalitarianism, the Rawlsian philosophy framework is not inherently incompatible with strong private property rights and a limited role for state redistribution.[58]

---

[56] Tomasi, *Free Market Fairness*, p. xiv.

[57] Epstein, R. A. (2002, November 27). Rawls Remembered: An Appreciation from the Right. *National Review*. https://www.nationalreview.com/2002/11/john-rawls-remembered/.

[58] Epstein shows how individual autonomy and private property may be defended 'by an astute application of the veil-of-ignorance technology... Therein lies the greatness of Rawls.

Thomas Sowell for his part seeks clarity of definition, pointing out that we often seek fairness or equality without considering precisely the nature of our claim. Sowell argues that most people are troubled by inequality, including champions of free markets like Adam Smith whose concern for the poor in his moral philosophy is well known. For those who regard inequality as problematic, equality would surely be a worthwhile ideal if governments had the omniscience and omnipotence to inveigle cosmic justice from the universe. But unfortunately governments do not have the wisdom or power to implement cosmic justice, and they cause great untold harm to the economy and to society in the attempt.[59] Sowell suggests that instead, we should consider carefully the staggering costs of pursuing Rawlsian redistributive justice, in particular the cost to liberty, peace and prosperity. In Sowell's analysis, the political contestation between socialist and conservative, between classical liberal and progressive, is not about whether socio-economic inequalities should concern us (which they do) but rather what is to be done about them and in particular the degree of coercion that is justifiable to bring about greater equality. Sowell, like Hayek, is critical of the tendency to treat the outcome of spontaneous market order or natural misfortune as 'just' or 'unjust'. Hayek opposes coercive legislation not primarily because the equal outcomes it seeks to engineer are unworthy goals per se, but because the means adopted to bring about equal outcomes are ultimately totalitarian in the extent to which they sacrifice individual liberty. Hayek sees no way to enforce equal outcomes without sacrificing liberty, and considers the defence of liberty to be a fundamental purpose of the rule of law. To that extent Hayek did not necessarily consider the differences between his position and that of Rawls to be substantial, being no more than 'verbal' differences of definition, method and emphasis.[60]

In his relentless pursuit of finding the right way to design political and social institutions, he articulated a system that could be used with great power to defend a set of political and social arrangements that he had no intention of defending': in Rawls Remembered.

[59] Sowell, *Cosmic Justice*.

[60] For discussion see DiQuattro, A. (1983). Rawls and Left Criticism. *Political Theory, 11*(1), 53–78.

Egalitarian ideals may also be challenged by classical liberals on the practical ground that they intrude too far into the scope of individual discretion. If racism is said to denote any situation that could be perceived as racist, and jokes or banter may or may not be hate speech depending on how they made the listener feel (was one amused?), then there can be no objective or rational evaluation of personal sensitivities and feelings and no agreement as to whose truth supersedes another person's truth. Perhaps Buckingham Palace, finding itself caught up in fraught family disagreements about who said what to whom, and when and why and how, and whether that amounted to racism against the Sussexes, was wise simply to remark that 'recollections may vary'.[61] Similarly the varied reactions to the recent race discrimination report commissioned by the conservative UK government sparked heated debate amounting almost to an inter-black civil war, as different groups of black British people could not agree on whether the UK is racist or not. One cohort of black people convinced that western civilisation is systemically racist complained of feeling 'gaslighted' by the cohort of black people convinced that the UK is the best country in which to live. Slanging matches ensued on television and in the Twittersphere, followed by the unedifying spectacle of ethnic minority MPs on both sides of the House of Commons debating who should give whom lessons on being *authentically* black. To adapt Antony Flew's logical fallacy to the context of this particular spat, the claim was that 'no *true* black person would vote conservative'.[62] Such disputes cannot easily be resolved by rational debate. There are too many subjective influences shaping our view of fairness and opportunity in the societies in which we live. The idea of racial justice is unsuited to legislative prescription precisely because it is a subjectively imagined concept that defies the principle that law should be objective, certain and predictable. As will be shown later in discussing its operation in the context of employment, it is also incompatible with

[61] Ward, V. (2021, March 9). The Queen: Harry and Meghan's Racism Claims Will Be 'Taken Very Seriously'. https://www.telegraph.co.uk/royal-family/2021/03/09/analysis-will-three-paragraphs-enough-extinguish-flames-meghan/.

[62] Flew describes a person convinced that 'No Scotsman would do such a thing!' who reacts to seeing a Scotsman doing that precise thing by declaring that 'No *true* Scotsman would do such a thing!'

other aspects of the rule of law such as the presumption of innocence and the importance of intention in establishing legal culpability.

This brief overview is by no means exhaustive of the landscape of classical liberal perspectives, but it suffices to illustrate the diversity of approaches to equality in classical liberal thought. Some scholars might well endorse equality as an important component of justice, but raise concerns about the extent to which equality is pursued, the means adopted to promote it, the justifications offered or the countervailing costs. They might for example insist that favouring specific groups with extra 'equality' rights is justified so long as the law does so with the aim of equalising their *opportunities* and refrains from promoting equal *outcomes*. We shall see later that these perspectives have all played a valuable role in framing the legislative framework and constraining some of its wildest excesses. Yet these perspectives may be described as largely concerned with differences of degree or emphasis. They do not challenge the importance of equality, per se, in the conceptual framework of liberalism, nor do they confront directly the fundamental assumptions of egalitarianism.[63]

Murray Rothbard adopts a more radical perspective, denying that inequality is unfair. Unlike the classical liberal perspectives outlined in the preceding paragraphs, Rothbard does not ground his opposition to egalitarianism in utilitarianism or efficiency, nor even in the idea that total equality is unattainable or that classical liberalism is more conducive to productivity. Rothbard's approach is rooted in the ideals of justice and individual liberty. He is concerned not simply with whether egalitarianism works in practice, but also whether it is a sound theory, based on true principles, and whether it is ethically and morally justifiable. If it is not morally justifiable, then the objection to egalitarianism is more fundamental than a concern with the effectiveness of the means or the cogency of the goal. It is also more fundamental than a concern with democratic failures or the weakness of the social contract, for even if we achieved unanimous consent on the goals of make-believe equality, and everyone voluntarily accepted socialist values, we would still in such

[63] Gordon, D. (2017). Wrestling Reality from Rawls. In *An Austro-Libertarian View Vol. II: Political Theory*, p. 58.

circumstances be adopting objectively bad values. Fundamentally, if egalitarian principles are unjustified then the progressive ideologies that aim to achieve equal outcomes are, by the same token, unjustified. Thus before evaluating the effectiveness of social justice equalisation schemes a prior question must be asked: 'should equality be granted its current status as an unquestioned ethical ideal?'[64]

To understand better the significance of Rothbard's critique it may be helpful to contrast it with other influential perspectives. It has been seen that Rawls regards equality as the default position, so that in his theory of justice is the deviations from equality require to be justified and corrected.[65] Sowell, writing from a classical liberal perspective, views this default position with some sympathy; he observes that 'even those few writers who have tried to justify inequalities on merit grounds are nevertheless conceding that inequalities are things requiring justification' adding that 'virtually no one regards these inequalities as desirable in themselves. If the world had chanced to be more equal than it is, it is hard to see who would have had any grounds for complaint, much less just grounds'.[66] Rothbard, by contrast, views egalitarianism as a 'revolt against nature' which ought not to be taken as the default position in analysing society and social interaction.[67] For Rothbard the default position is not inequality but diversity rooted in 'the ineluctable facts of human biology; in particular, the fact that each individual is a unique person, in many ways different from all others'.[68] Rothbard treats the study of liberty—libertarianism—as a 'discipline which touches closely on many other areas of the study of human action: economics, philosophy, political theory, history, even—and not least—biology'.[69] As such, inequality reflects the 'variety, diversity, differentiation' of nature and does not call for justification. Rothbard writes:

---

64 'Egalitarianism as a Revolt Against Nature,' p. 5.

65 Rawls 'thinks that people do not deserve to profit from their superior abilities, because these are arbitrary from the moral point of view. If so, Rawls claims, equality is the default position and any departure from it requires justification': Gordon, D. (2017). One Flew over Equality. In *An Austro-Libertarian View, Vol. II*, p. 85.

66 *Cosmic Justice*, pp. 5, 6.

67 *Egalitarianism as a Revolt Against Nature*, p. v.

68 Ibid., p. xvii.

69 Ibid., p. xvii.

> Equality of all men—the egalitarian ideal—can only be achieved if all men are precisely uniform, precisely identical with respect to all of their attributes. The egalitarian world would necessarily be a world of horror fiction—a world of faceless and identical creatures, devoid of all individuality, variety, or special creativity. Indeed, it is precisely in horror fiction where the logical implications of an egalitarian world have been fully drawn.[70]

Indeed, given the diversity of human nature and market activity, the claim that calls for justification is the expectation that opportunities and outcomes in contexts of diversity ought to be equal.

In thus confronting the fundamental assumptions and ethical basis of egalitarianism, Rothbard's theory is radical. It is also radical in another sense, namely that it is not based principally on the standard reactionary arguments identified by Hirschman. As mentioned earlier, the standard way to oppose equality measures is to show that they are impractical, ineffective in meeting their stated goals, inadvertently give rise to a host of perverse incentives, and hurt those whom it is intended to help by undermining their self-reliance, self-determination, resilience and economic independence. These arguments are developed to great effect by scholars like Epstein and Sowell and will be examined in considerable detail in this book. Hirschman depicts this form of argument as a set of typical objections to progressive dreams: it is customary to argue against progressive legislation on grounds that it hurts those it is intended to help (which Hirschman calls the perversity thesis), socialism does not work (the futility thesis) and the cost of social engineering outweighs the benefits (the jeopardy thesis).[71] By categorising these arguments into three 'identical lines of reasoning' typically put forward in social justice debates, Hirschman depicts this form of argument as a reflex response with which reactionaries meet all progressive proposals. He implies that critics of the progressivist agenda react predictably in instinctive ideological opposition to the demands of socialism, which would cast doubt on the cogency of their arguments. As Gordon explains, 'the main point

---

[70] Ibid., p. 5.

[71] Hirschman, A. O. (1991). *The Rhetoric of Reaction: Perversity, Futility, Jeopardy*. Harvard University Press.

of Hirschman's polemic is that these arguments have been used again and again. If conservatives always trot them out, must we not suspect that the arguments are not altogether advanced in the cause of truth?'[72] But as Gordon points out, Hirschman's lines of reasoning just state the possible ways a policy proposal can be opposed by those who question whether the means are likely to achieve the stated goals, and any critique of a policy would be expected to resort to one or other of these grounds of opposition:

> His three theses, perversity, futility, and jeopardy, are all cases in which conservatives allege that measures they oppose will not achieve their ends. But, unless you argue that the aims of a proposal are flawed, that is virtually the only way you can oppose it. Almost any argument opposed to any proposal will take this form, so long as the aims of the proposal themselves are not subject to attack.[73]

Nor does Hirschman address critiques that fall outside his classification system, such as Rothbard's argument that egalitarian progressivism is unethical.[74] Moreover Hirschman concedes, as indeed he must, that if or when these arguments are true, they are devastating. Unless we are altogether to abandon intellectual inquiry and reasoned debate then we must persist in posing these questions: does equality law advance the cause of racial minorities? Does it work effectively in enhancing racial equality? Do the costs, including hidden and unintended costs, outweigh the benefits? These questions are explored in the book, but the book also addresses the deeper underlying concerns raised by Rothbard which may be summarised as follows.

First, egalitarianism revolts against nature by exhibiting disdain for human diversity and difference. As Flew argues, a disdain for difference leads in turn to a disdain for the classical notion of justice based on desert. The principle of desert envisages difference because it requires

[72] Gordon, D. (2017). Tea for One. In *An Austro-Libertarian View: Essays by David Gordon, Vol. III*, p. 6.

[73] Gordon, D. Tea for One, p. 7.

[74] 'He ignores another "rhetorical strategy" of free-market advocates and conservatives, the contention that leftist measures are immoral'. Gordon, D. Tea for One, p. 7.

'rendering to everyone their due' which will in turn inevitably produce varying outcomes: 'Their due, of course, will be their several and presumably often different deserts and entitlements – moral deserts and moral entitlements if we are talking about morals; legal [deserts] and legal [entitlements] if we are talking about the positive law'.[75] The idea of desert is central to the classical ideal of justice, thus in the classical ideal 'any conception that either rejects the notions of desert and entitlement or holds that those of everyone are in all respects, and without regard to any differences between individuals, equal, cannot be a conception of justice'.[76] If individual human beings are different then it is not unfair for them to have unequal endowments, and fairness requires neither that such endowments must be made equal nor that everyone must be granted an equal opportunity to do what others are able to do. By the same reasoning, conferring equal outcomes on all regardless of desert would be unjust. The incompatibility between a disdain for human diversity and the classical ideal of justice is central to Rothbard's rejection of egalitarianism.

The diversity of nature, and the wrongfulness of artificially equalising things which are naturally different, thus plays a central role in Rothbard's argument. It is because people are different that liberalism offers no promises that everyone will enjoy equal opportunities in life, but promises only the opportunity to strive towards our highest ideals and values. We may not all be the smartest boy in the schoolroom or the prettiest girl in the pageant, but the ideal of individual liberty makes possible a whole world of pursuits open for our enjoyment.[77] At the conceptual level, the ideal of having the opportunity to pursue

[75] A. Flew, Enforced Equality—Or Justice? p. 33.

[76] Ibid.

[77] Mises explains: 'Equality of opportunity is a factor neither in prize fights and beauty contests nor in any other field of competition, whether biological or social. The immense majority of people are by the physiological structure of their bodies deprived of a chance to attain the honors of a boxing champion or a beauty queen. Only very few people can compete on the labor market as opera singers and movie stars. The most favorable opportunity to compete in the field of scientific achievement is provided to the university professors. Yet, thousands and thousands of professors pass away without leaving any trace in the history of ideas and scientific progress, while many of the handicapped outsiders win glory through marvelous contributions': Mises, L. v. (2012). *Human Action: A Treatise on Economics* (p. 276). Martino Publishing (Original work published 1949).

the good life is distinct from the comparative issue as to whether that opportunity is 'equal' to the opportunities pursued by others. Thus the notion of equality of opportunity means nothing more than that everyone is entitled to the equal protection of the law: 'no one should be prevented by arbitrary obstacles from using his capacities to pursue his own objectives'.[78]

One might readily endorse access to basic needs such as education and health, or acknowledge the essential role played by schools and hospitals, without thereby committing oneself to an ideal of equality and indeed without committing oneself to a particular view of the role of the state in supplying basic needs. Access to education or health care, key determinants of the racialised experience, are important not merely by comparison between different races or ethnic groups but for the broader implications for individual liberty and human capabilities.[79] As will be seen later in the discussion of relative inequality, overall progress and attainment are more significant than comparison, disparities and gaps. The moral concern is for all to have sufficient resources, not for all to have equal resources, a principle which Harry Frankfurt terms 'the doctrine of sufficiency'.[80] The distinction between sufficiency and equality may seem at first glance to be overly nuanced, as some might argue that it is only through comparison that we can ascertain whether any person's basic needs are being sufficiently met. Poverty is a relative concept. Poor in Botswana means lacking clean drinking water, while poor in Britain means lacking a laptop and broadband with which to home-school during lockdown. Understanding relative poverty in a

[78] Friedman, M. (2018, March 8). What Does "Created Equal" Mean? *Hoover Institution.* https://www.hoover.org/research/what-does-created-equal-mean (Original work published 1990).

[79] 'The mistaken belief that economic equality is important in itself leads people to detach the problem of formulating their economic ambitions from the problem of understanding what is most fundamentally significant to them. It influences them to take too seriously, as though it were a matter of great moral concern, a question that is inherently rather insignificant and not directly to the point, namely, how their economic status compares with the economic status of others. In this way the doctrine of equality contributes to the moral disorientation and shallowness of our time.' Frankfurt, H. (1987). Equality as a Moral Ideal. 98 *Ethics, 21,* 23.

[80] The distinction between these two levels of concern lies at the heart of some of the critiques of egalitarianism: 'The fundamental error of egalitarianism lies in supposing that it is morally important whether one person has less than another regardless of how much either of them has.' Frankfurt, H. (1987). Equality as a Moral Ideal. 98 *Ethics, 21,* 34.

comparative sense is certainly relevant in evaluating human welfare. But the distinction between evaluating human flourishing and measuring comparative outcomes also has far reaching implications for law and legislation. The egalitarian focus on comparison and equalisation causes equality legislation to be institutionalised as a socially-constructed moral code binding those who might well support sufficiency through private charity without in any way being committed to mandatory equalisation schemes. Thus the issue is not whether kindness and charity ought to be directed towards the vulnerable and disadvantaged, but whether it ought to rely on individual choice and community spirit rather than legislative coercion.

A final point to address in understanding libertarian perspectives on equality is the egalitarian disdain for human ambition. To be more precise, it is not ambition in itself that is derided by egalitarianism, but the implications and outcomes of ambition in particular its association with economic growth and progress. Ambition is not encouraged by the social justice discourse because, as will be seen later in the discussion, it comes uncomfortably close to accusations of victim-blaming and lack of empathy for those lacking personal ambition. After all nobody ever had the 'ambition' to subsist on state welfare; government largesse is linked to victimhood and disadvantage, not to ambition. Further, there is little distinction in the public discourse between ambition as a desire to strive towards achievement and reward, and the notions of materialism, greed and selfishness with which socialists associate capitalist free markets. Egalitarians suppose that economic considerations and social well-being are mutually exclusive, and therefore embrace rhetoric that prioritises emotional altruism above economic prosperity. In his moral foundations theory Haidt explains this inclination as reflective of a care/harm moral paradigm in which caring for others or avoiding harm to them is seen as the overriding moral duty in a fair and just society.[81] This aligns with the progressive idea that 'rights' ought to be framed as positive duties—such as the duty to care for those who are vulnerable—unlike the classical definition of a right that entails negative duties—the duty not to cause

---

[81] Haidt, J. (2012). *The Righteous Mind: Why Good People Are Divided by Politics and Religion*. Penguin Books.

harm to others. Policies which can be framed directly as a way of caring for others, for example social welfare support, thus take priority over policies which have only indirect effects on 'caring' such as creating jobs.

In addressing these concerns, the premise of this book is that productivity and wealth creation are important not merely for their own sake but for their connectedness to individual liberty and human flourishing. The link between productivity and human flourishing has become obscure, or at least overlooked, over time, so that it is often supposed that those who pursue economic 'progress' are somehow lacking in 'morality'. It then seems to follow that socialists motivated by moral concerns can roll out their equalisation schemes without being unduly concerned about the implications for economic productivity.[82] Adam Smith's depiction of the market shows the error in delinking economic productivity from human well-being. Smith's famous analogy about appealing not to the benevolence of the baker but to his self-interest, sounds intolerable to modern virtue-signallers. No baker outside the annals of Randian fiction would be so reckless as to announce that he bakes bread to make money. He does it, of course, to feed the poor, to help society and to keep all our communities safe. Even Ikea solemnly informs us that it sells flatpack furniture to express its 'humanistic values' and its 'aim to be inclusive'.[83] The Financial Reporting Council advises corporate boards of directors to 'invite greater diversity and not only improve board and corporate performance but also unleash our full potential as human beings'.[84] This matters because we tend now to suppose that signalling benevolence and rising above self-interest is more socially acceptable than being productive.[85] The reality that the Smithian baker promotes the well-being of

[82] '"Progress" unguided by humanism is not progress': Pinker, S. (2019). *Enlightenment Now: The Case for Reason, Science, Humanism, and Progress* (p. 12). Penguin Books.

[83] Jolly, J. (2021, June 15). Brands Pull Ads from GB News TV Channel over Content Concerns. *The Guardian*. https://www.theguardian.com/media/2021/jun/15/brands-pull-ads-from-gb-news-tv-channel-over-content-concerns.

[84] Financial Reporting Council. (2021, July). *Board Diversity and Effectiveness in FTSE 350 Companies*. https://www.frc.org.uk/getattachment/3cc05eae-2024-45d8-b14c-abb2ac7497aa/FRC-Board-Diversity-and-Effectiveness-in-FTSE-350-Companies.pdf (p. 5).

[85] 'It is not from the benevolence of the butcher, the brewer, or the baker that we expect our dinner, but from their regard to their own interest. We address ourselves, not to their humanity but to their self-love, and never talk to them of our necessities but of their advantages.' Smith,

society without being driven by a deliberate intention to do so (his desire being simply to bake and sell the bread) is increasingly obscured by the social pressure to express a commitment to social responsibility, so that self-interest wherever it may be detected is deemed to be synonymous with greed, selfishness and dishonesty and thus not worthy of being disclosed in polite society. We denounce the Smithian baker for his self-regarding motives while overlooking the value we gain from his commitment to his tradecraft. We are more concerned with evaluating the morality of his stated motives, how practised he is in the language of emotional intelligence and 'unleashing our full potential', than with the incentives driving him successfully to pursue his trade and keep the bread baskets in stock.

Continuing with the Smithian analogy, in prioritising redistribution over productivity we suppose that productivity can 'take care of itself' without the need for government intervention, while redistribution needs concerted state action. There is always more for the government to do in implementing redistributive schemes, but somehow or other (the particular mechanisms are considered to be of little relevance to public policy) the baker will always rise each morning and find a way to bake his bread without state input. Perhaps he bakes on autopilot. He cannot help it. Baking bread is in his blood. He does not worry about property taxes, wage regulation or trade licence fees, nor does he mind being denounced as a profiteer when he responds to rising demand by raising his prices. He would not mind being compelled to hire workers to meet a racial quota. Even if he might have preferred to hire only friends and family, who happen to belong to his own race, he will not fold up his business just because he is forced to hire some workers of a different race. He just endlessly bakes delicious baguettes to feed the hungry. That being the case the only question that need concern public policy would be how to distribute the bread equally. Thus encroachment upon individual liberty does not unduly trouble the proponents of equality who suppose productivity to be ubiquitous—the baker will carry on baking regardless of incentives or disincentives, so there will always be bread to

---

A. (1993). *An Inquiry into the Nature & Causes of the Wealth of Nations: A Selected Edition*, Vol. 1 ch. 2. (K. Sutherland, Ed.) (p. 21). Oxford University Press (original work published 1776).

distribute. Logically, if there is no bread in the first place there will be nothing to distribute, but economic logic has no influence in a worldview governed by the moral imperatives of equality because achieving the goals of equality would justify any decline in productivity. A bread shortage, should that result, would be deemed to satisfy the demands of social justice if there was no inequality with some having more bread than others. The government would be called upon once more to ensure equality in bread rationing.

This prioritisation of equality above all else, is, in that sense, a denunciation of the value of individual liberty, reason, common sense, and ultimately as Rothbard says a 'revolt against the ontological structure of reality itself'.[86] The focus on redistribution presumes that 'the technological and material appurtenances of our economy could be preserved even if the intellectual foundations on which they are based were destroyed'.[87] The set of priorities identified by social justice, focusing on redistribution while ignoring productivity, fails to grasp the reality that productivity depends on the underlying framework of economic freedom. The delineation of individual rights and freedoms matters precisely because 'the quantity of things produced in a capitalist society is not independent of the manner in which production is carried on'.[88] It is wrong to suppose that we could take or leave liberty and still enjoy all the wealth that springs from, presumably, the government's paper money printing press. Everybody benefits from the wealth and prosperity produced in free enterprise societies, and thus egalitarians do not generally claim to be opposed to productivity in itself but rather are concerned about the priority accorded to productive activity and with unequal wealth distribution. They may be willing in principle to encourage economic progress and prosperity, but only subject to the self-defeating proviso that account is taken of distributive implications by reference to race, sex, class and an expanding range of other parameters by which it is proposed that central planners should reallocate opportunities to where they are most needed in the interests of justice, through coercion if necessary, with the blasé

86 Rothbard, *Egalitarianism as a Revolt*.

87 Mises, *Liberalism*, p. 60.

88 Ibid., p. 42.

presumption that this will not unduly affect productivity. This ignores the role of liberty in productivity and progress. As Mises points out, if we destroy the liberal foundations of free enterprise, prosperity inevitably falls:

> The ultimate and most profound of the fundamental insights of liberal thought is that it is ideas that constitute the foundation on which the whole edifice of human social cooperation is constructed and sustained and that a lasting social structure cannot be built on the basis of false and mistaken ideas.[89]

For these reasons, rather than blithely presuming the ideal of equality to be self-evidently justified without closely examining its underlying ethical foundations, the onus is on egalitarians to justify their equalisation schemes. Rothbard argues that equality mandates which fly in the face of reality are not ethical because 'correct ethics must be in accord with human nature'.[90]

Egalitarians, who often take great umbrage at the suggestion that human beings are natural creatures, might argue that we do not have to live according to our nature. They remind us that we are more sophisticated than, say, lobsters. Human nature is not immutable. We need not be guided by our frail human nature in pursuit of the good but should seek to improve upon our natural predilections. These arguments are to an extent quite reasonable. Many people join religious and other social groups precisely because they do not want to be slaves to their natural predilections but would strive to be better than they are. Less sugar, more exercise. Certainly we can all behave better if we set our minds to it, and it is tempting to use legal mandates to steer us all in the right direction. The law could easily nudge us along with a few moderately painful sanctions—nothing unreasonable, not like the gulag—just a few carefully tailored penalties to focus our minds on the goal. Financial compensation or reparations for present or past inequalities could serve as useful reminders of the equality ideals to which we should all

[89] Ibid., p. 119.
[90] Ibid., p. vi.

aspire. Why stop there? As we collectively try to be better people why not harness the legal system to keep us all on the straight and narrow? Unless we can offer persuasive answers to these questions, there is no reason to oppose the quest for total equality. As Gordon asks, 'Why not try to counteract inequality whatever its source?'[91] Gordon is right to point out that if the logistics, costs and excesses were all that would be at stake in the overweening equalisation programmes, there would be no valid reason not to make the attempt to pursue egalitarian ideals. After all, as Gordon argues, 'Egalitarians think that equality has intrinsic value: they advocate it for its own sake, not just to forestall bad consequences'.[92]

Thus the relationship between law and equality must be examined on its own merits. The 'Rhodes must fall' movement illustrates the hazards of responding to an ideological quest for equality with arguments rooted in cost and practicality. The British government patted itself on the back for a 'very British coup' in saving Rhodes by introducing a costly and time-consuming consultation process to forestall the toppling of statues. Oriel College Oxford, custodian of the Rhodes statue, announced that it very much wished Rhodes to fall, as demanded by those who consider the statue to be violent, but balked at the costs of the new procedural prerequisites. There was much rejoicing in the land. Everyone congratulated the government for refusing to be cowed by those who would destroy British culture. But before long the Oxford equality activists were back, threatening to go on strike until Rhodes comes down.[93] This illustrates well the hazards of pointing to the costs of meeting equality mandates as a basis for opposing egalitarian claims. If the statue of Rhodes is indeed a source of violence to ethnic minorities, then procedural safeguards are no guarantee of its endurance—and why should they be? If such cultural icons are indeed harmful then cost alone should not be a bar to their destruction.

The principled debate cannot be evaded. As Rothbard cautions, 'if one side is granted ethics and the "ideal" from the start, then that side

[91] Gordon, D. Wrestling Reality from Rawls. In *An Austro-Libertarian View, Vol. II*, p. 57.

[92] Gordon, D. Don't Dream the Impossible. In *An Austro-Libertarian View, Vol. II*, p. 148.

[93] Badshah, N. (2021, June 10). Cecil Rhodes: Oriel College Faces Teaching Boycott over Refusal to Remove Statue. *The Guardian*. https://www.theguardian.com/education/2021/jun/10/oriel-college-faces-teaching-boycott-over-refusal-to-remove-rhodes-statue.

will be able to effect gradual but sure changes in its own direction; and as these changes accumulate, the stigma of "impracticality" becomes less and less directly relevant'.[94] Thus it is important to emphasise that impracticalities and overwhelming costs are not the worst that results when law attempts to override our essential human nature. Instead, no sooner are a few steps taken down that road than tyranny follows: 'Everywhere in nature we find inequality. Attempts to remake human beings so that everyone fits the same mold lead inevitably to tyranny'.[95] Personal choice, freedom of conscience and freedom to associate or disassociate are sacrificed when the law, public institutions and 'teachers and preachers of morality'[96] embark on a project to realise their egalitarian dreams. In that light this book engages with the central justification for egalitarian theories in legislative policy.

In explicating the nexus between equality and justice Gordon poses two key questions which this book sets out to address: 'Does justice ideally demand equality? Are differences in abilities among people in some sense unfair?'[97] These are profound questions that cannot be answered comprehensively within the confines of a single book, but the aim here is to offer a partial response focusing on fairness and justice as depicted within the legislative framework, and specifically as that framework operates in the context of employment regulation. That may seem to be an unduly narrow focus for an inquiry into equality and fairness, but employment regulation constitutes perhaps the most visible locus of the exercise of economic freedom as a component of individual liberty. If we understand better the impact of law upon economic freedom in the employment context that may suggest helpful answers to some of the broader questions about the interplay between freedom, equality and justice. In framing the scope of this argument it may also be observed that race is not the only legally protected characteristic, and it may be questioned whether it is worth analysing race without reference to the

[94] *Egalitarianism as a Revolt*, p. 1.

[95] Ibid., p. vi.

[96] Hayek, F. A. (2013). *Law, Legislation and Liberty: A New Statement of the Liberal Principles of Justice and Political Economy* (p. 230). Routledge (Original work published 1973).

[97] Gordon, D. (2017). Wrestling Reality from Rawls. In *An Austro-Libertarian View Vol. II*, p. 58.

other protected grounds. Again this may be justified by reference to centrality of racial diversity to understanding employment regulation. Race was one of the first grounds to be protected (along with sex) by antidiscrimination legislation and thus offers a useful focus for a discussion of contemporary equality legislation. Compared to other protected characteristics, race has played a dominant role in the development of this legislation since its earliest inception in the civil rights era of the United States. The context of employment has in turn occupied the centre stage in understanding racial equality and the racial discrimination.[98] Therefore by studying race discrimination in the context of employment we gain insight not only into the challenges posed by racial inequality but also into the operation of equality legislation more generally.

1.4 Premises of the Argument

Having offered an overview of the broader context of our discussion, this part of the Introduction sets out the essential premises on which the argument in the book is constructed. As earlier observed, the book argues that equality legislation and the egalitarian foundations of that legislation are inimical to justice. The book rejects the idea that state intervention is justified if it is designed to promote equality, arguing that the presumed worthiness of a legislative goal does not justify such intervention if its ethical foundations are unsound. We argue that legislative policies conferring special rights and privileges on selected groups to the exclusion of others, in a bid to equalise socio-economic outcomes, lack any sound moral or ethical justification and offer nothing more than a superficial appearance of moral idealism. To those who ask 'By what right are you proposing to employ the machinery of the state to impose on everybody, or more often it is everybody else, your own

[98] 'Employment is perhaps the single most important measure of life-chances. It is at the centre of most discussions not just of racial equality but of social justice generally.' Modood, T., Berthoud, R., Lakey, J., Nazroo, J., Smith, P., Virdee, S., & Beishon, S. (1997). *Ethnic Minorities in Britain: Diversity and Disadvantage* (p. 5). Series: PSI report (843). London: Policy Studies Institute.

personal ideal?'[99] the egalitarian would answer that the wondrous vision of cohesive communities bound by fairness and equality is no imposition because *everyone supports it*. The purpose of the much derided virtue-signalling is precisely to show that everyone supports the public pursuit of moral virtue. Our laws are said to be derived from unanimous, or at least democratic (which is the next best thing) support. The legal framework is therefore said to reflect the outcome of some form of social contract, and we are entreated to respect and uphold our legal duties even if we have different opinions about what the law should uphold. Nobody is entitled to storm the Houses of Parliament, or Capitol Hill, just because they disagree with the law.

But it is a basic principle of the rule of law that encroachment on fundamental rights cannot be justified by reference to majority agreement in favour of violating such rights. Thus it does not suffice for egalitarian principles to appeal to democratic mandates for moral validation. To those who value truth, reason, logic and doing what they believe to be right according to the dictates of their conscience, it is not acceptable to identify what is just or fair by reference to a majority vote or popular opinion. It is true that many horrors have been perpetrated in the name of doing what one believes to be 'right' and every demagogue and charlatan professes himself to believe that he is doing the right thing, but this is no reason to rule out individual conscience as relevant to ascertaining the qualities of the good life, nor to imposing through legislative mandates one particular worldview of what is 'right' on those who have reason to disagree. On the contrary, it highlights the importance of testing political claims not by reference to the labels they bear such as 'justice' or 'fairness' but by standards and ideals such as individual liberty that have stood the test of time. The need to revisit the philosophical foundations of social justice in the context of promoting equality therefore becomes imperative.

The philosophical arguments against egalitarian idealism can be constructed on a number of grounds, and this book draws upon four interrelated grounds: that egalitarianism undermines social cohesion by encouraging envy and resentment, it destroys individual liberty, it leads

99 Flew, Enforced Equality—Or Justice? p. 39.

ultimately to totalitarianism, and it is, in sum, unethical and unjust. Racial justice and special preferment of disadvantaged groups are said to be necessary for the most laudatory motives, but in addition to lacking sound ethical foundations the egalitarian vision of social justice undermines equality under the law and destroys the individual liberty which animates economic freedom. The book offers a different basis on which to understand progress for racial minorities, highlighting the importance of formal equality before the law in defending the freedoms that undergird peaceful exchange, social cohesion, progress and prosperity.

The central argument here is not simply that the demands of equality are inappropriately framed, nor that they in some sense go 'too far' in their pursuit of social justice. Nor is this merely an extended complaint about the excesses of the 'wokism', 'political correctness' or 'cancel culture' that blight our daily interactions. The more pressing task is to answer the egalitarians who insist that they are prepared to sacrifice free speech, prosperity, even happiness, if that is what it takes to be kinder, more generous, more empathetic, to those who are suffering. It should be remembered that these are often the same people who are prepared to sacrifice human existence itself in order to promote the ends of social justice: the rights of the environment, the welfare of animals, the needs of future generations. The egalitarian agenda is in that sense profoundly antihuman. Rothbard explains:

> An egalitarian society can only hope to achieve its goals by totalitarian methods of coercion; and, even here, we all believe and hope the human spirit of individual man will rise up and thwart any such attempts to achieve an ant-heap world. In short, the portrayal of an egalitarian society is horror fiction because, when the implications of such a world are fully spelled out, we recognize that such a world and such attempts are profoundly antihuman; being antihuman in the deepest sense, the egalitarian goal is, therefore, evil and any attempts in the direction of such a goal must be considered evil as well.[100]

Egalitarian theories of redistributive justice offer a beguiling vision of a world where all are equal. All people of good will wish for fairness and

[100] *Egalitarianism as a Revolt*, p. 8.

equality to prevail, and therefore find this vision superficially appealing. But closer analysis reveals this vision to be constructed on the premise that glorious ends justify tyrannical means. The reality of this Utopia is ultimately 'antihuman' in denying the nature of human diversity and human interaction. Rothbard states the case powerfully:

> Since their methodology and their goals deny the very structure of humanity and of the universe, the egalitarians are profoundly antihuman; and, therefore, their ideology and their activities may be set down as profoundly evil as well. Egalitarians do not have ethics on their side unless one can maintain that the destruction of civilization, and even of the human race itself, may be crowned with the laurel wreath of a high and laudable morality.[101]

In pursuit of goals of the highest worthiness egalitarians are hardly likely to be troubled by matters such as the loss of free speech or economic freedoms, which they regard as utterly trivial. The inherent attractiveness of their moral ideals *easily* overcomes the demands of reason or rationality. As will be seen later, they have no concern for the ethical implications of persistently bombarding ethnic minorities with messages of hopelessness and futility, insisting that oppressed minorities lack free will and their only path to self-esteem or self-worth is through identity politics and restricting the freedoms of others. They remain committed to the pursuit of their moral ideal, in this case the social, financial and political equality of all people, even when it is crystal clear that the means chosen patently cannot produce the desired end. Indeed, the more unworkable their methods are shown to be, the more determined they become to strive more valiantly towards their preferred ideal. This very human desire to strive towards moral ideals is powerful. People will often do whatever it takes to meet their goal if they consider their goal to be worthy of the attempt. Sowell may be right to point out that cosmic justice is unattainable, but governments do not generally detain themselves unduly in philosophical inquiries before promising voters that they will attain the unattainable within the next two to five years. It is no

[101] Ibid., p. 20.

wonder that *Mission: Impossible* so captures the popular imagination, as striving relentlessly towards unattainable goals without regard for the consequences is but the flip side of one of humanity's most admirable traits: our fortitude and resilience, our determination to pursue our moral ideals and highest goals even in the face of adversity. As Nozick writes, 'It is quite difficult to resist the allure of the "ideal situation", to avoid hoping and believing that things will manage to work out better this next time'.[102]

But life is not a Hollywood set. Our desire to pursue goals that help us to feel that we are good people too often overrides the objective search for truth or the identification of principles that work in practice, which in Rothbard's view are two sides of the same coin: principles that are true, work, and principles that are not true do not work. Untrue principles may give a short term appearance of success, long enough to cover perhaps an illustrious political career, but they always end in failure sooner or later.[103] In proposing grand equalisation schemes egalitarians do not require their ideals to be underpinned by any objective truth, as they consider truth to be a subjective construct—your truth, my truth, etc.—that must be set aside in order to arrive at a reasonable moral consensus. In upholding fairness, Rawlsian liberals are therefore not concerned with the objective correctness or truth of ideas or moral principles.[104] Indeed, they would regard undue concern with 'truth' as a sign of unreasonableness or maybe even religiosity, and thereby a threat to peace and social stability in raising the prospect of warring factions seeking the dominance of their religious, moral or political 'truth'. Having thus set aside any concern for truth, what appears to the rational observer to be hypocrisy is to them merely an emanation of overlapping 'truths'. If the moral ideals they proclaim do not match the underlying facts, they would explain that as merely a reflection of the

[102] Nozick, R. (1990). *The Examined Life: Philosophical Meditations* (pp. 283, 284). Touchstone.

[103] Niemietz, K. (2019). *Socialism: The Failed Idea That Never Dies.* Institute for Economic Affairs.

[104] 'The question whether the opinions that overlap in this consensus are correct or true, and whether those reasons are valid or sound, is to be set aside by public reason, i.e. in decision-making on the fundamental questions of political life and legislation.' Finnis, J. (2007). *On Public Reason* (Notre Dame Legal Studies Paper No. 06–37; Oxford Legal Studies Research Paper No. 1/2007). http://ssrn.com/abstract=955815.

importance of promoting moral values without regard to any particular version of truth.

This book takes a different view, proceeding on the premise that not all ideals have equal value. Ideological claims, moral values and social visions must be evaluated by reference to whether they are based on objective truth rather than accorded an 'immunity from criticism'; as Rothbard writes:

> While candor in proclaiming one's values may be admirable, it is surely not enough; in the quest for truth it is scarcely sufficient to proclaim one's value judgments as if they must be accepted as tablets from above that are not themselves subject to intellectual criticism and evaluation. Is there no requirement that these value judgments be in some sense valid, meaningful, cogent, true?[105]

One way to test the truth of ideals is by evaluating them against principles whose validity has been objectively tested over hundreds of years. This is the method by which we know that socialism does not work—by observing it to have been tried and failed several times. True principles withstand the test of time, when evaluated in the long run. The classical tradition draws upon the wisdom of the ages precisely because time offers a vast laboratory in which ideas are tested so that we have evidence of what works and what does not, and we can see the results or consequences of false premises. Despite protestations that the track record of failed socialist experiments were not *real* socialism because real socialism has never been tried, we can see that the only practicable forms in which socialist ideals have been implemented have ended in misery and tyranny.[106] Thus Rothbard also cautions that ideals worth pursuing must be not only ethical but also practicable, capable of being achieved in real world conditions rather than merely a vision of what could be achieved in ideal circumstances:

---

[105] Rothbard, *Egalitarianism as a Revolt*, pp. 3, 4.

[106] 'Mises and Hayek demonstrated incontrovertibly that a socialist economy cannot work; to make matters worse, the attempt to establish such an economy makes likely the onset of a totalitarian order …[but] rationality is not a trait much in evidence among the socialistically inclined. If reason speaks against socialism, is not the solution obvious: out with reason!': Gordon, D. (2017). Finding Meaning. In *An Austro-Libertarian View, Vol. 1*, pp. 361–362.

> If an ethical ideal is inherently 'impractical,' that is, if it cannot work in practice, then it is a poor ideal and should be discarded forthwith. To put it more precisely, if an ethical goal violates the nature of man and/or the universe and, therefore, cannot work in practice, then it is a bad ideal and should be dismissed as a goal. If the goal itself violates the nature of man, then it is also a poor idea to work in the direction of that goal.[107]

Before concluding this introductory chapter, some further comments on the scope of the study should be mentioned. In challenging the ethical foundations of egalitarianism the book examines the implications of some of the most influential philosophical ideas, but the book does not of course attempt to develop a complete or even partial theory of liberal justice. Nor does the book offer a comprehensive philosophical treatment of liberalism or attempt to survey the entire field. The aim is not to resolve the philosophical debates about the meaning of justice or to reconcile the broad spectrum of classical liberal perspectives on freedom and equality. The difficulty of embarking on such an enterprise is compounded by the tendency for the underlying assumptions of the different positions to remain implicit, especially when their proponents regard their premises as too self-evident to require explicit exposition. Further complexity is added by commentators disagreeing on what precisely different thinkers espoused. Rather than attempt generally to unravel these types of philosophical contestations this book focuses on a rather different, but related, field of inquiry, namely the philosophical foundations of legal doctrine and the underlying rationales influencing the jurisprudence of equality legislation. Although the book has made explicit its conceptual premises and the notions of liberty which it propounds, it is not directly concerned with the conceptual disputation surrounding ideas of justice and equality on which there is a vast literature that is not canvassed here. Instead the book aims to clarify our understanding of the role of law in liberal market societies by evaluating how law harnesses the concepts of justice and equality to frame legal rules in contexts such as employment when specific disputes arise for legal settlement. The book is therefore concerned with how we frame

[107] Ibid.

legislative goals, how we justify the steps we take to achieve those goals, and the role of law and legislation in enforcing social and moral ideals. The discussion focuses primarily on the legal and policy framework in the UK, but the conceptual framework and examples are relevant in understanding the law in other common law jurisdictions.

1.5 Overview of the Book

This chapter has set out the conceptual framework of the book and identified the premises of the argument to advanced. The book is concerned with the academic discourse on racial equality, a field of inquiry which has expanded over the past few decades to encompass many facets human action: philosophical, economic, political and sociological. The book is in that sense an interdisciplinary study, primarily focusing on legal doctrine but also drawing upon ideas in philosophy and political economy in order to examine more closely the egalitarian principles underpinning the legal framework and its implications for society. The book does not attempt to survey the field generally, nor to review all that has been written from different perspectives, but focuses on the core legislative framework and how the ideas which underpin and justify that framework may be understood from a classical liberal perspective. This final section offers an overview of the essential structure of the discussion in the ensuing chapters. Rather than summarise the precise content of the book it may be more helpful to highlight the key themes to be explored and how those themes support the argument advanced in the book.

Chapter 2 discusses in more detail the apparent moral consensus around contemporary liberal tenets of social justice. The chapter explains the reasons for rejecting Rawls's premise of 'public reason' as the appropriate starting point in evaluating the interplay between freedom and justice in contexts of racial diversity. Rawls's public reason treats substantive equality as an essential component of distributive justice, while this book rejects the premises underlying both substantive equality and distributive justice. The chapter argues that in the absence of unanimity on what constitutes 'justice' or 'fairness' people must be free to disagree concerning their moral obligations, leaving each person free to follow the path that seems right. Rather than engage in an endless clash of deeply held moral ideals, or attempt to compel others to follow moral ideologies with which they fundamentally disagree, the chapter suggests a more fruitful approach. The chapter makes the case for regulating public life less through legislative mandates and more through standards and mechanisms that allow the greatest possible scope for individual decision-making and freedom to pursue different conceptions of the good. The chapter depicts the 'war against racism' as being, far from a unanimous liberal position, one that masks deep philosophical and ideological disputation. While socialist ideology considers social engineering to be the proper function of state power, classical liberalism takes a different view. The egalitarian desire for substantive equality, far from being a pure desire for fairness, is rooted largely in comparison, envy and resentment. These are not worthy sentiments. On the contrary they have been regarded since time immemorial as vices. The preoccupation with disparities and comparative rates of progress between different racial groups transforms envy from an unworthy vice into a virtue—labelled 'social justice'—that demands vindication through legal claims. But not even conditions behind the Rawlsian 'veil of ignorance' can transform vice into virtue. Egalitarian worldviews are purely subjective, and there are good reasons to reject them as a basis for legislative policy. Egalitarian schemes have no power to improve the lives of the disadvantaged; on the contrary, as Sowell argues, such schemes search for unattainable value in those with greater endowments and seek to appropriate that value through coercive means in pursuit of a superficial make-believe equality.

Chapter 3 evaluates the basis of the claim that equality law is needed to correct and atone for historical grievances and to reverse past discrimination. Slavery and colonialism were oppressive and exploitative, and the claim is that this legislation can help to expiate that evil and reverse its residual harms. Yet the anti-racism drive is no longer about emancipation or freedom; it seeks instead to have racial difference explicitly embraced by the institutional framework, to have racial identity acknowledged in public discourse, and for race to be a prime determinant in allocating public resources. In that context the claims for state-sponsored equity have assumed a more amorphous character, with concrete goals for material and financial reward increasingly supplemented by the general aim of keeping people safe from suffering emotional and psychic harm said to be caused by racism. The chapter argues that it is wrong to conflate racial disparities with racial discrimination and economic inequality. Various studies are examined which identify multiple causes of socio-economic inequality that have nothing to do with racial discrimination. Inequality, like most complex social phenomena, has several contributing factors: not only ethnic and family origins but also education, cultural attitudes, demographics, geography, history, and labour market conditions, plus unmeasurable personal factors like character, industriousness and resilience. None of these factors is, by itself, deterministic and the studies surveyed do not attempt to delineate the relative weight of each factor given the wide contextual variations. The chapter makes the case that the value of economic freedom and prosperity ought not to depend simply on comparisons and statistical disparities between different identity-based groups, but must draw also upon other related ideals and values of the good society including the recognition that, ultimately, our fortunes are all linked. Any growth in a society's prosperity and abundance means a growth in opportunities for all members of that society. This does not depend on a claim that markets are perfect, treat everyone perfectly fairly, and produce perfect equality, but rather a claim that free markets have proved over time to be the most reliable path to prosperity.

Chapter 4 evaluates some of the key arguments generally advanced to justify antidiscrimination legislation. This legislation is often defended on the basis that without equality protection most people would immediately embark on unfairly discriminating against others—a belief in the generally malign nature of human beings who would set about oppressing those outside their own racial group if the law did not force them to behave better. It is also said that even where people show kindness to one another the legislation is needed as an aspirational standard or guideline, to nudge them, in the manner of an indulgent but firm parent, to remember their manners and make the guests feel welcome. It is also inordinately costly, in that it overlooks the wider unintended effects of antidiscrimination legislation. Three main effects are highlighted: the tendency for antidiscrimination legislation to expand in scope over time, the perverse incentive structure created by the legislative framework including its implementation by the courts, and most importantly the implications for economic liberty. The chapter examines in more detail how the legal framework addresses these challenges in the context of the employment contract. Disparities in employment, wages and income provide an instructive case study in understanding the quest for equality. It is through employment that most people engage in productive activity, earn an income, pursue their career aspirations and participate meaningfully in social and economic life. The chapter argues that while the law stops short of creating a free-standing right not to be discriminated against, when read in light of the egalitarian ideals underlying the growing policy focus on 'equity' it can be seen that the law in practice mandates *unequal* treatment as a means of equalising racial outcomes. While the classical ideal of equality requires fair rules of the game and the absence of arbitrary barriers to participation, political pressure to advance equity effectively requires an extensive programme of wealth distribution. In arguing that there is no right not to be discriminated against nor a right to have one's interests advanced by the state this chapter sets the stage for the discussion in chapter five of the role of free enterprise in achieving progress for racial minorities.

Chapter 5 reasserts the importance of economic freedom as a component of individual liberty in promoting wider participation in economic life for racial minorities. The chapter argues that such progress is most effectively achieved through freedom, not in spite of or at the expense of freedom. A market-oriented approach to resolving the challenges of racial inequality must reflect the underlying normative values of individual liberty. Liberty ultimately enhances human life. Where market participation plays the dominant role in shaping socio-economic outcomes, society as a whole benefits from encouraging cooperation through voluntary exchange. The chapter argues that our freedom and ability to make choices, to exercise free will, to exercise individual agency or autonomy in ordering our own lives, to experience self-realisation or self-actualisation, is inherent in everyone's humanity and a necessary component of living a meaningful life. It is wrong to suppose that ethnic minorities care nothing for economic freedom or living a fully human life, and wish only to complain about historical grievances while demanding financial retribution against others. To be the author of one's own life and to experience a sense of pride and self-worth in one's own achievements however humble they might be is not a privilege reserved only for the rich and famous. Nor does living a meaningful life depend on how much wealth one's group enjoys compared to other groups, as is supposed by egalitarians preoccupied with measuring group disparities. The individual liberty defended by classical liberalism represents an important aspect of what is valuable in the human experience, what it means to be fully human, constraints and challenges included. To say that one lacks free will or self-responsibility because of their disadvantaged race or because of racial discrimination or because of unhappy historical legacies, is to deny members of disadvantaged groups an important facet of their own humanity. It amounts to a defeatist approach to life. Classical liberalism may not promise to construct a world with no unfairness and no social problems, but it promises to resolve pressing social problems more effectively than the alternatives and has proved over time to be more effective than egalitarian schemes in yielding the sought-after economic gains without destroying society in the process. The argument is not that classical liberalism is a philosophy with no drawbacks, but that even with its drawbacks it yields better outcomes for racial minorities than progressive ideologies. The reasons are rooted in the importance of economic freedom for human flourishing.

Chapter 6 concludes by summarising the core message of the book, which is that we are not called simply to decide whether 'liberty' should trump 'equality' in an abstract sense, but to address a deeper and more concrete concern about the meaning and value of these ideals for the rule of law.

2

Liberalism and Equality

The starting point in understanding the policy framework of racial justice and other forms of social justice is to reiterate the importance of formal equality in classical liberalism. It is often stated in the public discourse that social justice demands racial equality, with little careful consideration of what is meant by equality. Nor is the matter clarified by distinguishing between opportunity and outcome, as the social justice discourse slips seamlessly from 'opportunity' to 'diversity' to 'disparities' to 'inequalities' and 'inequities', resulting always in new proposals for wealth redistribution. In adopting the language of 'inequity' the claim made by proponents of legislative interventions is that formal equality does not suffice to meet the demands of justice. The contemporary conceptualisation of social justice identifies a just society by reference to substantive or material equality, with the automatic designation of wealth inequality as an injustice. Something more than equality is demanded, requiring concerted effort by government to eradicate inequality and achieve 'equity'. A typical expression of this requirement is reflected in President Joe Biden's January 2021 announcement of his intention to pursue 'a comprehensive approach to advancing equity for

W. Njoya, *Economic Freedom and Social Justice*, Palgrave Studies in Classical Liberalism, https://doi.org/10.1007/978-3-030-84852-1_2

all, including people of color and others who have been historically underserved, marginalized, and adversely affected by persistent poverty and inequality'.[1] Against that background, the aim of this chapter is to evaluate the liberal democratic consensus surrounding contemporary tenets of social justice. The chapter explains the reasons for rejecting Rawls's premise of 'public reason' as the appropriate starting point in understanding the meaning of justice.

As Kukathas argues, the justification for the state playing the primary role in implementing distributive justice is that 'the state should be guided by a substantive view of the good life (which it may justifiably promote)' in contrast to the classical liberal position which holds that 'the state should remain neutral about the good life'.[2] To extrapolate the classical liberal position on the good life in contexts of racial diversity this chapter evaluates and defends the classical ideal of justice based on formal equality. The argument is that whatever political claims can be made in support of 'affirmatively advancing equity', such claims cannot be founded in a theory of justice. The Rawlsian stipulation that equality is self-evidently worth promoting in order to uphold social justice precludes the very inquiry which the book aims to conduct. To clear the slate for a subsequent analysis of formal equality and achieving progress through market participation this chapter argues that in the absence of unanimity on what constitutes 'justice' or 'fairness' people must be free to disagree, leaving each person free to follow the path that seems right. Classical liberalism offers a theoretical framework within which to respect this philosophical diversity.

Contemporary social justice discourse deems classical ideals of equality and justice to be unsuited to modern demands of racial equality. To address that concern this chapter considers the meaning of equality and justice in the classical tradition, explaining the value of these ideals and why they are worth defending. Classical liberalism treats individual

---

[1] The White House. (2021, January 20). *Executive Order on Advancing Racial Equity and Support for Underserved Communities Through the Federal Government*. https://www.whitehouse.gov/briefing-room/presidential-actions/2021/01/20/executive-order-advancing-racial-equity-and-support-for-underserved-communities-through-the-federal-government/.

[2] Kukathas, C. (2003). *The Liberal Archipelago: A Theory of Diversity and Freedom* (p. 5). Oxford University Press.

liberty as valuable in itself, as an emanation of individual self-ownership. Racial equality, and the legal endorsement and promotion of its collectivist, socialist, racialist visions, threatens liberty by threatening the concept of the individual. Individualism recognises the broad diversity of perspectives within and between different ethnic groups, genders, and other identity-based 'communities' in relation to social ideals and the pursuit of the good life. Diversity of opinion, moral values and the best way to pursue happiness are fatally obscured by preoccupation with group outcomes. Classical liberalism looks to the benefits of individual liberty as a prerequisite to human flourishing and prosperity. The classical ideal of liberty upholds formal equality without granting special favours to one group or another on the basis of race, class, wealth, or any other personal characteristics. As Mises explains:

> The liberals of the eighteenth century, guided by the ideas of natural law and of the Enlightenment, demanded for everyone equality of political and civil rights because they assumed that all men are equal...What is imperishable in man – his spirit – is undoubtedly the same in rich and poor, noble and commoner, white and colored.[3]

The influence of formal equality in shaping the ideals of justice and fairness has evolved over a long history.[4] It is necessary to address one of the objections sometimes heard for abandoning the lessons of history including classical interpretations of justice and fairness, namely that ideas from an age when the importance of racial sensitivity had not been appreciated ought no longer to be studied. Calls to 'decolonise the syllabus' suggest that ideas should be selected for study based on the racial or cultural identity of the author. That being the case it seems to follow that influential classical scholars should be disregarded due to the outmoded, insensitive or even racist language that may be found in their texts and correspondence, or because they were known to have ancestors or friends who profited from slavery, or because in some other way they

[3] Mises, L. v. (2005). *Liberalism: The Classical Tradition* (B. B. Greaves, Ed., p. 9). Indianapolis: Liberty Fund (Original work published 1927).

[4] 'Historically, liberalism was the first political movement that aimed at promoting the welfare of all, not that of special groups'. Ibid., p. xxii.

have fallen short of modern standards of politeness and courtesy. For example, David Hume wrote in his *Essays* published in 1777 that 'There never was a civilized nation of any other complexion than white, nor even any individual eminent either in action or speculation'. We might choose, then, not to study Hume in the same way as some choose not to listen to the music or enjoy the art of classical composers and artists, many of whom would not be classified as paragons of virtue if judged by reference to modern sensibilities including some who could perhaps be described as downright unpleasant. Yet progress in life requires that we build upon what is already known not only in science, culture and the arts but also in philosophical thought, ethics, morality, and in choosing the personal codes by which to live our lives. Choosing not to draw upon what is already known, trying to 'reset' our understanding of the world by redefining the principles of natural law to suit changing tastes and fashions, throwing out the dictionary and making up new meanings for words, is not progress. That approach would amount to complaining about being left behind while choosing to fall even further behind, knowing and understanding even less of the world, as the wheel of human progress continues to turn.

At the time of writing, scientific advancements do not enable us to travel back in time to advise those who lived centuries before us to mind their language, to be a bit more sensitive, to respect racial diversity. Nor, looking ahead, are we able selectively to stop the march of time to enable groups who are lagging behind others to catch up. As long as there is time, there will be differential ideas, abilities, ambitions and fortunes, which will always enable some to race ahead of others in the immediate and shorter term leaving everyone else to catch up in due course and at different speeds.[5] This might seem at first sight a painful state of affairs, and it is one that often embroils the great 'left-behind' in envy and resentment, yet it is eventually resolved by a longer term perspective on human progress.[6] Much has been said about the exponential rise in

[5] 'There is in man, in so far as he is a thinking being, an inherent desire for the improvement of his material condition. This impulse cannot be eradicated; it is the motive power of all human action.' Ibid., p. 148.

[6] Deaton, A. (2013). *The Great Escape: Health, Wealth, and the Origins of Inequality*. Princeton University Press.

living standards, and the relative abundance of the modern world. Similarly, attitudes towards race have evolved to make public life and market transactions easier than at any time in history, due in no small measure to the internet. A recent European Commission Report on *Discrimination in the European Union* found that despite the general perception that discrimination is widespread, an overwhelming majority (92%) reported feeling 'totally comfortable' with the idea of having a person of a different race in an elected position and said (86%) they would be 'totally happy' with the idea of their child being in love with a black person.[7] We have rational grounds to be optimistic, to go forward as best we can, choosing either to tolerate, if we must, or to embrace, if we wish, or simply to ignore, if we prefer, all kinds of human diversity. By drawing upon what is valuable from the wisdom of the past we may thereby maximise our ability to live together in peace. Exposure to a diverse range of ideas empowers us to understand and interact with the world and the people around us from all walks of life, not just those who happen to share our race or cultural background. For that purpose, whether people have used our preferred form of words is less important than whether what they say is true.

2.1 From Formal to Substantive Equality

The principle that all people are free and equal often gives rise to the expectation that justice requires each person to have the capacity to do what others are able to do. This expectation is often expressed in the demand for governments to guarantee equal opportunities for all. But freedom and equality for all people in the classical tradition means only that 'They are free in that they need permission from no other person to act. They are equal in that there is no natural political authority of one

[7] Evans, M. D. R., & Kelley, J. (2019). Prejudice Against Immigrants Symptomizes a Larger Syndrome, Is Strongly Diminished by Socioeconomic Development, and the UK Is Not an Outlier: Insights from the WVS, EVS, and EQLS Surveys 4. *Frontiers in Sociology*. Retrieved from https://www.frontiersin.org/articles/10.3389/fsoc.2019.00012/full.

person over another'.[8] Justice according to the ideals of classical liberalism requires not that everyone must be equal in how they live their life but that the law must grant equal rights to all in virtue of their humanity. Law must not favour one or other group, granting rights to special interest groups to the exclusion of those outside the group or allowing any individual to dictate how another must live his life. This principle constitutes the essence of formal equality. As Mises explains, liberty depends on upholding formal equality before the law:

> The liberals maintained that with the elimination of all the artificial distinctions of caste and status, the abolition of all privileges, and the establishment of equality before the law, nothing else stands in the way of the peaceful cooperation of all members of society, because then their rightly understood, long-run interests coincide.[9]

Formal equality is essential to the rule of law.[10] It means that law ought not to confer special privileges upon some and not others. This idea is inherent in the very notion of liberalism: 'Liberalism addresses itself to all and proposes a program acceptable to all alike. It promises no one privileges'.[11] Formal equality does not attempt to equalise the human condition. It aims to ensure that there are no artificial barriers to market participation or legal obstacles preventing anybody from pursuing his own happiness. Thus formal equality does not permit the legal exclusion of certain groups from buying property or entering into contracts. Formal equality ensures that all can enforce their legal rights equally. From this it can be seen that formal equality supplies the basis of the objection to segregation and apartheid, legal regimes which assign rights and liabilities according to race.

---

[8] Tomasi, J. (2012). *Free Market Fairness* (p. 5). Princeton University Press.

[9] Mises, *Liberalism*, p. 125.

[10] 'A meaningful human rights statute will surely protect all individuals equally, and equal protection of the laws (to refer to one clause of the Fourteenth Amendment adopted in 1868 in large part to give constitutional grounding to the 1866 Act) can be afforded only through some system of formal equality such as the 1866 [Civil Rights] Act provides'. Epstein, R. A. (2002). *Equal Opportunity or More Opportunity: The Good Thing About Discrimination* (pp. 2, 3). Commentary by Simon Deakin. Civitas. Retrieved from http://www.civitas.org.uk/pdf/cs18.pdf.

[11] Mises, *Liberalism*, p. 123.

Under formal equality general rules of law implement an ethical ideal focusing on fair process rather than equal outcomes.[12] Formal equality, treating like cases alike, is conducive to peace and cooperation because everyone has confidence and expectation that the same law will apply to all, a simple idea which reflects the most basic principle of fairness. As Flew explains, the classical ideal of justice requires equal treatment of like cases, and unequal treatment of unlike cases. Formal equality means that 'everyone is equally entitled to his day in court', but it does not demand that all litigants should be awarded equal outcomes. Flew explains:

> Any rules of justice, like any rules at all, must, to be rules, be applied in the same way, and hence equally, to all those to whom they are applicable. But this is a very different thing from saying that, to be just, you have to treat everyone in the same way, in all respects without exception. Nor is there any doubt but that justice requires equality before the law, in the sense that all offenders must be treated in the same way with no one privileged because of color, relationship to the dictator, or anything else of a similar nature. But any system of what purported to be criminal justice that refused to treat offenders in any way differently from nonoffenders would – as Kant might have said – contradict itself as a system of criminal justice.[13]

The contemporary legal framework in liberal market jurisdictions has departed from this conceptual framework of formal equality, seeking to supplement it with substantive equality. This conceptual and juridical shift is illustrated in the discussion that follows by reference to substantive equality in employment regulation.

Beginning with formal equality, the early race and sex discrimination legislation required that no employee should be treated less favourably

---

[12] 'Equal treatment…has nothing to do with the question of whether the application of such general rules in a particular situation may lead to results which are more favourable to some groups than to others: justice is not concerned with the results of the various transactions but only with whether the transactions themselves are fair': Hayek, F. A. (2013). *Law, Legislation and Liberty: A New Statement of the Liberal Principles of Justice and Political Economy* (p. 141). Routledge (Original work published 1973).

[13] Flew, A. (1986). Enforced Equality—Or Justice? *Journal of Libertarian Studies, 8*(1), 31–41, 34.

than another on grounds of their race or sex. This is a declaratory principle of formal equality, that does not purport to create new substantive rights but simply requires that irrelevant considerations (the race or sex of the employee, where that is not relevant to the decision) should not influence hiring, firing or promotions. Formal equality would also prohibit racial or gender segregation and apartheid, systems that distinguish legal claims by reference to race or sex. Antidiscrimination law based on formal equality is therefore declaratory in much the same way as human rights instruments declaring that all human beings are created equal and entitled to equal protection of the law. In that context disparate treatment or direct discrimination on grounds of race, which entails treating people less favourably because of their race, would be unlawful subject to the usual prerogatives of ownership and freedom of contract and the attendant principles of private law.

The key point to make here about formal equality is that it does not abrogate or override fundamental rights and freedoms including private property or freedom of contract. As will be discussed in Chapter 4, which offers a more detailed analysis of discrimination in employment, formal equality does not entail a free-standing, general or independent right not to be discriminated against.[14] Instead it protects a right that may be described as procedural in the sense that it confers protection from detriment in the exercise of the natural rights that vest in all human beings. To give an example, we all have the right to private property, and must not be subjected to discrimination in the exercise of that right. No jurisdiction should establish legal rules preventing certain races from owning property, living in specified areas, or participating in commercial life. Conversely, in the absence of vested property rights, the right not to be subjected to disparate treatment does not entail a right to go anywhere one pleases even when that constitutes a trespass, or to have any job one desires even though the employer does not wish to offer it, nor does it confer immunity from being fired where the employer seeks lawfully to terminate the relationship. Such claims would infringe upon the rights, freedoms and prerogatives of others. Antidiscrimination law based on formal equalityis therefore negative in its formulation, denoting

[14] Section 4.3 of Chapter 4 offers more detailed discussion of the legal framework.

a right *not* to be prevented from the exercise and expression of one's own rights and freedoms rather than a positive right granting the power to override the freedoms of others.

Classical principles of formal equality are often criticised as insufficient in defending modern formulations of human rights. Human rights are conceptualised variously as general rights to dignity and inclusion, including the right to feel that one is treated equally as a valued member of society or, as commonly expressed in the equality discourse, the right to feel welcome. From this broad formulation of human rights the argument follows that 'the right to equality should be responsive to those who are disadvantaged, demeaned, excluded, or ignored'.[15] From that point it is but a short step to promoting the view that groups who are disadvantaged should take priority in the definition and delineation of human rights and legal entitlements. Other people's rights take second place to the imperatives of making the excluded feel welcome. It can be seen that this conceptualisation of equality does not entail any form of natural right in the classical liberal sense, but rather represents a political or philosophical claim in the nature of a wish, a desire, an aspirational vision of those who believe that socio-economic rights are synonymous with fundamental human rights. Fundamental human rights, as understood in international law, therefore entail an extra set of positive rights superimposed onto the natural rights that vest in all human beings. For example the European Human Rights Commission advises public bodies to focus on specific equality outcomes:

> An equality outcome is a result which you as an authority aim to achieve in order to further one or more of the needs mentioned in the general equality duty…an equality outcome should further one or more of the following needs: eliminate discrimination, advance equality of opportunity and foster good relations. By focusing on outcomes rather than objectives, this specific duty aims to bring practical improvements in the life chances of those who experience discrimination and disadvantage.

[15] Fredman, S. (2016). Substantive Equality Revisited. *International Journal of Constitutional Law, 14*(3), 712–738. See also Barnard, C., & Hepple, B. (2000). Substantive Equality. *Cambridge Law Journal, 59*(3), 562–585.

> So in practice, you might find it helpful to think of equality outcomes as results intended to achieve specific and identifiable improvements in people's life chances.[16]

In that formulation we have a natural right to pursue our own happiness, *plus* a right to have the state implement improvements in our life chances. The improvement of people's life chances seems to be the worthiest possible function of state power, until it is remembered that a way must be found to implement it which ultimately entails some form of wealth redistribution—taking from those who have more, without their consent, to give to those who have specified protected characteristics. Precisely the types of measures described by Sowell as make-believe equality. For example, if we aspire to create a society in which nobody feels 'demeaned, excluded or ignored' we may frame that as a right for those with protected characteristics not to be subjected to harassment including microaggressions such as failing to make eye contact with those who are different from us.[17] Any claim based on a right to enjoy the same quality of life as others may in this sense be framed as a human right. Thus for example the United Nations defines the imperative to provide broadband access to all communities as a 'digital human right' in which all people globally have equal access to the internet and are able to spend equal amounts of time online.[18] Digital human rights are defined as essential to global justice. The terminology of rights and justice signifies that these are not mere aspirations or ideological visions of the meaning of our common humanity, but legal mandates which states have a duty to implement and enforce. This notion of a right to equality defined as a fundamental human right underpins the legislative concept

[16] Equality and Human Rights Commission. (2016). *Equality Outcomes and the Public Sector Equality Duty: A Guide for Public Authorities in Scotland* (p. 10). https://www.equalityhumanrights.com/sites/default/files/equality-outcomes-public-sector-equality-duty-scotland.pdf.

[17] 'Oxford University has apologised for saying that avoiding eye contact could be "everyday racism" after it was accused of discriminating against autistic people. The claim was included in a list of "racial micro-aggressions" in an equality and diversity unit newsletter. But the university was criticised for being "insensitive" to autistic people who can struggle making eye contact.' https://www.bbc.co.uk/news/uk-england-oxfordshire-39742670.

[18] United Nations. (2020). *Roadmap for Digital Cooperation.* https://www.un.org/en/content/digital-cooperation-roadmap/assets/pdf/Roadmap_for_Digital_Cooperation_EN.pdf.

of substantive equality. Substantive equality as defined in equality legislation shifts the focus from due process in the protection of rights, to mandating equal outcomes by prohibiting disparate impact or indirect discrimination. The focus shifts away from formal equalityin the defence of vested rights towards ameliorating situations where racial disparities persist despite everyone being subject to the same rules and requirements. The policy discourse of equality therefore centres on addressing socio-economic disparities rather than facilitating opportunity.

This departure from formal equality, a shift grounded in highly politicised notions of human rights, has its roots in the early civil rights debates in the United States. The civil rights reforms of the 1960s faced considerable opposition from those concerned about 'the risk of some hitherto unimaginable federal government infringement' although at the time supporters of the legislation generally denied that their proposed law would attempt to equalise outcomes: 'when Florida Democratic senator George Smathers worried that attempts to equalise school enrolment might lead to busing, his Pennsylvania Republican colleague Hugh Scott scoffed, "Does the senator not agree that there is nothing whatever in the bill which relates to the transportation of schoolchildren by bus from one district to another? I find nothing in the bill which pertains to any such provision"'.[19] The very suggestion that children might be bused to and fro to implement the civil rights reforms or that employers might be required to implement hiring quotas was regarded as some sort of wild conspiracy theory. Legislators who pushed through the civil rights reforms insisted that they were only concerned to ensure equal opportunities, to level the playing field, and to counteract the overt racial hostility of Jim Crow by passing legislation 'to make those bad Southerners behave'.[20] The supporters of this legislation were complacent and optimistic as politicians often are, secure in the knowledge that they will

[19] Caldwell, C. (2020). *The Age of Entitlement: America Since the Sixties* (p. 22). Simon & Schuster.

[20] Caldwell, *The Age of Entitlement*, p. 18 et seq. 'Most Americans, liberal as well as conservative, saw the race problem as something distant. It had to do only, or mainly, with the exotic culture of the South, where segregation was legal. The sociologist Alan David Freeman wrote… "I can recall distinctly the response of my own naively liberal consciousness…The Law is now going to make those bad Southerners behave." Outside the South, white people seemed to believe it would be a simple matter to get rid of segregation', p. 21.

be long gone from office by the time the chickens come home to roost. It does not appear to have been within their contemplation that the project would ultimately require meeting concrete demands to provide the jobs, money, education and housing which civil rights activists clearly expected as the outcome of these reforms:

> The mostly Northern whites who legislated against Jim Crow saw themselves as making a grand and magnanimous gesture, cutting a heroic figure. They would affirm the moral principles on which the Constitution rested by extending its legal principles to a region where they had never really been applied.[21]

As Caldwell shows, what began as a moral opposition to segregation was rapidly transformed, through civil rights legislation, into a behemoth requiring armies of 'bureaucrats, lawyers, intellectuals, and political agitators to become the "eyes and ears," and even the foot soldiers, of civil rights enforcement'.[22]

> A year after the Civil Rights Act [1964] passed Lyndon Johnson announced that it was time for the 'next and most profound stage of the battle' which he described as a battle for 'not just equality as a right and a theory but equality as a fact and equality as a result'.[23]

Caldwell describes this as 'the mightiest instrument of domestic enforcement the country had ever seen', arguing that the scale of the civil rights reforms was nothing short of a constitutional revolution whose impact was to redefine not only the constitutional foundations of the rule of law but also the cultural and demographic foundations of Western society.[24] To those who had suffered long years of oppression, the Civil Rights

---

[21] Ibid., pp. 24, 25.

[22] Ibid., p. 9.

[23] Ibid.

[24] 'It can fairly be described as the largest undertaking of any kind in American history. Costing trillions upon trillions of dollars and spanning half a century it rivals, in terms of energy invested, the peopling of the West, the building of transcontinental railways and highways, the maintenance of a Pax Americana for half a century after World War II, or, for that matter, any of the wars the country has fought, foreign or civil': ibid.

Act was not a simple matter of desegregation and enforcement of the civil rights granted to them by earlier legislation, as clearly new legislation would not be needed merely to enforce previous legislation, but amounted in their view to a constitutional revolution whose outcome was that 'race was invested with a religious significance'.[25]

> Black people, and the most zealous among the civil rights activists of all races, saw whites as having entered a guilty plea in the court of history, and thus as repudiating the moral posturing on which the good name and the good conscience of their constitutional republic had rested.[26]

For purposes of our discussion the issue here does not concern the implications of these political trends for the US, on which views may reasonably differ. Progressive thinkers may deem this to be a worthwhile investment of trillions upon trillions of dollars, and may view this constitutional revolution as a triumph to be celebrated. Such matters are rightly the subject of political debate, and indeed Caldwell does not attempt to decide which interpretation of the civil rights reforms had the better argument.[27] But the point to be made here concerns the overtly political goals of equality legislation, and the curious results of extending the fallout of a very American revolution to all corners of the globe with American 'critical race theory' assuming dominance as the only acceptable lens through which race is henceforth to be analysed. Shelby Steele observes:

> Here we see redemptive liberalism's great ingenuity: it seized proprietorship over innocence itself. It took on the power to grant or deny moral legitimacy across society. Liberals were free of the past while conservatives longed to resurrect it, bigotry and all. What else could 'Make America Great Again' mean? In this way redemptive liberalism reshaped the moral

[25] Ibid., p. 10.

[26] Ibid., p. 25.

[27] 'These are matters of perspective. There is no point in describing one interpretation as morally "right" or "wrong". We can say, though, that where the black consensus differed from the white consensus, it was blacks' views that were more congruent with the reality of what would be required, and what would be effective, in bringing racial equality about', p. 25.

> culture of the entire Western world with sweeping idealisms like 'diversity,' which are as common today in Europe as in America… Racism and bigotry generally are the great driving engines of modern American liberalism. Even a remote hint of racism can trigger a kind of moral entrepreneurism.[28]

Political debate can never be closed off in a democratic society, therefore any ideological position whose goal is to transform the cultural and demographic foundations of society would expect to be met with robust debate. Yet by depicting egalitarian ideology as being merely concerned with enforcing basic legal rights, a false impression is created of objectivity, unanimity and consensus which can then be relied upon to preclude any debate: after all, there can be no 'debate' concerning the enforcement of basic legal rights. Who would object to a project designed to protect human rights? This strategy, planting the egalitarian flag on the high moral ground of human rights, is reflected in the free speech debates when it is said that there can be no 'debate' about anti-racism; by framing the issue as a matter of the right to equality it is relocated beyond the scope of debate. If we do not 'debate' whether we should commit crimes of murder or false imprisonment against our neighbours, we should not 'debate' whether it would acceptable to cause them harm by committing microaggressions against them. By conflating the right to life, liberty and equality in that way, we imbue equality with the same moral status as life and liberty. This is important in understanding the claims often made about viewpoint diversity. Debate on economic regulation and social ordering is vital in a free society. As Pennington argues, 'the strength of democracy rests on its ability to organize experiments with alternative social models and to reduce conflict. By ensuring that divergent voices are heard, democratic mechanisms facilitate learning and can sustain support from those losing out from any specific decision'.[29] But proponents of Rawlsian liberalism view the importance of such debate as perhaps appropriate in the political arena but not in the

[28] Steele, S. (2018). A Sick Hunger for Racism. *Hoover Digest*, pp. 158, 159.

[29] In Robust Political Economy and the Priority of Markets. *Social Philosophy and Policy, 34*(1), 1–24, 18, drawing upon Knight, J., & Johnson, J. (2007). The Priority of Democracy: A Pragmatist Approach to Political Economic Institutions and the Burden of Justification. *American*

arena of basic human rights. There is no viewpoint diversity on whether all human beings have a natural right to life and liberty, therefore by defining substantive equality as a basic human right progressive ideology is able conveniently to extract itself from the legitimate arena of political debate. In this way the shift from formal to substantive equality in the legal framework has served to mask, and to shield from political disputation, a transformational shift from enforcing basic legal rights to enforcing an overtly political and socialist ideology under the banner of 'equality'.

Under this mask the discourse of equality has over time eroded the distinction between the policy goals of equal opportunity and equal outcome. In the United States, as envisaged by the first Civil Rights Act in the nineteenth century following emancipation, equal opportunity would guarantee the rights to vote, to own property, freedom of contract and freedom of association for all regardless of race or creed or other station in life. It would preclude laws assigning both detriment and preference on a discriminatory basis. But as Caldwell argues it is unlikely that the concept of 'opportunity' employed in the 1960s civil rights legislation ever meant anything less than 'outcomes'. The caution voiced in the 1960s civil rights debates that legislation designed to protect equal opportunities would risk undermining the presumption of innocence soon proved to be prescient:

> I feel that the regulations, lawsuits and Federal pressures placed upon private business by this title are utterly unacceptable in a free economy, particularly since these pressures can be placed upon any firm at any time in presuming the firm guilty until it proves itself innocent.[30]

This is precisely how the legislation soon operated. Moreover it is likely that this was always the intention, given that prior civil rights legislation had already enshrined formal equality so the only meaningful purpose of the legislation introduced in the 1960s was to conflate the idea of equal opportunity with the growing expectation of equal

---

Political Science Review, 101(1), 47–61 and, Knight, J., & Johnson, J. (2011). *The Priority of Democracy*. Princeton University Press.

[30] Senator Tower, 110 Cong. Rec. 9024 (1964); quoted in Epstein, *Forbidden Grounds*, p. 192.

outcomes. That is clear from the academic and juridical explanations of the antidiscrimination principle.[31]

Caldwell explains the legacy of the 1960s civil rights era as in many ways an outcome of US foreign policy, with the ideas underlying the Civil Rights Act of 1964 being commended as the best system to 'manage' ethnic and marginalised groups. He describes how the Act was sold to the American public as a means of safeguarding equal opportunities as a step towards the classical ideal of equality. Nobody would object to that. Thus the ideal emphasised the right to participate in public life on an equal footing with which everyone agreed. But, as Epstein also points out, the freedom of contract and right to own property had already been achieved. It is not surprising then the 1964 Act was understood by the victims of oppression as a promise of something more: equal outcomes designed to remedy historical wrongs. The disjunction, even if only in terms of perception, between 'opportunity' and 'outcomes' was a logical extension of the priority placed on the legislative pursuit of equality as an end in itself. From this point the deviation from the classical ideal of equality become increasingly entrenched. It is clear from Caldwell's study that whatever may have been the original intentions of the civil rights movement, it soon began to drive a legislative shift from a process-based conception of justice to one based on distributive results. This shift was surprisingly swift, a matter of months in some cases.[32] While affirmative action was initially framed with ideals of racial equality, it soon translated into 'quotas and goals and timetables' designed to measure the 'results' of equality policies.[33] The focus began

---

[31] 'The effect of antidiscrimination laws – and, indeed, for many who understand this, the laws' very purpose – is not so much to protect members of a specified group from discrimination, from being treated less favourably than others because of their status (which nearly everybody agrees would be wrong and foolish), as to exempt them from the reasonable standards and requirements that apply to others': O'Shea, M. L. (1999). *A Cure Worse Than the Disease: Fighting Discrimination Through Government Control* (p. 235). Hallberg.

[32] The emphasis was accordingly transferred 'from a focus on the rights of minority individuals to the preferential treatment of minority groups. In less than a decade, the goal had shifted from equal opportunity to statistical parity': Riley, J. L. (2014). *Please Stop Helping Us: How Liberals Make It Harder for Blacks to Succeed* (pp. 147, 148). Encounter Books.

[33] 'It is not written in the bill that there must be a quota system, but the net effect of the [statute] would be that employers, in order to keep themselves from being charged with having discriminated, would, in time, have certain people working for them to meet the color

with removing barriers to entry into employment and other aspects of economic life, but once translated into law it soon became necessary to build upon it in ways that have created intractable regulatory problems.

The prioritisation of equal outcomes has now assumed the dominant role in the equality discourse. This explains why the intentions of those accused of discrimination, whether innocent or hostile, are altogether irrelevant in establishing legal liability: it is the inequality of the results that matters most for legal liability, not the worthiness or otherwise of the intentions behind the unequal result. Under principles of substantive equality the law aims explicitly to produce equal outcomes through special privileges designed to 'reverse discrimination' through 'positive action' and 'affirmative action' offered in compensation for historical oppression and residual group disadvantage.[34] Those in the public sector have specific duties actively to encourage progress for underrepresented racial groups, while the sphere of the public sector is itself so broadly defined as almost to erase entirely the boundary between public and private transactions.[35] As the equalisation of outcomes assumes increasingly greater priority, public discourse continually identifies new ways to promote equal outcomes. The ascendant concept of 'equity' denotes the eradication of racial and other group disparities in hiring, promotions and income all of which are closely monitored to ensure that they are equally distributed between different groups.

2.2 From Equality to Equity

Equity as a cultural ideal has abandoned any pretence of being concerned with equality. Equity is to be achieved by closing income and attainment gaps and compensating for historical disadvantage. Equity relies explicitly on legislative mandates, diversity training and monitoring

---

qualifications, the religious qualifications, the creed qualifications, and so on' (Senator George Smathers, 110 Cong. Rec. 8500 (1964): cited in Epstein, *Forbidden Grounds*, p. 187.

[34] Fredman, S. (1997). Reversing Discrimination. *Law Quarterly Review, 113*, 575.

[35] Discussed in more detail in Sects. 4.4 and 4.5 of Chapter 4.

behaviour and language to ensure that it is inclusive, adopting enforcement methods that extend into many spheres of private life including matters of conscience. The concept of equity rejects formal equality on grounds that treating everybody equally would heap more unfair advantage on those who already have an advantaged position in life. The egalitarian conviction is that human beings ought as much as possible to enjoy equal social and material status which can be achieved through wealth redistribution. Luck egalitarians have long argued against merit as a basis of making decisions, on grounds that merit inherently favours those with educational or other social advantages including the good fortune of being born into a supportive family or living in a good school district. The argument is that treating people equally is only fair if they started out equal in the first place. Given that different races do not start out with equal fortunes, it therefore seems fair for the law to treat those who are disadvantaged more favourably than those who are advantaged. As people are differently situated in life, some are unable to achieve the same progress as others through no fault of their own; a child from a wealthy family begins life with a different starting point from a child living in deprivation and thus it is said to be unfair to treat both children equally. For the luck egalitarian, being fortunate in the sense of being endowed with natural attributes or talents that others lack, is itself a source of unfairness and injustice. Thus productivity, success or good fortune are depicted as inherently unjust and unfair to those who are underprivileged.

Formal equality offers equality in the eyes of the law with no guarantee of *achieving* equality. Egalitarians argue that formal equality is therefore not 'real' and is in fact meaningless. When people demand equality they do not simply claim the right to throw their hat in the ring but they in fact hope and expect ultimately to *become* equal with those around them. They expect not simply to have the same rights or the same chance to have a go as everyone else on a level playing field, but to have the playing field tailored to mitigate their relative weaknesses. The law is then harnessed to make all people *be* equal in fact, and experience equal lives. The hope and expectation is that legislation can reverse-engineer a fair and equal world by equalising the starting point through measures which reverse discrimination thereby ensuring that nobody enjoys better life chances than others and correcting the situation if anybody appears to be privileged above others.[36] Favouring the disadvantaged is expected to equalise the fortunes of both advantaged and disadvantaged.

By challenging the classical ideal of equality the notion of equity reflects an expectation that market interventions can be tailored to produce equal levels of success. As Rothbard argues, the goal of this concept of equity is to equalise the human experience, which is a 'nonsensical goal' to the extent that it is inherently unattainable.[37] It establishes a moral ideal that 'can only be achieved if all men are precisely uniform, precisely identical with respect to all of their attributes. The egalitarian world would necessarily be a world of horror fiction—a world of faceless and identical creatures, devoid of all individuality, variety, or special creativity'.[38] It presumes that in the absence of discrimination the socio-economic outcomes of all peoples, races and cultures would be equal regardless of input or context.

> Since egalitarians begin with the a priori axiom that all people, and hence all groups of peoples, are uniform and equal, it then follows for them that any and all group differences in status, prestige, or authority in society must be the result of unjust 'oppression' and irrational 'discrimination.'[39]

The realities of human diversity prompt us to value and pursue different ends and outcomes. We have different priorities, hobbies, values, preferences—different conceptions of the good. Variation in biological traits and natural endowments, together with the influence of environmental and cultural factors including educational and family background, guarantee that our life experiences and outcomes will not be

[36] Fredman, Reversing Discrimination.

[37] 'The challenge must take place at the core — at the presumed ethical superiority of a nonsensical goal': Rothbard, *Egalitarianism as a Revolt*, p. 5.

[38] Ibid., p. 6.

[39] Ibid., p. 10.

uniform.[40] Where merit is unequal results inevitably vary.[41] Equality engineered through redistribution would hardly be 'real' but rather artificial, contrary to nature and to reality; 'Nature never repeats itself in its creations; it produces nothing by the dozen, nor are its products standardised. Each man who leaves her workshop bears the imprint of the individual, the unique, the never-to-recur'.[42] It is a pipe dream, a 'revolt against nature' to expect law to engineer equal outcomes. In reality 'egalitarian distribution without regard for individual merits and demerits is inequality rather than justice'.[43]

Moreover, as Sowell has argued, institutionalising unequal treatment by favouring disadvantaged groups and relegating privileged groups to the back of the queue is bound to provoke hostility and resentment precisely because there is no consensus on what amounts to 'disadvantage' or 'privilege'. As Sowell points out, these descriptions vary greatly from one individual to the next regardless of race, and vary for each individual over time so that the same person may be disadvantaged while young and privileged when older, or a millionaire today and bankrupt tomorrow. Superficial equality produced through arbitrary points of comparison is moreover unstable because when law favours one group above others, the overlooked groups immediately begin jostling for similar favours. Regardless of the grounds for favouritism, a law that favours one group over others ultimately yields inter-group conflict: 'Whoever denies rights to a part of the population must always be prepared for a united attack by the disenfranchised on the privileged'.[44] Regardless of the ground selected for favouritism, each group has an incentive to argue that the selected ground applies equally or even more closely to them than to other groups. Thus the protected ground of

[40] 'We must face the fact that the preservation of individual freedom is incompatible with a full satisfaction of our views of distributive justice': Hayek, F. A. (1958). Individualism: True and False. In *Individualism and Economic Order* (p. 22). University of Chicago Press (Original work published 1948).

[41] Thus 'egalitarian distribution without regard for individual merits and demerits is inequality rather than justice.' De la Mora, G. F. (1987). *Egalitarian Envy: The Political Foundations of Social Justice* (p. 95). Paragon House.

[42] Mises, *Liberalism*, pp. 9, 10.

[43] De la Mora, *Egalitarian Envy*, p. 95.

[44] Mises, *Liberalism*, p. 10.

'religion' soon expressed more broadly as any 'philosophical belief' soon came to include vegans and nudists. If disadvantage is the key to entitlement, then each group promotes itself as the most disadvantaged, or at least as being equally disadvantaged with other disadvantaged groups, and everybody tries to shoehorn themselves into one protected group or other. It is rational to compete for recognition in the victimhood stakes when victimhood grants priority in the eyes of the law. Selecting particular traits for special protection risks encouraging resentment from those who are excluded and intersectional civil war as different groups scramble for privileged access to scarce resources. This is reflected in the expansion of protected grounds to cover an increasing proportion of those who claim to be unfairly left out. Seeking immediate advancement for one's own group merely invites others to seek advancement for their group. The goal is inherently impractical. Equal outcomes cannot be legislatively engineered without extracting an inordinate price in its encroachment upon other fundamental values. As Kukathas argues, the attempt to equalise outcomes requires that diversity be suppressed and dissent from equalisation programmes be discouraged. Thus attempting to equalise outcomes 'does not bring about equality but simply creates different inequalities'.[45]

The outcome of these developments is that the classical ideal of justice, with its insistence upon formal equality, no longer plays a role in the policy framework of substantive racial equity. Formal equality appears on the face of it to be inadequate to the evolving political demands for equality of lifestyle, based ultimately on equality of income and wealth. Formal equality has been discarded for its inability to advance progressive dreams. In thus disregarding formal equality much of value to the rule of law has been lost.

In defending the classical ideal of justice based on formal equality it is important to make explicit the ideals underlying that concept of justice. Justice in the classical sense is described by Flew as 'an essentially backward-looking notion' because it reflects an outcome following upon our acts or omissions as expressed in ideas of reward and desert rather

---

[45] *The Liberal Archipelago*, p. 215.

than emanating from the grant of gifts and favours.[46] Justice in that sense emanates not from vague aspirational notions of human rights but from the concrete reality of human acts and omissions. Flew denotes this simply as justice. Not 'racial' justice or 'social' justice or 'historical' justice or 'political' justice or 'global' justice but plain 'old-fashioned, without prefix or suffix' justice, which means 'rendering to everyone their due'—we get what we deserve, we earn our reward, we all have the same rights, and vindicate those rights through the same legal process before the same courts.[47] Rendering to everyone their due results not in equality, but in inequality of both claim and reward. As Flew's analysis shows, there is no reason to suppose that people living different lives and engaging in different transactions will have the same entitlements and returns. They will have what is due, and 'their due, of course, will be their several and presumably often different deserts and entitlements – moral deserts and moral entitlements if we are talking about morals; legal [deserts] and legal [entitlements] if we are talking about the positive law'.[48] These notions are clearly regarded as untenable by progressive conceptualisations of 'forward-looking' justice by which the state allocates or distributes entitlements according to moral guidelines on group entitlements ascertained through political decision-making.[49]

The notion of political justice is especially significant in debates surrounding race relations, a context where social justice is said to demand resource allocation according to vulnerability, disadvantage and grievance rather than desert. In the desire to implement progressive justice, the notion of desert is eschewed: it is said that those who have natural talents do *not* deserve those talents and therefore do *not* deserve to keep the fruits of their labour.[50] Rawls for example argues that the

[46] 'Justice is an essentially backward-looking notion, concerned with people getting and being able to keep their several and presumably often different deserts and entitlements-deserts and entitlements we have antecedently acquired by being what we are and have been, and by doing or refraining from doing what we either have done or have refrained from doing.' Ibid., p. 31.

[47] Ibid.

[48] Ibid.

[49] Ibid.

[50] 'Protagonists of this Procrustean ideal would, if they were both clear-headed and frank, sacrifice the propaganda advantages of presenting it as a kind of justice. Instead, and taking a leaf from the book of the orthopsychiatrists and other self-styled penal progressives, they would

state is justified in reallocating the fruits of our labour to more just ends because our natural talents are 'accidents of natural endowment' which are not morally deserved.[51] In the theoretical framework of Rawlsian liberalism the most advantaged do not 'deserve' their personal attributes or advantages but have them purely as a result of luck in the great lottery of life since nobody chooses their race, family, personality, talents or traits such as intelligence, creativity or even attractive appearance, all of which correlate with socio-economic advantage. Luck egalitarians argue that this shifts the fruits of valuable human attributes from the absolute moral control of the individual who might unjustly keep all the advantages of his unearned natural skills and talents, to the purview of social control which enables public officials to ensure fair distribution in the interests of those who are less well off.

There is some debate as to whether Rawls is a luck egalitarian, but as Gordon points out Rawls exhibits elements of luck egalitarianism in suggesting that 'people do not deserve to profit from their superior abilities, because these are arbitrary from the moral point of view'.[52] While Rawls did not regard the initial distribution of luck as fair or unfair—Rawls would agree that the situation to which we are born is blameless—nevertheless he would subject the subsequent unfolding of unequal fortunes as amenable to socially oriented redistribution to produce fair outcomes by ameliorating the position of those who started out as the least advantaged. The Rawlsian reasoning is that while it is not inherently unfair to be born with great musical talent, for example, it is fair for society to redistribute wealth earned through such talent, so that the least well off among those born without musical ability should be able to share in some of the outcomes of the wealth of musical talent in society. In this example the luck egalitarian would deem it to be fair to take wealth from the musician who earned it, because he did not 'deserve' the talents with which he was born and it was sheer luck that

mount a bold and radical onslaught on the very notion of justice – denouncing the whole business as antique, gothic, reactionary, and – what is the truth – irreducibly backward-looking.' Ibid., pp. 31, 32.

[51] Rawls, J. (1999). *A Theory of Justice*. Belknap Press (Original work published 1971).

[52] Gordon, D. (2017). One Flew Over Equality. *An Austro-Libertarian View: Vol. II: Political Theory* (p. 85). Mises Institute.

he happened to be born with such talents. In this way, as Gordon points out, 'Rawls has moved from the contention that the category of desert does not apply to natural endowments to the much more controversial claim that these endowments are undeserved'.[53] Thus the issue is not whether the vagaries of life are fair or unfair in an abstract sense, but whether it is justified to take contested notions of fairness as the basis for redistributive legislative regulation of economic life.

By contrast, in Smithian moral philosophy advantage gained through virtues such as moderation, courage, temperance, thrift, industry, prudence, self-discipline, self-responsibility and self-respect, among others, cannot be deemed unjust since that advantage constitutes the reward or return from virtue. This applies not only to wealth or savings earned through one's own industry and frugality, but also the fruits of these virtues devised to members of one's family or community through inheritance or through charitable gifts. The Smithian virtues are in themselves important moral values in conceptualising the good. It is true that these virtues are not equally upheld in all cultures, and indeed have come to be viewed as a form of cultural imperialism that is oppressive to those whose cultures embrace indolence as a perfectly viable path to the good life. Yet the fact that Smithian virtues undoubtedly shape economic outcomes must be, if we prefer better economic outcomes to worse economic outcomes, in itself good reason to prefer these virtues to sloth and idleness. On that basis market participation may be deemed to be inherently 'moral' and 'just' even though it operates unequally and produces unequal outcomes, as the morality or justice of any outcome must be evaluated by reference to the virtues that produced them. If virtue and morality cannot produce unjust outcomes then it cannot be 'unfair' or 'immoral' for one person to prioritise industry and thrift while others do not, nor does it become immoral or unfair or unjust if the thrifty person ends up accumulating more wealth, or even if that person chooses to devolve that wealth to their own children. In a free society each person elects to pursue his own conception of the good, and therefore if the outcome is unequal to that created by others who chose a different path that outcome is in no sense rendered unjust by the

---

[53] Ibid.

resulting disparity. Nor is one person's pursuit of virtue rendered unjust where another person's non-pursuit of that virtue is not the result of personal fault, even though a luck egalitarian might argue that thriftiness often runs in families or cultures and nobody chooses the family into which they were born.

It is clear, then, that justice in the classical liberal sense is not a construct bestowed by state largesse in a manner independent of individual input, but is contingent on human agency and thus responsive to our own actions. By contrast, designating justice as 'social' or 'racial' or 'global' is more appealing to progressive liberals with its forward-looking applications and its flavour of the new, the improved, the sophisticated. This goes a long way in explaining the appeal of contemporary social justice and the challenge to be met in defending the classical ideal. The classical ideal of justice also faces further hurdles in the public popularity contest because it focuses on the individual, which implies notions of self-responsibility with which many people feel uncomfortable. Political justice, by contrast, goes easier on the personal conscience by focusing on collective group claims. Political group-justice avoids the bracing need for self-responsibility and allows people to join groups that can more easily mount newsworthy political crusades to demand government interventions requiring no personal effort on their part. That the government will do something to fix injustice is regarded as a comforting thought by those who have lost sight of the longer term, have failed to identify the true drivers of success in life, and perhaps have little interest in the nature of reality.

2.3 Rawlsian Impartiality and Room for Debate

The argument thus far has outlined some of the contentious issues in understanding the meaning of justice, in particular concerning the distinction between formal and substantive justice, the role of the state, and the specific goals set out to be achieved. In this part of the discussion we expand on the argument that these contentious issues are amenable to reasoned debate. Nor can debate be closed off simply by applying the label of 'human rights' to the political preference being expressed. For those engaged in these debates it may seem to be self-evident that there is much to be debated, and much value to be gained from doing so, in understanding the interplay between freedom and justice. Yet the academic discourse is dominated by liberal scholars who take the view that the importance of equality in meeting the demands of social justice is settled and all that remains to be debated is the practicalities and scope of state-led equity programmes. This is notably the case for that subset of liberal scholars in fields such as employment law for whom it is convenient to suppose that we are all Rawlsians now and anyone who departs from the Rawlsian view of justice need not be heard. It is important, in understanding the debated terrain, to highlight that many fundamental liberal principles remain deeply contested with no prospect that they will ever be settled because they reflect strongly held underlying ideologies. Disputation and debate is not unfortunate; on the contrary, it is essential to the richness of life, to advancing knowledge, and to expanding our understanding of the world. From all the permutations of socialism to the different strands of libertarianism and much in between, justice remains contested. For example, in modern liberal democracies all who describe themselves as liberals would in principle value individual liberty and other fundamental human freedoms, but not all liberals would accord priority to economic freedom. The ideal of economic freedom is regarded with particular scepticism by progressive or left-leaning liberal philosophers.[54] Nor do we all share a common vision of the just society or hold uniform opinions on the moral and distributive implications of free markets.[55] Debate also surrounds the moral provenance of capitalism and the institutions of private property. For example, Adam Smith's moral philosophy is regarded by some as central to the meaning of economic freedomand individual liberty, while treated in other parts of the discourse as having nothing relevant to say

[54] The term 'progressive' here denotes liberal thinkers who lean left in their politics: 'New liberals, modern liberals, liberal democratic theorists, prioritarians, sufficientarians, egalitarians of various stripes, or – at their most enthusiastic – high liberals; for now I use the term left liberals to refer to them all. Speaking generally, left liberals are skeptical of the moral significance of private economic liberty': Tomasi, *Free Market Fairness*, p. xiii.

[55] On the morality of capitalist markets, see Devine, D. J. (2021). *The Enduring Tension: Capitalism and the Moral Order*. Encounter Books.

on questions of morality, or perhaps deemed to be relevant to moral debates only to the extent that it can be re-interpreted through the prism of egalitarian interventionism.[56] On all these issues, there is much insight to be gained from discussion and debate.

Concerning the debate about the importance of economic freedom, progressive liberalism adheres to Rawls's theory of distributive justice which 'rejects the idea that the economic rights of capitalism [primarily property rights] have any essential connection to liberty'.[57] Thus there is a deep and unbridgeable schism between contemporary social justice theories which underplay the importance of economic freedom, and classical liberalism which regards private property as the bedrock of free enterprise and the motor driving the engine of productivity, abundance and prosperity. Progressive liberals consider equality to be the paramount ideal in a just and fair society, and since economic freedom does not necessarily produce equality they would argue that freedom must yield to the determined pursuit of equality. To many progressive liberals socio-economic equality and power precede the enjoyment of freedom, so that it would be pointless from their perspective to pursue freedom without equality being established as a precondition. These different perspectives within the broad church of liberalism mean that liberal scholars lack a uniform or shared approach to the demands of justice in contexts of racial diversity. In the discussion that follows we outline the main principles of social justice which claim adherence to the Rawlsian philosophical worldview, or which display Rawlsian theoretical constructs in their concept of distributive justice, in order to examine how Rawlsian ideas have shaped the discourse on racial equality and to establish the parameters of disputation between classical and progressive scholars. The aim is not to present generally the framework of Rawlsian liberalism, with which readers will no doubt be familiar, but to highlight some of the principles which have influenced the racial equality debates, the reasons why those principles have been influential, and identify some of the philosophical problems they raise.

[56] For a critique see Otteson, J. R. (2016). Adam Smith on Virtue, Prosperity and Justice. In J. A. Baker & M. D. White (Eds.), *Economics and the Virtues: Building a New Moral Foundation* (p. 72). Oxford University Press.

[57] Tomasi, p. xv.

Rawls sets out to derive a theory of justice with which all reasonable people would agree: 'one conception of justice is more reasonable than another, or justifiable with respect to it, if rational persons in the initial situation would choose its principles over those of the other for the role of justice'.[58] To formulate objectively just and fair rules within this initial situation Rawls posits a theoretical model within which our knowledge of our own position is constrained by 'restrictions it seems reasonable to impose on arguments for principles of justice' in order to exclude factors that may lead to bias in favour of our own position. In Rawls's original position 'no one knows his place in society, his class position or social status, nor does any one know his fortune in the distribution of natural assets and abilities, his intelligence, strength and the like'.[59] In Rawls's example, if we are wealthy we may be inclined to regard a welfare tax as unjust; if we are poor we would consider it to be just. Following the 'difference principle' we should aim to maximise the position of the least well off in society. We would expect any reasonable person to regard this as the fairest approach if they had no information as to whether they personally might occupy that disadvantaged position. Rawls's original position has much to commend it as an approach to understanding the demands of fairness. The basic idea is that if we reflected on the possibility that we might well end up on the wrong side of the tracks we would focus on ameliorating conditions in the poorest location, in cognisance of the risk that we might well occupy it ourselves. By deliberating behind the veil of ignorance, the consensus thus struck would be objective, impartial and unbiased, being uninfluenced by race, class, fortunes or misfortunes, or personal attributes such as skills and talents. The veil of ignorance is an intellectual device that encourages objectivity by positing rules that would be of benefit to all, including the least advantaged, not just subjectively beneficial to the decision-maker and biased according to his personal situation or private predilections. This would in principle have the advantage of avoiding the endless squabbling over the meaning of justice which has historically fuelled hostility, violence and

[58] Rawls, *A Theory of Justice*, pp. 15, 16.

[59] Ibid., p. 11.

even war, with each political group seeking to enforce the dominance of its own subjective and idiosyncratic beliefs.

Rawlsians are thus primarily concerned with justice as fairness to all. They are concerned that if left to their own devices, the rich would trample callously over the poor, or abandon them to their fate, unless they were metaphorically reminded to consider the world they would wish to live in if they were poor. It is a reasoned and intellectual version of saying 'there, but for the grace of God, go I', expressing the moral counsel to put oneself in the other person's shoes. A mature and reasonable person is able to think of others and not just of himself, to be empathetic and able to foresee the impact of his actions on others. This is, in one sense, the 'reasonable man' known to the law of tort as Lord Atkin's neighbour principle:

> Acts or omissions which any moral code would censure cannot, in a practical world, be treated so as to give a right to every person injured by them to demand relief. In this way rules of law arise which limit the range of complainants and the extent of their remedy. The rule that you are to love your neighbour becomes in law, you must not injure your neighbour; and the lawyer's question, Who is my neighbour? receives a restricted reply. You must take reasonable care to avoid acts or omissions which you can reasonably foresee would be likely to injure your neighbour. Who, then, in law, is my neighbour? The answer seems to be – persons who are so closely and directly affected by my act that I ought reasonably to have them in contemplation as being so affected when I am directing my mind to the acts or omissions which are called in question.[60]

It is right that the legal framework should recognise a duty not to cause harm to others, through deliberate fault or through negligence or weakness, or sheer recklessness in failing to consider the impact of our conduct on others. This is part of the intellectual and moral context in which to understand Rawls's original position—as an intellectual devise that

[60] *Donoghue v Stevenson* [1932] UKHL 100.

encourages us to think of the least well off in making rules to govern human conduct.[61]

The moral imperative of being other-regarding is therefore not unique to Rawls. As Mises observed, it is intrinsic in civilised society that we should consider the implications of our decisions for the general welfare and avoid the endemic self-centeredness in which 'He who espouses the institution of slavery never stops to reflect that he himself could be a slave'.[62] Human beings often tend to be self-regarding and to perceive the world from their own vantage-point. We also, as Mises further observed, tend to be preoccupied with our immediate and short-term prospects. We tend to consider only our immediate best interests or the benefits to be derived for our own race or tribe or other group, sparing little thought for the long term implications including the rights of others or the welfare of society: 'The great mass of people do not inquire what will happen the day after tomorrow or later on. They think of today and, at most, of the next day. They do not ask what must follow if all other groups too, in the pursuit of their special interests, were to display the same unconcern for the general welfare'.[63] It is essential to liberty that we should consider the general welfare. The exhortation to put one's subjective preferences aside in considering the demands of justice is therefore indispensable. Rawls's theory of justice also shares with classical liberalism a concern that having regard to the general welfare should not undermine the importance of individual liberty. Rawls cautions that 'Each person possesses an inviolability founded on justice that even the welfare of society as a whole cannot override. For this reason justice denies that the loss of freedom for some is made right by a greater good shared by others'.[64]

In deriving principles of justice and fairness Rawls departs from classical liberalism in prioritising 'equal basic liberties' followed by 'the

[61] These ideas are reflected in Rawls's original position, which as Epstein observes 'has a certain kinship to Adam Smith's notion of the "impartial spectator" developed at length in *The Theory of Moral Sentiments*. To Rawls, ordinary individuals would never be able to get a sense of the just structure of social institutions if they only looked at the world from their limited perspective.' Epstein, R. A. (2002, November 27). Rawls Remembered.

[62] Mises, *Liberalism*, p. 40.

[63] Mises, *Liberalism*, p. 137.

[64] Rawls, *A Theory of Justice*, p. 3.

distribution of wealth and income'.[65] On this two observations may be made. First, Rawlsian liberalism excludes private ownership of the means of production or unconstrained contractual freedom from the scope of basic liberty.[66] Second, there is freedom to own, produce and contract, but only to the extent compatible with a basic equality of wealth and other social advantages. When racial equality debates are interpreted within this framework, it is said that the urgency of achieving racial equality as a component of basic liberty justifies encroaching upon individual liberty, so that the commitment to individual liberty as a component of justice surrenders, in its implementation, to social priorities such as ensuring the greatest benefit to the least advantaged (the difference principle) and fair access to equal opportunities. While income and wealth need not be equally distributed in Rawls's theoretical framework, they must be distributed in a manner that benefits everyone. Thus inequality should only be tolerated if it benefits or at least does not harm the least advantaged. For example, unequal pay may be tolerable to the extent that higher pay acts as an incentive to the least advantaged to work harder.[67] Beyond that, justice as fairness requires a program of redistribution from the most advantaged to the least well off.

Rawls acknowledges that there are matters on which we may continue reasonably to disagree as free and equal moral beings, including matters relating to personal property or falling within the personal sphere which are unlikely to place us in any significant advantageous social position compared to others. Even the most totalitarian communist societies permit personal ownership of, say, one's pen or toothbrush. But the personal sphere, like the scope of liberty, is relatively narrowly defined in Rawls's theory compared to the classical ideal. The scope of matters that

[65] Ibid., p. 53.

[66] 'Of course, liberties not on the list, for example, the right to own certain kinds of property (e.g., means of production) and freedom of contract as understood by the doctrine of laissez-faire are not basic; and so they are not protected by the priority of the first principle': Rawls, *A Theory of Justice*, p. 54.

[67] Gordon, D. 'According to Rawls, inequalities can benefit the worst off through their incentive effects. If people can increase their wealth or income beyond the norm, they will produce more; and part of the increase can be taxed away to help the poor.' Don't Dream the Impossible. In *An Austro-Libertarian View: Vol. II: Political Theory*, p. 151.

fall to be subjected to 'public reason' is correspondingly broad, encompassing matters that potentially place us in a position to be significantly better off than others or to produce outcomes which are likely to be disadvantageous to the least well off. From this perspective factors that may make us much better off than the least well-off, and which will not benefit the disadvantaged in any meaningful way, thus ought properly to be deliberated upon through public reason. It follows that just as we would not reasonably expect to be permitted a personal opinion on whether to infringe others' rights, such as an opinion on whether or not it would be acceptable to murder that annoying neighbour who has trespassed once again across our lawn, we should similarly not expect reasonably to be permitted our own opinions on whether billionaires should amass wealth while others languish in poverty and deprivation. That free market allocation permits disproportionate amounts of wealth to coexist with socio-economic inequality is thus viewed by the reasonable Rawlsian observer as a matter of similar gravity to other social and moral wrongs which reasonable people would regard as unjust. Thus it follows, for Rawlsian liberals, that wealth beyond a certain basic level should be publicly regulated as a social asset and subjected to redistributive policies.

In their critique of Rawls's notion of public reason George and Wolfe address the delineation of this construct of reasonableness, showing several ways in which the terms of the Rawlsian consensus only mask deeper layers of dispute. For example, they note that to satisfy the requirements of public reason an argument must be publicly stated, openly debated, and widely accepted by reasonable people. That seems all very well, until we consider the definitional questions underlying these terms. For example, we do not all agree on how much acceptance is required for a perspective to be accurately described as 'widely accepted'. How will wide acceptance be measured, and how widespread need it be? What are the requirements for debate to be described as 'open'? How will 'reasonable' people be identified? George and Wolfe ask:

> Are we to construct some idealized figure – something like law's 'reasonable man' - i.e., a person of 'average' intelligence with an 'average' education (whatever that would mean)? What are the standards according

> to which such an idealized figure should be constructed? Or is it that the arguments should be intelligible to well-educated people, who would then serve as representatives of all those who share their views, though perhaps to widely ranging degrees of sophistication? If so, how should we define 'well-educated'? And then we might ask whether the well-educated people of a given society or era might not accept as rational some pretty irrational positions.[68]

As George and Wolfe point out, 'What are from the liberal viewpoint mere "popular prejudices" may or may not truly be prejudices' and by the same token 'what are truly prejudices can masquerade as rational judgments'.[69] There is no widely accepted common sense meaning of terms like 'justice' or 'fairness'.[70] Thus labels such as 'just' or 'fair' or even 'reasonable' will not get us very far without closer scrutiny of the content of the ideas to which the labels apply. It is necessary to examine closely the truth, cogency and implications of the underlying values. Even without declaring what is wrong or right, true or untrue, matters with which Rawlsians are not directly concerned, it is clear that there still remains significant scope for serious debate that cannot be precluded or avoided by stating that the principle fails the test of 'public reason'. Rawls's definitional framework is itself highly value-laden. Defining the terms of what is, or is not, commonly agreed upon is a critical prerequisite to any public debate, and to insist that social outcomes are not legitimate if they are 'unfair' or 'unjust' merely begs the question by co-opting uncontested moral labels like 'justice' 'equality' and 'fairness' to apply exclusively to one's preferred ideologies. George and Wolfe are right to argue that the liberal doctrine of public reason remains unsatisfactory. It is

[68] George, R. P., & Wolfe, C. *Natural Law and Public Reason*, p. 53.

[69] Ibid.

[70] 'If liberal public reason is adopted as a standard, those who are most adept at manipulating language and symbols – members of what Irving Kristol labels the "knowledge class" – are going to end up with a disproportionate share of the power to define what can and cannot be admitted into public discourse and decision-making on the most fundamental issues facing a society': ibid.

> ultimately implausible and, in any event, an intellectually unhelpful doctrine. Its measures are unclear. It is difficult to square with the complexities of human knowledge. It is easily susceptible to partisan manipulation, especially by comprehensive liberals whose partisan interests, after all, it almost always serves. On the whole, we would be better off without it.[71]

There are further disputed characteristics of Rawls's reasonable man. He wishes to avoid risks such as 'the risk that, having acknowledged principles favouring activities in proportion to their intrinsic value, he might turn out to have preferences and criteria of excellence that could accordingly be treated as trashy and insupportable', or 'risk turning out to be abandoned at the bottom of the social heap'.[72] He is self-regarding in prioritising his well-being in all potential states of the world and is primarily motivated to safeguard and bolster his own position. He would not want to end up at the bottom of the scrap heap of life because he would not relish the challenge of working his way up with the attendant grave risk of failure. He seems predisposed to envy and jealousy, hence his desire to avoid ending up with substantially less material wealth than other people. His primary motivation is risk aversion rather than charity, so the only incentive that would motivate him to help the poor is the theoretical possibility that he could end up himself being poor. In this way we discover that the reasonable man is a socialist. He favours positive rights and social comforts which are guaranteed by the state, which in turn requires a legislative framework designed to implement wealth redistribution. It can therefore be seen that just as the underlying scope of public reason may be contested, people's concept of what is just or fair 'will almost certainly replicate their substantive moral disagreement regarding the underlying matters in dispute'.[73] A socialist will regard unequal wealth distribution as obviously 'unfair' while a free-market idealist would regard the question whether wealth distribution is fair or unfair with the same lack of moral concern as the question whether

---

[71] Ibid.

[72] Finnis, J. (2011). *Human Rights and Common Good: Collected Essays, Vol III* (p. 74). Oxford University Press.

[73] George, R. P., & Wolfe, C. *Natural Law and Public Reason.*

naturally occurring phenomena like stones or trees are 'fair' or 'unfair'. For example, it has been seen that the socialist regards natural ability as arbitrary and the resulting unequal outcomes as morally unjustified, yet if naturally occurring phenomena like intelligence or ability are neither just nor unjust, it could reasonably be argued that the outcomes to which ability gives rise are in turn morally neutral.

It must be concluded then that the Rawlsian view of redistributive justice, and the discourse of social justice to which it lends moral and ethical credence, is not as *objectively* reasonable as it seems. It has therefore failed to persuade the entire flock of liberals into its fold. For a scheme of justice that set out to achieve consensus, and to propose a political process through which we can all agree upon a reasonable social contract, this is serious. Unlike the classical liberal predilection to live and let live, the Rawlsian liberal cannot simply 'agree to disagree' because their goal is to arrive at a reasonable consensus. Gordon writes:

> Our aim, Rawls holds, should not be a mere modus vivendi with those who profess other conceptions of the good. Rather, we should seek a stable society in which people decide disputed questions by democratic discussion.[74]

Gordon highlights that a strategy of imposing Rawlsian values on those who disagree would be inconsistent with the moral high ground on which Rawlsian high liberalism has planted its social justice flag: 'Given [Rawls's 'fact of reasonable pluralism'] it would be wrong for the holders of one conception to impose their views on others; respect for others requires that we defend our political views with reasons others could acknowledge'.[75] Yet to live according to the tenets of Rawlsian liberalism and let others live according to classical liberal values would be intolerable to the Rawlsian. It would be tantamount to conceding failure: failure to arrive at a consensus, failure to persuade everyone, perhaps even a failure in the procedural systems of democratic decision-making and in the achievement of a stable constitutional order. Rather than

[74] Gordon, D. (2017). A Libertarian Rawls? *An Austro-Libertarian View, Vol. II*, p. 361.
[75] Ibid.

concede to such failure, Rawlsian liberals are given to pretending that we are all in agreement, insisting that there is no dispute, that we all uphold redistributive justice and the priorities of identity politics, and that the 'culture wars' are simply a myth fabricated by mischievous journalists.[76] They resort to affecting innocent surprise at the notion that there might be any dissenting opinions, or that such opinions are in any way being actively discouraged through 'a system of public shaming known as 'cancel culture', which its adherents carry out ruthlessly while repeatedly denying its existence'.[77] The assault on viewpoint diversity is not a simple matter of one or two celebrity academics whose high-profile public lectures have been cancelled. It is a broader and further-reaching intolerance of dissent in the liberal ranks.

> They insist that they are not 'cancelling' anyone, but merely 'holding the powerful to account'. But when a supermarket employee loses his job for a joke he posted on Facebook, it doesn't feel much like a valiant blow against plutocracy and the ruling class. Cancel culture is not, as its proponents claim, aimed at the most powerful in society. It is a method of systematically smearing ordinary members of the public for failing to toe the line. This takes the form of humiliation through online censure, and direct contact with their targets' employers in order to deprive them of a livelihood.[78]

Yet it is necessary for a Rawlsian to affect unawareness of anything like public shaming of those who disagree with their social justice and equalisation schemes, because high Rawlsian liberalism does not defend a strategy of brow-beating its opponents into submission, threatening that dissent has 'consequences' or simply locking dissenters out of the academic citadel and pretending they do not exist. It is politic for liberals

---

[76] Furedi, F. (2021). The Free-Speech Crisis Is Not a Right-Wing Myth: Those Denying the Existence of Cancel Culture Are Often in Its Vanguard. *Spiked*. https://www.spiked-online.com/2021/03/12/the-free-speech-crisis-is-not-a-right-wing-myth/.

[77] Doyle, A. (2021, January 1). Ignore the Gaslighting—Cancel Culture Is Real. *Spiked*. https://www.spiked-online.com/2021/01/01/ignore-the-gaslighting-cancel-culture-is-real/. For an example of this reality see Smith, E. (2020, February 22). The University 'Free Speech Crisis' Has Been a Right-Wing Myth for 50 Years. *The Guardian*. https://www.theguardian.com/commentisfree/2020/feb/22/university-free-speech-crisis-censorship-enoch-powell.

[78] Ibid.

to feign a lack of awareness that this is precisely the brow-beating strategy that has now been embraced, in violation of its own high liberal tenets. Frank Furedi writes:

> Just listen to them. In a piece entitled 'The myth of the free-speech crisis' Guardian journalist Nesrine Malik waves away people's 'overblown fears of censorship', and argues that those defending the principle of free speech are only doing so because they want to normalise 'hate speech or shut down legitimate responses to it'. As she sees it, her attack on free speech is really an attack on the 'racism and prejudice' that is supposedly advanced in its name.[79]

2.4 Warring Liberals

John Finnis highlights some of the ways in which the dominant philosophical view aligns with Rawlsianism, in the sense that the dominant view regards 'adherence to Rawls's principles of justice [as] the only or main way to get what it is rational to want in the way of (a) expressing one's nature and (b) securing from one's fellows the esteem necessary for one's self-respect'.[80] At a superficial level, it is true that if we assume agreement on the meaning or definition of terms like fairness and justice and what it means to be reasonable, we could on that basis identify a set of principles which all reasonable people would consider to be just. For instance it is easy to agree that murder or slavery are unjust; nobody who tried to defend the right to commit murder or the right to own slaves would deserve respect for their position.[81] Yet even taking clear examples of crimes that (hopefully) none of us would condone, there is still

[79] Furedi, F. (2021). The Free-Speech Crisis Is Not a Right-Wing Myth: Those Denying the Existence of Cancel Culture Are Often in Its Vanguard. *Spiked*. https://www.spiked-online.com/2021/03/12/the-free-speech-crisis-is-not-a-right-wing-myth/.

[80] Finnis, J. *Human Rights and Common Good: Collected Essays, Vol. III*, p. 74.

[81] As Robert George and Christopher Wolfe argue 'respect may sometimes be owed to persons who in general exhibit reasonableness and good will, but not to some position they have adopted, which one regards as so deeply misguided and wrong as to be unworthy of respect': *Natural Law and Public Reason*, p. 51.

ample scope for fierce philosophical disputation about the precise activities falling within the ambit of murder (is euthanasia murder? Is abortion murder?) or slavery (are workers in capitalist societies wage slaves? Do firms in the gig economy treat their workers as slaves?[82] Do workers have the right to 'work from home' because they are not slaves?) Reasonable people disagree about these types of questions, and neither side of the debate can be dismissed out of hand as unreasonable nor can further insight be gained on how to resolve these issues to everyone's satisfaction by saying that we all agree murder or slavery to be wrong. Thus outlining the scope of moral debate, defining clearly the issues on which we may reasonably disagree and delineating the boundaries of what falls within these definitions, will always remain highly contested.

This contestation surrounding deeply held moral values suggests that justifying redistributive mandates in Rawlsian terms would amount to imposing one conceptions of the good onto those who have a different conception of the good. Nor does Rawls's 'overlapping consensus' permit us to identify a range of subjective views with which we all agree as a basis for legal mandates, as the Rawlsian social consensus can only be arrived at if we exclude the views of those whose moral code fails to meet his standards of public reason. We might suppose that excluding unreasonable views is not only acceptable but in fact desirable, and this would indeed be the case if we could all agree on what amounts to a reasonable view. The ongoing debates about free speech and the increasing polarisation of politics illustrate that agreement on this point is however highly unlikely. Approximately half the liberal world now considers the other half to be utterly and inexplicably unreasonable. Each side claims that the other is divisive and authoritarian and intent on 'gaslighting' them. Yet for either side of the liberal divide to dismiss their opponents' views as unreasonable would exclude large swathes of the population from the bounds of reasonable consensus.

In the liberal debates there is now little meaningful engagement between 'free market' liberals who regard private property rights as an essential component of economic liberty, and 'democratic' liberals

[82] For discussion see 'I'm my own boss...': Active intermediation and 'entrepreneurial' worker agency in the Australian gig-economy. Barratt, T., Goods, C., & Veen, A. (2020). *EPA: Economy and Space, 52*(8), 1643–1661.

who prioritise a form of social or distributive justice that requires state encroachment upon property rights and individual liberty. Free-market liberals 'see liberalism as a doctrine of limited government power and wide individual economic freedom' while democratic liberals define distributive justice in a way that demands 'direct government involvement in the lives of citizens, most notably in economic affairs'.[83] There is little common ground between the two liberal camps, and it is unlikely that any compromise, where such may be possible, would be meaningful given that such a compromise would require one or both sides to abandon their core commitments. As Kukathas argues, a compromise arrived at by stripping an ideal 'of much of its substantive content' is unlikely to substantiate a robust theory, yet retaining that content in any meaningful way would 'run the risk of having a theory which commands the loyalty of only a small subset of its audience'.[84] A free market liberal would no more compromise the commitment to private property than the progressive liberal would compromise the commitment to distributive justice. To pursue social justice priorities that put peaceful coexistence at risk is untenable to classical liberalism, while progressive liberalism would be unwilling to risk undermining their visions of redistribution and equalisation. Nor are the two demands symmetrical. Private property protection demands no positive duties from anyone; it defends rather than undermines liberty. Distributive justice by contrast demands from others what one does not have, and thereby undermines liberty. The priority of equality in the progressive worldview demands not merely *social* obligations to be observed by those who so choose as a matter of courtesy but prescriptive mandates binding on all members of society. Thus for example it is said that free speech must be 'courteous' in order to make people of marginalised races feel welcome and valued in society, a demand which far exceeds the duty of tolerance. In the context of formal equality, the law does not require free speech to be courteous or inoffensive, nor does it impose on anyone a duty not to 'ignore' others. Tolerance entails only a negative legal duty not to cause harm to others not a positive duty to show them courtesy or even listen to

[83] Tomasi, *Free Market Fairness*, p. 2.

[84] *The Liberal Archipelago: A Theory of Diversity and Freedom*, p. 6.

them whenever they wish to speak.[85] The progressive perspective rejects negative duties to do no harm, arguing that negative duties are insufficient for substantive equality and that the moral 'consensus' on social justice therefore requires a stronger legal framework based on positive obligations.

The two liberal positions are thus fundamentally oppositional. Classical liberalism prioritises liberty, while Rawlsian progressivism undermines liberty in order to prioritise equality. This is not merely a theoretical debate about whether the two positions can be reconciled, as argued by those who point out that the two positions are not mutually exclusive and need not require trade-offs. It is also a political debate about which position ought to take priority. From a perspective of political philosophy, Kukathas highlights the fact that the issue in dispute lies precisely in the attempt to frame a theory of justice in contexts of political, philosophical and cultural diversity to be upheld as a consensus and backed by the state, when the moral imperatives of justice in relation to diversity lie beyond the realm of consensus and should therefore lie beyond the realm of law. Justice, as backed by the state and implemented by law, can only properly concern itself with formal equality and with rights and liabilities that apply equally to all. It is relatively easy to tolerate the existence of dissenting views which one is free to ignore and is not compelled to fund or join, while it is relatively difficult to tolerate dissenting views that are redefined and reformulated as binding legal obligations based on a reasonable 'consensus' with which one may strongly disagree.

In relation to philosophical diversity, there is little room for compromise between those who place the highest priority on liberty and those who would postpone the priority of liberty to redistributive goals. It is difficult for them even to be congenial or polite to each other. This

[85] Courtesy may be a moral obligation, but not one that is the appropriate subject of mandatory edicts as is commonly heard in modern discourse: 'We have thousands of students and staff from different backgrounds and countries. They are all entitled to feel welcome and valued. So we are providing a safe way to report concerns and help tackle bullying and harassment while raising awareness that small, often unintentional gestures can be upsetting. As is set out in our policy on freedom of speech, the university expects everyone to be tolerant of the opinions of others, while remaining courteous.' Professor Eilís Ferran Pro-Vice-Chancellor for Institutional and International Relations, University of Cambridge. https://www.telegraph.co.uk/opinion/2021/05/23/letters-surging-demand-gp-care-means-system-breaking-point/.

appears to trouble John Tomasi who has both progressive and libertarian friends and may therefore be classified as a 'bleeding heart libertarian'.[86] Being a professional academic his libertarian friends are vastly outnumbered.[87] Tomasi's theory of free market fairness attempts to identify liberal principles held in common by both progressives and libertarians, deriving a set of liberal principles 'erected atop footings sunk deep' in both progressive and libertarian ideals. Free market fairness encompasses a thick concept of economic freedom while also prioritising components of redistributive justice. Tomasi does not attempt to combine or straddle both strands of liberal thought or to achieve a compromise between them, but instead derives a 'genuine hybrid', a new theory of free market fairness which incorporates key themes from both liberal camps.[88] However, this theory of free market fairness emphasises ideal theoretic considerations while overlooking key constraints that arise in real world conditions and inevitably shape the contours of market capitalism.[89] Nor is his defence of market capitalism likely to persuade all his progressive friends, because no matter how much fairness is achieved through an application of the difference principle, they are reluctant to accept Tomasi's defence of private property rights or a thick concept of economic freedom.[90] Perhaps they sense that 'many of the words of Rawls are present in Tomasi's book, but not the music'.[91]

This throws into sharper relief the difficulties of arriving at a consensus for which the sacrifice of deeply held ideals would be required. As Gordon points out, 'Clearly, you cannot at the same time consistently be both a classical liberal and a high liberal' committed to substantive

[86] Maloberti, N. (2015). Rawls and Bleeding Heart Libertarianism: How Well Do They Mix? *The Independent Review, 19*(4), 563–582.

[87] 'Some of my best friends are libertarians', he announces, which is a problem because 'most of my professional friends and colleagues, by far, are left liberals': *Free Market Fairness*, pp. xi, xiii.

[88] Tomasi's theory of 'market democracy' does not attempt simply to 'fuse' the two camps but to 'show how the board pieces of liberalism might be arranged in a different way' for those liberals who find some of the theories in *both* camps to be attractive: *Free Market Fairness*, p. xxv.

[89] Pennington, M. (2014). Realistic Idealism and Classical Liberalism: Evaluating Free Market Fairness. *Critical Review: A Journal of Politics and Society, 26*(3–4), 375–407.

[90] Fowler, T. (2015). Markets, Choice and Agency. *Res Publica, 21*(4), 347.

[91] Gordon, D. A Libertarian Rawls? *An Austro-Libertarian View, Vol. II*, p. 362.

equality.[92] To insist upon such an uneasy accord would be unsatisfactory and unsustainable. A more promising path lies in recognising that there are diverse reasonable perspectives on the fundamental tenets of the just society. Even if we suppose that most people would agree with Rawls's perspective it would not follow that his is the only reasonable position, nor even that his position is necessarily correct by reason only of it being intuitively appealing to those in search of a moral code who accept that proposed by Rawlsians. It is perhaps doubtful whether any philosophical position on such matters can be impartial in the sense that it does not inherently endorse one preferred conception of the good while excluding others, and it may be that the most we can do is allow freedom for each person to follow their own moral code. It may be, in other words, that consensus on fundamental moral questions is neither possible nor desirable.

By the same token, classical liberalism does not itself claim to be neutral or impartial in relation to its core ideals, or the sole arbiter of what is reasonable or true. The love of liberty is not a 'neutral' position. It is explicitly partial to liberty. It is difficult to see how any political philosophy can claim to be objective or impartial, while staking its impartiality on having a unique claim to the reasonableness of its ideology. One could for example make an explicit commitment to individual liberty and the rights and freedoms necessary to enhance individual liberty including a rich concept of economic freedom, without declaring it to be unreasonable for someone else to devote his life to promoting social welfare or whatever other ends that a person might choose to value. One might defend market participation while respecting the ascetic's choice to sell all he has, give his money to the poor, and repair to a remote mountaintop to find moral salvation in solitude. Each protagonist may seek to persuade his opponents of the value of his commitment to individual liberty or to social welfarism, without either one depicting his own position as a 'neutral' or 'impartial' worldview that provides the only reasonable perspective on the good life or the pursuit of justice.

As Gordon has argued, Rawls's point that people have different conceptions of the good can therefore be used against Rawls's own

[92] Ibid., p. 359.

account of distributive justice, to the extent that there is no agreement on the meaning content of justice and his proposed consensus is derived by the expedient of excluding perspectives which are meaningful to those who hold them. The only alternative is for the individual or group who wields power or who commands a majority of voters to impose their conception of 'the good' on everybody else including the dissenting minority. In a society that defends individual freedom to pursue different conceptualisations of what they consider to be right and just, any notion of 'social justice' imposed on the society as a whole, necessarily reflects the opinion of only part of society and is to that extent highly unstable as a basis of the consensus sought by Rawls. It is sometimes supposed that such an unsatisfactory 'consensus' is the only alternative to conflict and war. Rawls's veil of ignorance is a powerful theoretical framework precisely because it suggests within which to achieve social harmony, avoiding futile and destructive ideological battles. But failure to arrive at agreement or consensus on fundamental philosophical principles need not imply that violent conflict will inevitably result. As Gordon writes:

> Certainly [Rawls] is right that people in modern societies do not unite in accepting a comprehensive doctrine. But he at once takes a false step. He assumes that, unless its situation is somewhat palliated, a society whose members have clashing beliefs faces disaster. But why assume this? Why cannot people with differing beliefs live together, even if each person refuses in public debate to dilute his own beliefs? Why, for example, should a natural-rights libertarian put aside his views just because he knows that egalitarians in his society do not share his beliefs? Why should he not attempt to defend his beliefs as best he can?[93]

We are not faced with a choice either to arrive at a consensus or else wage destructive war upon each other. Ideological wars are always wrong, regardless of whether the ideology is theist or whether it is the ideological adherence to 'social justice'. The methods of liberalism lie only in the exchange of ideas, in debate and in persuasion. Thus people may seek objective truths founded in natural law without setting out to coerce others to embrace what they believe to be true. Alternatively one may

---

[93] Rawls's Ballet. In *An Austro-libertarian View, Vol. II*, p. 91.

sacrifice his own personal goals and devote his own life to the good of society without attempting to coerce the radical individualist who prioritises the pursuit of his personal happiness into taking a vow of poverty. Nor need either of them succeed in persuading the other or establishing a framework of consensus. Nor need they even be friends or be forced to extend courteous remarks to each other. This is the beauty of freedom, that people can engage in peaceful coexistence and exchange without converting each other to their preferred moral or political ideologies.

Coming to an agreement or compromise in political or philosophical debate is widely regarded as the hallmark of being reasonable, the idea being that if we are all reasonable people we should be able to agree on basic principles. Thus failing to agree with one's ideological opponents, or failing to persuade them to abandon their opposition, failing to show courtesy to all whom one encounters, is often taken to imply that one or other of the parties is being wilfully trenchant or obstinate. But there is an alternative approach to understanding disagreement, a more honest approach of delineating clearly the issues on which we choose to agree to disagree, with cogent reasons for the position we choose to take. The attempt to arrive at a political and philosophical consensus on the demands of justice by agreeing on our shared values through public reason seems to offer a beguiling alternative to endless quarrelling over idiosyncratic values and subjective beliefs. But when people disagree on their conception of the good a way must be found to coexist peacefully, which in the absence of mutual agreement calls for mutual toleration.

In sum, the moral foundations of social justice are disputed. The dominant interpretations of social justice reflect highly contested egalitarian theories rooted in moral justifications which defy consensus. The diversity of modern society renders meaningful consensus elusive. As Kukathas argues, 'In a world of moral and cultural diversity one of the subjects over which there is dispute, even conflict, is the subject of justice. Different peoples, or groups, or communities, have different views or conceptions of justice'.[94] The Rawlsian consensus is achieved only on terms that exclude vast swathes of political and philosophical thought. Rather than consensus, therefore, we may choose peaceful

[94] Kukathas, *The Liberal Archipelago*, p. 6.

coexistence and voluntary exchange, to support cooperation through voluntary interaction and thereby to maximise productivity for our mutual benefit.

2.5 Legislating for Racial Equality

Although there is no social or political consensus around wealth redistribution as a policy goal, in principle everyone is committed to justice and fairness—nobody of good will would be against justice and fairness. Yet deeper investigation of equality concerns soon reveals that although equality is expressed as a concern with fair opportunity, it soon shifts seamlessly into the redistribution of the material wealth and political power that are seen as measurable indicators of progress in attaining the desired equal opportunities. The reasoning is that we would expect equal opportunities to lead to equal outcomes, thus opportunities which do not yield equal outcomes are *not*, by that definition, equal opportunities. This is reflected in the notion of 'equity' which requires an extra boost for those who start from a disadvantaged position in life. In this way socialist ideologies devoted to the equalisation of wealth are shrouded in a cloak of equality and depicted as unanimous moral ideals upheld by all reasonable people. This creates the impression of a consensus surrounding equality legislation. Equality legislation is thereby turned to the pursuit of ends which would not enjoy such widespread support if those ends were clearly and honestly stated. Social justice activists are often motivated by ideological goals quite different from what their supporters might imagine. As demonstrated by the foregoing discussion justice is a deeply value-laden label easily wielded to support fine-sounding social goals with little clarity on what precisely its proponents intend by their declarations of commitment to justice. Nor is clarity achieved merely by setting up equality as the ultimate goal, when it is not clear whether the aim is to treat like cases alike or whether the goal is to equalise things that are not alike. Rarely do proponents of equality intend to achieve absolute equality in all things, but even specifying equality of a minimum of goods required to live a good life, as proposed for example by Rawlsian philosophers, still leaves open a wide field of disputation concerning what precisely we intend to equalise and how we shall determine whether the equalisation goal has been met. How much equality is enough, and how shall we know when that goal has been accomplished?

Many liberals deny that these contestations are relevant in the context of racial equality. After all, the primary concern in the context of race is that everyone should be respectful and courteous to those of different races, though we might perhaps disagree on what courtesy entails. For example we agree to respect each other's freedom of speech although we might disagree on the appropriate bounds of 'robust civility'.[95] Hence many liberals would welcome positive duties of 'courtesy' (why would any reasonable person not try to be courteous?), and building on that would happily embrace legal duties to be 'actively anti-racist', from which it seems to follow that some form of re-education and specialised training in critical race theories would help to support the effort to be courteous. Framed in this way, duties defined as an emanation of social justice are not perceived to be in any sense a threat to individual liberty.[96] Assuming that we all want to be good people, progressive liberals cannot conceive of any plausible reasons why anybody would object to undergoing mandatory training in how to avoid triggering ethnic minorities through carefree use of language, how to be a better person, a more evolved human being, a higher and more sophisticated emanation of the liberal.[97] Even the denizens of the House of Lords are expected to be good sports, to rise from their sick beds and convalescence homes to participate in mandatory training on matters such as sexual diversity,

[95] 'The UK already has a welter of laws restricting our right to speak freely so it is surprising that the government believes that to encourage free expression we need still more legislation… Many universities, such as Oxford, have adopted strong statements recognising that free speech will include speech that is sometimes shocking and even offensive, and that what is needed in higher education is intellectual exchange within a culture of robust civility.' Lord Macdonald of River Glaven QC, Warden, Wadham College, Oxford; former director of public prosecutions. https://www.thetimes.co.uk/article/times-letters-proposed-tariff-free-australian-trade-deal-xjtmfkfj8.

[96] Smith, E. (2020, February 22). The University 'Free Speech Crisis' Has Been a Right-Wing Myth for 50 Years. *The Guardian*. https://www.theguardian.com/commentisfree/2020/feb/22/university-free-speech-crisis-censorship-enoch-powell.

[97] 'High liberals see their political view as having emerged through an evolutionary process, a process that demonstrates the moral supremacy of their view': Tomasi, *Free Market Fairness*, p. 99.

'valuing everyone' and 'how to spot harassment'.[98] Why would they not wish to improve themselves by learning about sexual diversity and harassment, training which could help to make other people's lives better? The desire of all people to be good people, and more importantly *to be seen* as good people, means that concerns about the threat posed to classical liberal ideals by the policy framework of 'equity' are met with insouciance and a general lack of urgency even by many who would consider themselves to hold individual liberty in high regard. Unlike the threat of unemployment or starvation which rouses people into immediate action, threats to peace and prosperity from anti-racism measures seem rather amorphous and detached from the practicalities of daily life. Nobody will starve tonight simply because the statue of Edward Colston has been toppled into Bristol Harbour or the statue of Sir John A. Macdonald beheaded in Ottawa. Rhodes may or may not fall outside Oriel College Oxford, but life will go on with barely a flutter in the daily news.

These types of impositions on individual liberty are tolerated, indeed embraced, as they are designed to make the world more welcoming and inclusive to marginalised people—most noble intentions which appear to demand only a modest incursion on speech or behaviour. And classical liberals, with their live and let live ethos, are prone to minding their own business, overlooking slight provocations, tending only to fight a rear-guard action when its core tenets fall under serious threat. As Mises observes, freedom by its very nature does not regularly set out to impose itself on others or make any claims or demands upon them. There will be no campaign to prevent schools or corporations from spending money (assuming that it is their own money) on unconscious bias training schemes. The cause of liberty does not rally support for legislative programmes by which everyone may be corralled into obeying its edicts, nor does it wage aggressive wars against those who lack a taste for freedom to 'force' them to be free. The legislative programme of liberty is defensive, consisting in 'the denial, the rejection, and the

[98] Percival, R. (2021, April 26). Peers 'Treated Like Children' on £82,000 Taxpayer-Funded Harassment Training Course. *The Express*. https://www.express.co.uk/news/politics/1428130/house-of-lords-training-course-sexual-harassment-taxpayer-funded-james-roberts.

combatting of everything that stands in opposition to [its core ideals]'.[99] It seeks victory not through slogans and marches but with ideas and arguments.[100] It is ever on the back foot in the culture wars because it does not object to other people wishing to embrace whichever ideas they choose to pursue.

For these reasons progressives, with their soft-socialist dreams, have long made small-scale incursions and encroachments upon individual liberty. They have made huge leaps largely unopposed over several decades. Not for them the principle of non-aggression; on the contrary they regard it as their duty to rescue others from moral turpitude using aggression if necessary, for their own good. As they carry on with the unfolding of their social justice programmes they are understandably mystified by what appears to them to be a sudden and inexplicable objection to their antics. From their perspective, racial equality has always been the unifying ideal of civilised people. The defence of individual liberty, most notably in the realm of free speech, seems to them tangential. They do not agree that they are attacking free speech, because they see 'cancel culture' as simply an attack on racism. And we all want to wage war on racism, don't we?

We do not. First, many of us do not deem social engineering to be the proper function of state power. Second, we see ourselves as individuals, not as components of a racial or other collective unit. Third, we do not admire the egalitarian desire for equality, an ugly desire rooted largely in comparison, envy and resentment. Comparison and equalisation are antithetical to individualism.[101] Envy and resentment, rooted in a desire to have access to the same things as others, or the fear of being worse

---

[99] 'In this defensive posture, the program of liberalism – and for that matter, that of every movement – is dependent on the position that its opponents assume towards it.' Mises, *Liberalism*, p. 103.

[100] 'Rhetorical bombast, music and song resound, banners wave, flowers and colors serve as symbols, and the leaders seek to attach their followers to their own person. Liberalism has nothing to do with all this. It has no party flower and no party color, no party song and no party idols, no symbols and no slogans. It has the substance and the arguments. These must lead it to victory'. Mises, *Liberalism*, p. 151.

[101] '[True individualism] can see no reason for trying to make people equal as distinct from treating them equally.' Hayek, *Individualism: True and False*, p. 30.

off than others, are not worthy sentiments. These sentiments have been regarded as vices since time immemorial, and not even conditions behind the 'veil of ignorance' can transform vice into virtue.

2.6 The Politics of Envy

The intertwined motivations of justice and envy are difficult to distinguish in the political debates as justice and envy are often two sides of the same coin. The key attribute of envy is measuring progress by exclusive reference to the achievements of others. Rising standards of living are deemed to be irrelevant if they fall short of the standard of living enjoyed by others. The wealth gap becomes an injustice, in itself, as equal enjoyment of material goods becomes the expected measure of social justice. As Sowell observes, 'Ideological crusades in the name of equality promote envy, the principle victims of which are those doing the envying'.[102]

Fernandez de la Mora identifies the emotion of envy at the heart of egalitarian dreams.[103] The expectation that the human experience should be equal is sometimes expressed colloquially as the 'fear of missing out' when others enjoy advantages to which we have no access, or 'all in this together' when we suffer disadvantages from which others seem exempt. Those who bitterly harbour such sentiments assume them to be inherent in the human condition and thus universal, shared by all their fellow men. But egalitarian worldviews are purely subjective, and there are good reasons to reject them. De la Mora argues that envy is always to be regarded as a vice because it yields no value; on the contrary, it searches for unattainable value in those with greater endowments and seeks to appropriate that value through coercive means in pursuit of a superficial equality. By encouraging its adherents to devote their lives to seeking preferment to bring them up to the lifestyle they perceive others to enjoy, envy churns up frustration and desperate unhappiness. The envy and resentment which drive egalitarian schemes reflect what Shelby Steele

---

[102] *Cosmic Justice*, p. 77.

[103] De la Mora, G. F. (1987). *Egalitarian Envy: The Political Foundations of Social Justice*. Paragon House.

describes as 'a sick hunger for racism', devoting increasing amounts of time and effort in search of evidence of racism in order to justify a claim for preferment.[104]

According to de la Mora's analysis envy strikes hardest where a person not only lacks what others have, but even worse fears that he will never be able to attain the same advantages owing to what he perceives to be a deprivation from which he unfairly suffers. The problem then is not simply scarcity, which could be resolved in any number of ways, but scarcity compounded by deep emotions of fear and injustice which are less easily resolved.

> The essential condition for envy to arise is not an objectivity of scarcity, as so many think, but rather a subjective inability to have…In the majority of cases the problem of the envious person has nothing to do with the fact that some good is more or less limited, but rather for a lack of the necessary capacity to obtain it.[105]

Measures targeting particular races for preferment may be intended to redress historical imbalances, but they also encourage resentment not merely as a desire to achieve more at the expense of others, but also to have what other people are enjoying that one is currently lacking and, as de la Mora highlights, perceives no legitimate means of acquiring. This is particularly true in cases where the perception of one's own inability to achieve the desired social standing is attributed to belonging to the 'wrong' race, and the inability to change one's race then explains the sense of frustration and the recourse to compulsion to achieve what is perceived to be enjoyed by other races and groups of which one could never become a member without some form of coercion.[106] The

---

[104] Steele, S. (2018). A Sick Hunger for Racism. *Hoover Digest*, p. 158: 'The writer Walker Percy once wrote of the "sweetness at the horrid core of bad news." It's hard to witness the media's oddly exhilarated reaction to, say, the death of Trayvon Martin without applying Percy's insight. A black boy is dead. But not all is lost. It looks like racism. What makes racism so sweet? Today it empowers': p. 159. De la Mora also sees power at the root of envy: 'Social envy is born from the desire for power': *Egalitarian Envy*, p. 70.

[105] De la Mora, *Egalitarian Envy*, p. 69.

[106] 'Social envy is grounded in the belief that others are happier because of the position they occupy in the community due to their privileged birth or promotions.' Ibid., p. 70.

aggrieved person feels not so much that he envies others, but rather that he has been the victim of a grave injustice due to the historical antecedents of his group.[107] The fear of inability to achieve similar results for no fault of one's own is then easily translated into a noble desire for justice where one's lack of desired goods is attributed to the fact that others enjoy them—some are poor *because* others are rich.[108] It seems 'just' that we should acquire the object of our envy, where the reason for lacking it lies in factors we perceive to be beyond our control and thus beyond our ability to remedy. The reality that some people start life with advantages not enjoyed by others and the fact that some people have the advantage of belonging, for example, to a more industrious or well-established family or social community than others is then taken to be a justification for compulsory redistribution.[109] In that way the preoccupation with disparities and comparative rates of progress transforms envy from an unworthy vice into a virtue—justice—that demands vindication through legal claims. A policy goal of ensuring that identity-based groups participate in social and economic life on an 'equal basis' with other groups promises to remedy this frustration, but only compounds the problem by encouraging destructive politics rooted in envy, in which 'the envious one does not find dominant the desire to be more, but rather to make the other less; there is no will to improve, but rather to level all'.[110] De La Mora argues that this worldview does not yield any value; on the contrary, it searches for unattainable value in others and seeks to

---

[107] Ibid., p. 74.

[108] 'The envious feels sadness because he believes the good in others is the cause of his own misery. This belief is not objectively true': Ibid., p. 29.

[109] 'From the point of view of individualism there would not appear to exist even any justification for making all individuals start on the same level by preventing them from profiting by advantages which they have in no way earned, such as being born to parents who are more intelligent or more conscientious than the average. [Individualism] recognizes the family as a legitimate unit as much as the individual; and the same is true with respect to other groups, such as linguistic or religious communities, which by their common efforts may succeed for long periods in preserving for their members material or moral standards different from those of the rest of the population': Hayek, *Individualism: True and False*, p. 31.

[110] Identity politics too often reflects destructive motivations: 'the envious one does not find dominant the desire to be more, but rather to make the other less; there is no will to improve, but rather to level all:' De la Mora, *Egalitarian Envy*, p. 68.

appropriate it through coercive means, creating a heightened sensitivity towards grievance and oppression.

At the individual level few people would regard it as inherently unfair that they have a different level of income compared to, say, their next-door neighbour.[111] Income and attainment comparisons and concerns about disparities are linked to a strong sense of collective or group identity, for example the idea that all workers doing the same job should earn the same pay, that all workers in the same firm should earn a similar wage which should in turn reflect a proportionate percentage of the CEO's wage, that all races should exhibit equal levels of wealth, and many other ideas reflecting the conviction that it would be unjust for any group to earn much more than other groups. Thus the concept of 'justice' is transformed from a focus on what is fairly earned or deserved by each individual, into a socially and morally acceptable channel to express what are, in their roots, feelings of collective resentment at the perceived fortunes of other groups. As this resentment is collective, it takes no account of individual outliers—if white men as a group are 'privileged' then the individual white man who is disadvantaged is irrelevant to the analysis of the outcomes of his group as a whole, and so is the poor white boy who after all may one day rise to become a rich white man. Similarly, if black men as a group are oppressed then the individual black man who is a billionaire is irrelevant to the analysis. In this way the idea of social justice has to a great extent become inextricably conflated with the politics of collective envy.[112]

---

[111] '[True individualism] can see no reason for trying to make people equal as distinct from treating them equally'. Hayek, *Individualism: True and False*, p. 30.

[112] 'A contemporary disguise of collective envy is what is called 'social justice'… A fundamental postulate is established that the more just a society is, the more equal its members are in opportunities, position, and wealth; and immediately it is established that the party will fight without rest to achieve such "justice".' De la Mora, *Egalitarian Envy*, p. 93.

2.7 The Virtue of Individualism

The collective nature of group envy suggests another ground on which to reject egalitarianism, and that is on grounds of moral individualism. Individual liberty is a value worth defending based on the innate value of humanity and the diversity of human traits including all our follies and frailties. In legal philosophy, rights generally inhere in individual human beings or individual entities, not in groups. In political discourse we may refer to 'ethnic minority rights' but these rights vest in each individual member of the specified group, not in the amorphous group as a collective entity. As Epstein puts it, 'Each of us is an individual. The rights we are trying to protect are only those belonging to ourselves'.[113] Abstract duties devolved onto ethnic groups or artificial entities such as corporations ultimately require individuals to take specific action, if the right is to be at all meaningful.[114] Thus it is meaningless, from a legal perspective, to speak of 'quasi-collectivist' rights vesting in cultures or identity-based groups.[115] The notion of group rights is not only incoherent, but also liable to create division and inter-group hostility if rights are granted to some groups and not to others.

Egalitarians might argue that equality is not simply a matter of individual welfare but is also necessary in the interests of creating a better, more cohesive, society, especially in social and cultural contexts where many people consider group identity to be important. The challenge is that communitarian ideals like pursuit of 'the common good' ultimately require some form of legal constraint or coercion to ensure that everyone falls in line and aspires to live according to community values. Individual liberty inherently goes against this by eschewing coercion in all its

---

[113] *Equal Opportunity or More Opportunity?*, p. 1.

[114] 'The collectives on which we impose duties are comprised of individuals. Organisations do not act themselves; they act through individuals and for individuals, be they shareholders, union members or faculty and students. Consequently, in analysing the impact of the statute we must always follow a postulate of methodological individualism. We cannot simply pair human rights to a set of correlative duties on abstract bodies, hoping thereby to externalise their costs on no one in particular. We must trace the implications of the statute through the entity to the particular individuals on whom those duties will be imposed'. *Equal Opportunity or More Opportunity?*, p. 4.

[115] Modood, T., et al., *Ethnic Minorities in Britain*, p. x.

forms. Individualism upholds liberty for all, including, it must be said, those who have not devoted their lives to the pursuit of moral virtue as others consider that to be. Each person's natural rights as a human being do not depend on whether his neighbours consider him to be a good person and a morally upstanding citizen. Were it otherwise, none of our rights would be guaranteed. Individualism has therefore been criticised for being 'selfish' to the extent that human beings left free to pursue what they consider to be the good life often make choices of which other people may disapprove on grounds that those choices do not tend towards the common good, such as smoking or eating unhealthy food or, in our context, being impolite and failing to be courteous to those of other races. It is feared that individualism will lead to anarchy, and anarchy to social chaos.

Friedrich Hayek helpfully extricates individualism from its associations with selfishness and isolationism and situates the individual in society based on voluntary exchange with other individuals. Individualism does not connote the thoughtless and exploitative person who barricades himself in his castle, shuns social interaction and externalises the costs of his private activities onto society at large.[116] These interpretations are no more than a caricature, described by Hayek as 'the silliest of the common misunderstandings' of individualism in economic life. Nor does individualism simply denote the romanticised 'rugged individualism' reflected in the solitary and atomistic life of Robinson Crusoe, isolated on a desert island relying on nobody but himself for his daily existence. For Hayek, the role of individuals in constituting society relies on an accurate understanding of society, which in turn begins from an accurate understanding of individual preferences. He argues that it is not possible to understand societies 'as entities sui generis which exist independently of the individuals which compose them'.[117] Rather, the importance of social process, in particular market order, is

[116] See discussion in Herzog, L. (2013). *Inventing the Market: Smith, Hegel and Political Theory*. Oxford University Press.

[117] Ibid. Thus individualism in this context is better understood as that 'which regards man not as a highly rational and intelligent but as a very irrational and fallible being, whose individual errors are corrected only in the course of a social process, and which aims at making the best of a very imperfect material.' Hayek, *Individualism: True and False*, pp. 8, 9.

that it often improves on what might have been designed by a single individual: 'if left free, men will often achieve more than individual human reason could design or foresee'.[118] Hayek's notion of individualism maintains simply that 'there is no other way toward an understanding of social phenomena but through our understanding of individual actions directed toward other people and guided by their expected behaviour'.[119] Nor does Hayek's notion of spontaneous order rule out a role for democratic preferences or state interventions.[120] In this sense Hayek assigns importance to understanding the implications of individual actions for the way society is ordered; he is concerned with how to identify general rules for a legal system that would 'make man by the pursuit of his interests contribute as much as possible to the needs of other men'.[121]

This notion of individualism would be regarded by many people as common sense, reflecting the simple idea that the greatest forest is constituted by individual trees so the well-being of each individual matters for its own sake. Understood that way individual self-interest has nothing to do with greed or even selfishness in the sense of causing harm to others in order to gain advantage at their expense. Individual self-interest points instead to an important incentive in human life and in particular the aspiration towards personal ideals—the ideals of each individual as a human being rather than the ideals of one's race as a collective group. Within this theoretical framework incentives underpinning individual economic activity matter because the right incentives make each and every individual better off. In saying 'society? There's no such thing' Margaret Thatcher was expressing no more than the obvious point that society has no independent esoteric existence with interests

[118] Ibid., p. 11.

[119] Ibid., p. 6.

[120] Consistent with Epstein's view: 'Markets work best when property rights are secured by the state, when contracts are enforced, when fraud and duress are held in check, when monopolies are constrained, and when social infrastructure is available. All this activity takes government action; to create, as Coase suggests, the correct incentives to get the best out of individual self-interest. Within this general legal framework, the role for spontaneous order—a phrase that leaves me uneasy—should be best understood as demanding only that the state take no role in deciding (a) who should contract with whom, and (b) what the terms and conditions of their agreements should be': *Equal Opportunity or More Opportunity?*, p. 57.

[121] Hayek, *Individualism: True and False*, p. 20.

and duties detached from those of the individuals who constitute society. In understanding the functioning of markets, individualism does not imply that that the notion of 'society' is irrelevant to understanding the demands of justice. As Hayek points out, all justice is 'social' because it relates to interactions between individuals, rather than the isolated acts of an individual with no effect on anybody. Thus individualism is understood in relation to the idea of society as a network of interaction, exchange and cooperation between the individuals making up the society.[122] It follows that free markets are not constructed by 'isolated or self-contained individuals' because they rely on exchange, trust and 'voluntary and spontaneous collaboration of individuals:'[123] their 'whole nature and character is determined by their existence in society'.[124] The typical workplace, based on teamwork, cooperation and collegiality, is a good example of this. Thus a defence of individual rights does not undermine the importance of society—on the contrary, promoting individual liberty and free exchange is the best way to promote social cohesion. As Mises writes:

> The starting point of liberal thought is the recognition of the value and importance of human cooperation, and the whole policy and program of liberalism is designed to serve the purpose of maintaining the existing state of mutual cooperation among the members of the human race and extending it further. The ultimate ideal envisioned by liberalism is the perfect cooperation of all mankind, taking place peacefully and without friction.[125]

This brings us to the heart of the issue discussed in this book. As observed at the beginning of this chapter, racial equality, and the legal endorsement and promotion of its collectivist, socialist, racialist visions,

---

[122] Mises explains: 'Human society is an association of persons for cooperative action. As against the isolated action of individuals, cooperative action on the basis of the principle of division of labor has the advantage of greater productivity…All human civilisation is founded on this fact'. Mises, *Liberalism*, p. 1.

[123] Hayek, *Individualism: True and False*, p. 16.

[124] Ibid., p. 6.

[125] Mises, *Liberalism*, p. 76.

threatens liberty by threatening the concept of the individual. Individualism recognises the broad diversity of perspectives within and between different ethnic groups, genders, and other identity-based 'communities' in relation to social ideals and the pursuit of the good life. Diversity of opinion, moral values and the best way to pursue happiness are fatally obscured by preoccupation with group outcomes. A group cannot experience happiness or success. Society is happy only to the extent that it comprises happy individuals, and in final analysis the pursuit of happiness is unavoidably a deeply individual quest.

In this context individualism distinguishes itself specifically as a 'system which forms the alternative to socialism' in the political or ideological sense.[126] Socialism is a system which prioritises a dominant role for the state in wealth redistribution, as contrasted with reliance on free markets. While the distinction may in some cases be a question of degree, with some socialist states being more interventionist than others and much debate about what constitutes 'real socialism' (when socialist schemes fail we are often informed that it was not based on *true* socialism), we need not distinguish between degrees of market interventionism in order to explore the appropriate scope of law and regulation in contexts of racial diversity. Individualism in this context implies a preference for voluntary exchange over coercion.[127] This in turn leaves as wide as possible a 'sphere of responsibility' for individual decision-making over legislative diktat.[128] As will be seen in the ensuing chapters, the liberalising potential of competitive marketsassociated with human progress and flourishing is clear from the empirical evidence in various jurisdictions, and from economic studies showing that markets matter more than legal protections in promoting advancement of the marginalised. The interactions between individuals as members of society, such as trade or work relationships, are in turn central to understanding the

[126] Hayek, *Individualism: True and False*, p. 3.

[127] 'Much of what in the opinion of many can be brought about only by conscious direction, can be better achieved by the voluntary and spontaneous collaboration of individuals': ibid., p. 16.

[128] 'The essential point is not that there should be some kind of guiding principle behind the actions of the government but that government should be confined to making the individuals observe principles which they know and can take into account in their decisions.' Ibid., p. 18.

functioning of markets. By seeking closely to regulate private transactions equality legislation limits the individual sphere of decision-making. The purview of antidiscrimination legislation matters not simply because it gets some principles wrong or overextends in specified respects, but precisely because nobody is exempt from its application. By highlighting individual potential in place of the collective outcomes of class, group, or race, we avoid some of the hazards of setting an unrealistic standard of ensuring that everyone participates in social and economic life on an 'equal basis' in all cases without regard to context. We also expose some of the unintended consequences of 'one size fits all' equality policies, notably diminishing economic opportunities and increasing inter-group hostility as some groups benefit at the expense of others.

3

Racial Diversity, Discrimination and Prosperity

The discussion thus far has examined some of the ways in which progressivism cloaks itself with the moral authority to redesign the world and allocate rights and entitlements according to socialist ideals. This chapter turns to a closer consideration of the regulatory challenges posed by racial diversity and the perceived need to advance racial equality. The chapter argues that the public policy preoccupation with racial justice is concerned not with prosperity, but with providing a moral justification for wealth redistribution schemes. The arguments in favour of promoting racial equality begin with the idea that socio-economic inequalities are caused by various forms of injustice which call for redress. The proposed remedial system is implemented through various redistribution schemes which are said to justify increasing state control over wealth and income. By these steps the legislative basis of racial equality provisions is intrinsically linked not only to factors such as education, health and housing but also to disparities of income and wealth in a broader sense. The discussion in this chapter therefore considers the nature of wealth inequalities and the causal links drawn by egalitarians between inequality and injustice. The chapter highlights the absence of any objective evidential

W. Njoya, *Economic Freedom and Social Justice*, Palgrave Studies in Classical Liberalism, https://doi.org/10.1007/978-3-030-84852-1_3

basis establishing a link between discrimination and inequality. This exposes the weak moral and ethical foundations of wealth redistribution schemes. The notion of redressing historical grievance, which is increasingly offered by progressive politicians as the main justification for proposed racial justice schemes, is also shown to be unjustified.

Our discussion of prosperity in contexts of racial diversity draws a distinction between *relative* inequality and rising levels of prosperity. As adverted to in our discussion of the politics of envy, the key concern of egalitarian theories is not with socio-economic deprivation or lack of access to basic resources, but with inequality measured through statistical disparities. Historically the trajectory of rising prosperity across the board is undeniable.[1] Although the income gap between the richest and poorest may rise and fall in different contexts, in absolute terms more people are better off today than at any previous time in history. This includes access to consumer goods, rising standards of living, and better access to education and health care.[2] The widening scope of prosperity and the growing abundance of opportunities for advancement are shown to be predominantly the outcome of voluntary market interactions. For example Robert Higgs shows that the standard of living has been consistently raised by ethnic minorities through labour migration in pursuit of better opportunities, higher levels of education and literacy, developing broader skills and experience in diverse industries and occupations, property acquisition and the expansion of enterprise ownership. The

[1] Robert Higgs observes that 'By modern standards the average black of 1914 remained desperately poor; even by comparison with the whites of his own time he was poor indeed. Perhaps because he remained relatively poor the gains in his material well-being during the period 1865–1914 [following emancipation] have often been denied or minimized. But the evidence lends overwhelming support to a different conclusion: in fact, the first half century of black freedom witnessed major improvements in the level of living.' Higgs, R. (1977). *Competition and Coercion: Blacks in the American Economy, 1865–1914* (p. 117). Cambridge University Press.

[2] These gains are not necessarily reflected in the income tax data used to highlight income inequality, and thus wrongly give the impression that inequality is growing: 'the use of tax data instead of household survey data produces enormous illusory inequalities. Using tax data for the rich and survey data for the non-rich compounds the illusion.' Aiyar, S. A. (2017, October 11). Thomas Piketty Couldn't Have Been More Wrong About India: Just Look at the Data. *The Economic Times*. https://economictimes.indiatimes.com/news/economy/indicators/view-thomas-piketty-couldnt-have-been-more-wrong-about-india-just-look-at-the-data/articleshow/61032079.cms.

evidence is clear that much of this progress was attained in the face of overwhelming odds, through the efforts and persistence of marginalised people determined to get ahead.[3]

Understood against that background it is clear that the main driver of racial disquiet is not absolute poverty or an inability of black people to make progress, but the racial gap in wealth and income.[4] Inequality becomes in itself a condition that is deemed to be a source of suffering, with any improvement in material conditions considered to be irrelevant in light of the wealth gap. By highlighting statistical disparities and ignoring rising prosperity, political attention is diverted away from the real causes of inequality. Those who are falling behind are discouraged from attending to the real causes of their problems or from embarking on the path to progress, as they appear to be convinced that the problem lies in historical grievances and therefore the only solution lies in government reparations. Thus the issue in public debates is not the most effective way for racial minorities to make progress, but the quickest way to close the prosperity gap through equity schemes. The racial gap is depicted as an urgent problem, so that speed is deemed to be of the essence. Legislation in theory works faster than markets, thus redistributive laws are commended by egalitarians as the quickest method of social engineering.

This chapter shows some of the ways in which these egalitarian perspectives are short-sighted. Prosperity is not simply a matter of comparisons and gaps, but draws upon other related ideals and values of the good society, including the generosity of spirit that allows us to celebrate the fortunes of those around us because, indirectly, our fortunes are all linked. The worthiness of wishing well to other people even when they belong to a different race or culture does not come simply from being other-regarding, but also from awareness that a growth in prosperity and

[3] Higgs observes: 'That the stock of human capital expanded greatly in the first half century after emancipation is incontestable. That this larger stock yielded correspondingly greater returns to the efforts of the black labor force is equally evident' *Competition and Coercion*, p. 121.

[4] As Higgs observes, everything depends on whether we choose to observe progress or choose instead to measure the gap: 'Viewed in the context of its very low starting point and the serious obstacles and discouragements in the way of its increase, black property holding after 50 years of freedom appears substantial. Judged by the standards of white accumulation, it appears much less impressive.' *Competition and Coercion*, p. 122.

abundance means a growth in opportunities for all. As Sowell has emphasised, it is myopic and wrong to view other people's success as nothing but a source of grievance. Society as a whole benefits from encouraging voluntary exchange wherever feasible. We know that people are happier when they are involved in relationships and transactions they value, and become resentful and even hostile when forced to follow 'moral' codes they do not agree with in a bid to shortcut or bypass the path to progress.

The book so far has argued that egalitarian ideals lack a sound ethical foundation. Building upon that premise this chapter argues that legislative attempts to right historical wrongs are ethically unsound and harmful in the long term. This chapter therefore subjects to closer scrutiny the philosophical justification for the antidiscrimination principle that underpins the legal framework, in order to evaluate its suitability in achieving the progressive hopes and ideals which its proponents seek to advance. The chapter supports the purpose of the book in defending economic freedom by arguing that individual liberty enables prosperity and therefore obviates the need to feel trapped by historical disadvantage. The chapter begins by questioning whether historical antecedents cause racial minorities to be so vulnerable that special legal protection is needed to help them feel safe. The chapter then concludes with a discussion of the fortunes of racial minorities in free markets.

3.1 Safety First and 'Zero Tolerance' of Racism

The principle of racial equality was understood in the early civil rights movement as a quest for full and unrestricted participation of all races in social and economic life. Martin Luther King Jr.'s powerful speech reflects a political movement with concrete goals such as the right to vote, to earn a living, and not to have one's ability judged or be excluded from public life based on race.[5] The brazen injustices and cruelties of

[5] 'So even though we face the difficulties of today and tomorrow, I still have a dream. It is a dream deeply rooted in the American dream. I have a dream that one day this nation will rise up and live out the true meaning of its creed: We hold these truths to be self-evident, that

segregation and apartheid were plain to be seen. Much has changed since that time. The anti-racism drive is no longer about emancipation or freedom; it seeks instead to have racial difference explicitly embraced by the institutional framework, to have racial identity acknowledged in public discourse, and for race to be a prime determinant in allocating public resources. In that context the claims for equity made against the state have assumed a more amorphous character, with concrete goals for material and financial reward increasingly supplemented by the general aim of keeping people safe from suffering emotional and psychic harm said to be caused by racism.

Thus reports of racism in our universities are substantiated by reference to amorphous matters such as being made to feel unappreciated or undervalued, or feeling the need to work harder than others to earn the same level of reward.[6] Universities thus have a legal and moral duty 'to protect all students and staff from feeling unsafe, unwelcome and inferior'.[7] The reported racist experiences include 'being ignored or excluded from conversations or group activities' and other 'subtle and nuanced acts, often known as microaggressions' that are often, in cases of unconscious bias, unintentional, inadvertent and lacking any hostile motive such as a white student walking into the room and failing to sit next to a black student, or a white colleague raising their eyebrows while a black person is speaking.[8] The subtle and nuanced nature of microaggressions does not belie the very real sense of emotional harm they occasion:

---

all men are created equal… I have a dream that my four little children will one day live in a nation where they will not be judged by the color of their skin but by the content of their character. I have a dream today.' https://www.npr.org/2010/01/18/122701268/i-have-a-dream-speech-in-its-entirety.

[6] Equality and Human Rights Commission. (2019, October 23). *Tackling Racial Harassment: Universities Challenged*. https://www.equalityhumanrights.com/sites/default/files/tackling-racial-harassment-universities-challenged.pdf.

[7] University staff report 'being excluded and marginalised, overlooked for professional development, and facing hostile comments and stereotyping… Microaggressions are often shrugged off and harassment brushed under the carpet': ibid.

[8] Ibid.; see also Turner, C. (2021, May 20). *Cambridge Accused of Creating 'Police State' Where Dons Can Be Reported for Raising an Eyebrow*. https://www.telegraph.co.uk/news/2021/05/20/exclusive-cambridge-accused-creatingpolice-state-dons-can-reported/.

> Racial harassment can cause humiliation, isolation, loss of confidence and serious harm to mental health and wellbeing. Students who experienced racial harassment said they were left feeling angry, upset, depressed, anxious and vulnerable; 8% said they had felt suicidal. Staff reported experiencing similar impacts. Students and staff disengaged from core activities, to keep themselves safe or to prevent further erosion of their confidence and wellbeing, but at a cost to their studies or careers.[9]

Psychic safety therefore features prominently in framing the principles of racial equality. The legal framework responds to the threat of psychic and emotional harm by creating a range of civil and criminal offences arising from causing psychiatric injury to others, for example through hate-speech. In addition, public institutions have statutory 'safeguarding' duties towards vulnerable individuals and groups. For example the guidance on 'decolonising' schools is framed in terms of the duty of care to keep staff and students safe from psychological risk and harm.[10]

The issue then arises as to how such threats will be identified. In practice, this is defined largely by reference to the victim's perception. For example a government report on institutional racism in the UK police force (i.e. racism that is reflected not in any individual intention but in the procedures and practices of the institution) emphasised the 'perception' of racism in its findings, observing that it would be wrong for the police to draw a distinction between the 'perception' of racial minorities and the 'reality'.[11] Oddly for a murder inquiry, the language said to be 'unwittingly' used by the police (such as the use of the word 'coloured') and the lack of training in more sensitive racial descriptors was treated

---

[9] Equality and Human Rights Commission, *Tackling Racial Harassment*.

[10] 'How does the school/college enable staff and pupils to understand and vocalise how to keep themselves safe from everyday risks such as racist, sexist or homophobic abuse, sexual exploitation or grooming? Do staff and pupils feel safe and confident to report bullying and abuse? Does the school/college's approach to wellbeing and belonging understand the psychological harms caused to Black pupils from racism and the way racism is internalised?' National Education Union. (2021). *Framework for Developing an Anti-racist Approach, Theme 3: Power and Voice*. https://neu.org.uk/media/11236/view.

[11] February 1999. The Stephen Lawrence Inquiry. Report of an Inquiry by Sir William Macpherson of Cluny. Cm 4262-I. https://assets.publishing.service.gov.uk/government/uploads/system/uploads/attachment_data/file/277111/4262.pdf.

as significant evidence of 'institutional racism'.[12] Interpreted in that way the risk of being harmed by offensive words or conduct engages the institutional duty of care. Threats of harm abound. We are now deep in Alice's *Wonderland* where 'silence is violence' and ancient stone statues high above the parapets are perceived as threatening. Ideologues of all political hues declare their moral certainties to be an outcome of 'critical theories', as rationality and objective truth give way to emotionalism and subjective lived experiences. Subjective perceptions of racism have an important and very real perspective to share, as do all subjective life experiences, but without objective evaluation they constitute a weak and unstable basis for legal intervention. Words now mean whatever their ideological expositors declare them to mean.

By claiming not to feel safe in the presence of racist words and images a powerful moral and legal sanction is invoked. As Frank Furedi argues in his analysis of the 'culture of fear', framing offensive speech or conduct as 'intangible harms to the psyche' and conceptualising racial discrimination as a safeguarding issue 'is grounded in the recognition that safety enjoys a unique status as an uncontested value'.[13] Furedi also highlights the growing danger of 'conceptual creep', with the 'conceptual inflation of safe space' from the original notion of a designated physical location where people with legally protected identity characteristics could retreat to safety from a hostile world, to the prevailing idea of the world itself as a universal safe space wherein opinion should be sanitised and offensive speech eradicated. This is an 'inverted quarantine' in the sense that those at risk are not isolated for their own safety, but the world itself is constructed into a safe space by isolating and neutralising any threats to psychic well-being. Far from making people feel safer, the conceptual

[12] 'As to this officer's racism awareness it was established that he was accustomed to referring to black people as "coloured". He said to the Inquiry that he was not aware that this might be regarded by black people as insulting until he watched Mr Groves giving evidence on the screen at the Inquiry. This officer could not remember receiving any formal racism awareness training, although he said that he "seemed to remember some training in this regard when he was a probationer at Catford". This is yet another indication that the training of officers in this department of their activity and relationship with the community was almost totally lacking.' Macpherson Report, Para. 12.77.

[13] Furedi, F. (2018). *How Fear Works: Culture of Fear in the Twenty-First Century* (p. 233). Bloomsbury.

inflation of safety and harm and the depiction of the world and other people as threatening only heightens the perception of threat. Furedi explains:

> Yet precisely because support for an inverted quarantine is driven by the presumption that the world is unsafe, those devoted to the cause of safe spaces can never feel secure. Indeed, the very demand for safety contains an inner logic towards discovering more and more threats to fear.[14]

It is a typical feature of public accusations of racism that the alleged conduct focuses entirely on the harm caused to the victim rather than the nature of the threat. For example, King's College London apologised for causing 'harm' to its staff by expressing condolences concerning the death of Prince Philip, though the nature of the alleged harm was not disclosed.[15] Often reports of 'racist and sexist' words do not disclose the words themselves, because it is irrelevant what the actual words were if the victim reports that they felt them to be racist or sexist and suffered harm from hearing them. Those accused of causing offence might presume, quite reasonably, that objective analysis and the existence of 'plausible grounds for drawing those conclusions' should be relevant to establishing their culpability where a victim claims to feel unsafe due to their words or conduct.[16] But the absence of plausible grounds that might justify a feeling of being under threat, or the lack of any objective assessment regarding a conceivable risk of harm inherent in the situation, carry little weight in assessing liability for discrimination or breach of the institutional duty of care. The reason for this approach, as Furedi argues,

---

[14] Ibid.

[15] 'One of Britain's top universities has apologised for the "harm" caused to staff after they complained about being sent a photograph of Prince Philip who had a "history of racist and sexist comments"'. Fullerton, J. (2021, May 30). *The Telegraph*. https://www.telegraph.co.uk/news/2021/05/30/kings-college-apologises-harm-caused-staff-photo-tribute-prince/.

[16] "Regarding the selection of tweets which are variously described as 'triggering', 'offensive', 'bigoted', 'racist', 'misogynistic', and 'transphobic', you can see for yourselves that not a single one of them appears to give any plausible grounds for drawing those conclusions. Anyone who knows me would verify that none of those is anywhere close to an accurate or fair label for my political views'. University of Edinburgh lecturer responds to news that he has been 'exposed' as a racist by the BlackEd student movement. https://thetab.com/uk/edinburgh/2021/04/09/students-accuse-edinburgh-lecturer-of-spouting-racist-and-sexist-comments-70862.

is that the goal of the safety culture is to achieve a 'zero harm utopia' in which the risk of physical or psychic harm to those perceived as vulnerable, based on their perception that they are potentially at risk of harm, is reduced to zero. To that end, there must be 'zero tolerance' for the risk of causing harm through offensive speech or conduct. The question whether the conduct or speech complained of *in fact* caused harm, or could *objectively* be regarded as a threat, becomes irrelevant. Context is irrelevant in a zero tolerance world.[17] As Furedi explains:

> These are policies that are meant to be applied indiscriminately and punish without regard to circumstances. It spares judges and officials from having to think about the circumstances affecting a particular event and exempts them from exercising their capacity to discriminate and judge. In the case of zero tolerance towards offensive speech on campuses, it means sparing people the burden of having to draw their own conclusions about the merits of an argument.[18]

As will be discussed later, the law permits in some cases a defence of justification in racial discrimination claims. The doctrine of harassment also permits an objective evaluation of whether the conduct is reasonably likely to be perceived as racist. But in practice it is difficult, costly and embarrassing to mount such defences once a prima facie case of racism is established which means that in practice the principle of 'safety first' trumps the presumption of innocence. Confusion abounds. The language of psychic threat is now harnessed to express the generalised sense of bewilderment and despair expressed by those who fail to make progress, who fear that the solution lies beyond their control, and are convinced that the power to keep them safe lies in the realm of politically elusive social or institutional reform and other forms of government intervention. That in turn gives rise to the unsettling feeling of being cast adrift at sea, unsupported and unsafe in a hostile world, the increasing feeling that nobody is taking their fears seriously, and ultimately the urgent need for a safe harbour from racism. In these conditions the

[17] Furedi, F. (2018). *How Fear Works: Culture of Fear in the Twenty-First Century* (p. 232). Bloomsbury.

[18] Ibid.

notion of free-market participation evokes not freedom or opportunity but further risk of psychic harm. Anybody afraid to approach university life without special protections from being ignored or overlooked, and encouraged in this fear by institutional guarantees that anybody who shows them discourtesy, however inadvertently, will be treated with 'zero tolerance', is unlikely to approach participation in open markets with confidence.

The starting point in evaluating the influence of the safety-first culture on the law is the basic legal duty not to cause harm to others. The law of tort, for example, offers redress for psychiatric injury in the same way as it offers redress for physical injury or injury to property. Yet this depends, in each case, on the duty of care and the degree of harm in that particular case, and not simply on the victim's perception or the description of the type of harm suffered. There is an objective test in cases of psychiatric injury: there must, for example, be medical evidence of the injury or psychiatric evidence of the impact on mental well-being, rather than a mere claim to have felt shocked, offended, saddened, disappointed, or even seriously grieved. Yet the antidiscrimination safety-first principle departs from these standards of reasonableness by adopting a policy that amounts to zero tolerance for the prospect of people feeling unsafe because of their race, with little objective evaluation of the reasonableness of the perceived vulnerability. This heightened safety protection does not in fact offer actual safety—it only emphasizes the presence of danger. As Furedi argues, ratcheting up safety measures only compounds irrational fear:

> The demands of psychic survival and self-esteem are used as an argument for trading in freedom for the illusory goal of feeling safe…the culture of fear continually feeds itself. The act of trading in freedom does not make people feel safe. It heightens people's awareness of their lack of control over their lives and thereby enhances their sense of insecurity.[19]

Legal claims for compensation to redress emotional hurt or distress are not specific to discrimination claims, as anybody can seek redress for such

[19] Ibid., p. 236.

hurt under the law of tort if it amounts to psychiatric injury. But where it does not amount to a medically certifiable injury then there is no reason why emotional harm to one race should count more than emotional harm to another. The pursuit of psychic safety through increasing regulation of speech and conduct thus far exceeds the level of safeguarding that would ordinarily be regarded as reasonable. As Furedi argues, freedom is traded in for a feeling of safety, but paradoxically both freedom and the feeling of safety are lost.

3.2 Historical Grievance, Vulnerability and Victimhood

> History cannot be undone. Nor does conceiving of races as intertemporal abstractions have any such track record as to make it look like a promising approach to the present or the future.[20]

In the evolving progressive landscape of equity the contested ground is no longer how to ensure racial equality or eradicate harmful discrimination, but how to justify granting some races special legal privileges to compensate for historic wrongs—what was done to their ancestors by other people's ancestors. In order to justify such racial equity policies it is argued that these interventions are needed for two key reasons: to correct and atone for historical grievances and to reverse past discrimination. The idea is that equality legislation can help to expiate the evil wrought by slavery and colonialism and also reverse its residual harms. The ideas of historical grievance, victimhood and vulnerability are in this way weaved together in the wider narrative of safety and protection. This is further reinforced by Rawlsian theories of social justice which emphasise that the content of law should be governed by the needs of the weakest and most vulnerable in society. Not *all* the races who have suffered historic wrongs are selected for preferment through equity policies, as that might entail uncomfortable discussions about the historical

[20] Sowell, *Intellectuals and Race*, p. 121.

wrongs committed by the Egyptians, the Romans or the Vikings. Nor, as evidenced by the BBC questioning whether or not Jews are an 'ethnic minority', is there any genuine interest in historical grievances.

> Following his appearance on the show, Mr Cohen tweeted: 'I've just been on the BBC's Politics Live where the BBC literally just asked four non-Jews if they agreed with me that Jews are an ethnic minority. Imagine if I was black and four white people were asked to judge if I was a member of an ethnic minority. It would be as offensive.[21]

The real focus is on wealth redistribution, and historical grievance is selected to include only those historical events that will justify state interventions reallocating wealth from rich to poor. To qualify for policy protection, historical grievance must be coupled with vulnerability, and presumably Mr. Cohen did not strike the panel as sufficiently vulnerable. The focus of social justice is only on those 'ethnic minorities' whose victimhood is deemed to call for state intervention due to their inability to catch up without extra help funded by the public purse. The real concern is less with reversing historical disadvantage and more with identifying a secure platform for endless state interventions. To that end the policy priority must be with those considered to be incapable of raising themselves up by their own bootstraps, vulnerable groups for whom expecting them to resolve their own situation would amount to pointless 'victim-blaming' because they would not be able to fix their own problems.

Debates about inequality therefore carefully avoid implying that racial minorities must take steps to ameliorate their own socio-economic disadvantages. As Sowell highlights, the reluctance to look beyond discrimination for the causes of inequality is largely explained by reluctance to expect more from those who are already perceived to be suffering. For example in universities the issue of underperformance by black students is depicted as a form of double jeopardy—if they are unable to focus on their studies due to the demoralisation caused by racism, people ignoring

---

[21] Sheridan, D. (2021, March 1). BBC Criticised Over 'Offensive' Debate Asking Whether Jews Are an Ethnic Minority. *The Telegraph*. https://www.telegraph.co.uk/news/2021/03/01/bbc-criticised-offensive-debate-asking-whether-jews-ethnic-minority/.

them and making them feel inferior, and if they underperform in their examinations due to that inability to focus, it seems churlish and even needlessly cruel to suggest that if they worked harder at their studies, they might perform better. Such a proposal would appear not only to ignore the racism problem but also to double down by blaming the victims of horrid racism for their own underperformance. The desire to avoid victim-blaming also hampers rigorous scrutiny of the causes of inequality by ruling out any causal factors that may plausibly be within the control of the victim. It is surely more palatable to tell white students to 'check their privilege' than to tell black students to set aside their feelings and repair to the library to study for their exams. The unfortunate result is that white students are encouraged to study harder, while black students are encouraged to nurse their grievances and apply for exemptions. By treating the causal nexus between socio-economic disadvantage and discrimination as self-evident, any solutions that the victim would be in a position to implement are disregarded. Instead, presuming that inequality and failure are caused by discrimination allows blame to devolve more comfortably to society and institutions, with the government ultimately assuming responsibility for addressing the problem through, for example, targeted funding and further legislative interventions.[22] This approach is reflected in the slogans that anti-racism should target the racists, not the victims.

For these reasons Sowell sees in the policy goals of equity, or 'the quest for cosmic justice' as he terms it, the same pernicious principles as the old genetic theories of racial inferiority, in that both approaches derive the same policy prescriptions and justifications albeit for somewhat different motives: they both argue that economic progress is racially determined, that some races need more 'help' than others and cannot be expected to make progress unless somebody helps them, and that the role of the state is to implement the law along racial lines to achieve the best outcomes for

[22] As Sowell argues: 'No individual or group can be blamed for being born into circumstances (including cultures) that lack the advantages that other people's circumstances have. But neither can 'society' be automatically assumed to be either the cause or the cure for such disparities. Still less can a particular institution whose employment, pricing or lending decisions convey intergroup differences be automatically presumed to be causing those differences': *Intellectuals and Race*, p. 108.

disadvantaged races.[23] Sowell argues that it is no more scientific to treat statistical disparities between races as presumptive evidence of discrimination or other social injustices, than it was in a previous era to treat such disparities as evidence of genetic determinism. For example, different racial minorities emerge as both better and worse off than the majority in the same situation as with the well-known examples of black and Asian ethnic minorities in educational outcomes. Sowell argues that it would be just as intellectually dubious uncritically to attribute racial disparities to genetically determined intelligence, as it would be to attribute them to social injustice. Both of these conclusions are unscientific. Explaining racial outcomes by reference to genetic determinism led to unethical theories of eugenics; and no less so do explanations deterministically rooted in discrimination destroy innocent lives by spreading messages of pointlessness and doom.

Sowell's analysis of the effects of grievance politics highlights the range of unfortunate outcomes that result from drawing political links between historical oppression and inequality. That approach encourages a culture of victimhood in which it is fashionable to blame others for one's troubles, to avoid objective examination of the potential causes of disadvantageous outcomes, and thus to avoid following paths to success that others have trod. Linking socio-economic challenges to historical grievances is harmful because it implies that historically disadvantaged groups can never escape their history, that their history will forever determine their outcomes. Cultivating virtues such as industry and frugality has improved the fortunes of immigrant groups in many jurisdictions, showing that history need not determine life outcomes for successive generations. Effort and skill matter more in shaping life outcomes. Sowell is therefore critical of those who encourage disadvantaged groups to view themselves as victims of a cosmic injustice that in some abstract way misallocates resources between races, suggesting to marginalised communities that any disadvantage they suffer in life cannot be ameliorated unless the state takes charge of reallocating resources. The policy framework of equity is a Faustian pact between a state seeking more power to

23 Ibid.

seize and redistribute private wealth and the beneficiaries of that redistribution who need only testify to their own weakness and helplessness in return for special favours. As far as pacts go that may appear to be a worthwhile bargain for ethnic minorities, but in truth this option is not available to any human being wishing to live a fully human life. It is no surprise that the reports of anti-racism measures in universities grow more depressing from one year to the next. Far from reporting that ethnic minorities are thriving in their safe spaces and taking big steps to higher levels of success now that everyone is forced to be courteous to them, universities report increasing levels of severe mental health problems from the recipients of their special protections.[24]

But the purveyors of racial justice are unconcerned with the psychic costs imposed on those assigned to play the role of 'victim' in their evil cosmic theatre, relegated forever to the position of subsisting on state welfare and reparations in the new socially just form of charity, promoted to positions of influence through quotas and targets set aside for their race thereby casting aspersions on whether they are genuinely qualified for the role. Nor, as Sowell highlights, is this spurious form of racial justice concerned by its harmful unintended effects. If for example affirmative action policies promote privileged black children at the expense of underprivileged white children that is deemed to be justifiable in an intertemporal cosmic sense because any current injustice to white children is offset by the historical injustices perpetrated on black children by the forbears of the white children. Designating special legal rights based on race may have benign intentions designed to produce social justice, but the harmful outcomes of the contemporary benign racism will follow just as predictably as they did under the old hostile racism. It is not the motives or intentions behind race-based policies that are the problem, but the fact that institutionalised racial division whether ill or well-intentioned is wrong.

The moral imperative to address and correct historical wrongs also displaces the moral basis of individualism, the benefits of which were discussed in the previous chapter. The idea that groups of people are collectively harmed by the historical persecution of their race or tribe,

[24] Equality and Human Rights Commission, *Tackling Racial Harassment*.

and that this ought to be remedied through economic reparations and other corrective government policies, is based on a sense of 'collective' identity. The importance of collective racial identity plays the dominant role in communitarian perspectives of social justice. As Corey observes, identity politics is rooted in 'a loose application of Marxist class analysis' which explains economic outcomes by reference to exploitation and oppression of one social group by another. Neo-Marxist theories provide a useful conduit through which groups with a shared racial identity can forge their claims for preferment, and at the same time reinvigorate the centrality of conflicts of interest by framing 'justice' so as to prioritise certain races over others.[25] It is now customary, for example, to make reference to one's own racial identity before offering an opinion on race relations in public debate: '"It is so wrong to accuse people of colour who raise issues in relation to race of somehow inflaming feelings"', we hear, or 'I may be wrong on this factual issue, but you, white man, mustn't dare tell me so'.[26] Personal identity is also important in the conduct of official functions: 'I will be exclusively providing one-on-one interviews with journalists of color… As the first black woman mayor of Chicago, and the first openly gay mayor, my election in 2019 was hailed for breaking barriers to the halls of power that had existed in our city for generations'.[27] What used to be termed making ad hominem attacks is now called being 'identity-conscious', evaluating ideas by explicit reference to the racial identity of the speaker or intended audience. This need to express personal identity in public discourse is intended to lend or withdraw validity as appropriate in respect of the thoughts or feelings expressed. This understanding of personal identity is thus reflected in the duty to safeguard freedom of expression—the duty to safeguard personal identity gives rise to a duty to amplify and empower the voices of ethnic

[25] 'it arises primarily from the loose application of Marxist class analysis to non-economic factors combined with psychological and other theories of oppression, and proceeds in imitation of the American Civil Rights movement even when the nature of the freedoms being sought are not equivalent'. Corey, 'Liberalism and the Modern Quest for Freedom', p. 147.

[26] https://www.telegraph.co.uk/news/2021/05/25/people-dragged-sasha-johnsons-shooting-culture-wars-should-ashamed/.

[27] https://www.washingtonpost.com/context/letter-from-chicago-mayor-lori-lightfoot/89bc44f0-230f-40c4-89ea-5b5e5651d873/?itid=lk_inline_manual_13.

and other minority groups.[28] This view of group rights is framed as empowering to the oppressed, a way to lend voice to the voiceless, but it is not a sound foundation for legislative policy.

Identity politics promotes the contention that group advancement is only possible through achieving political power, and that it is pointless to enhance market participation for those on the periphery of power politics.[29] As Jason Riley highlights, the belief that economic progress depends entirely on political influence and attaining dominant political power is harmful because it persuades those with aspirations to improve their lives that working hard is pointless if they do not wield political power. Riley argues that ultimately, linking 'equality' to a quest for group-based political power reflects not a commitment to advancement of underprivileged groups but a desire for power for its own sake with no heed paid to the actual impact on group advancement, or even declining group fortunes. Riley shows that where group fortunes continue to decline despite increasing political power that suggests that the public policy debates may be losing sight of more important causal factors.[30] Conferring special protections on vulnerable groups may appear superficially to be a compelling initiative in the prevailing cultural ethos of safety, but insufficient attention is paid to the costs of entrenching a culture of vulnerability and grievance which is not only an unstable basis for a theory of justice, but is also likely to foment inter-group conflict. It provokes many to feel that their victimhood is persistently being ignored, that they are denied justice. Resentment against perceived injustice also tends to create new injustices of its own by holding people morally responsible for the perceived injustices of their racial ancestors. As Sowell cautions, 'there could hardly be a more deadly inspiration for a never-ending cycle of revenge and counter-revenge'.[31]

---

[28] 'Dear White People: Learn American History and Amplify Black Voices', https://emorywheel.com/dear-white-people-learn-american-history-and-amplify-black-voices/.

[29] Riley, J. L. (2014). *Please Stop Helping Us: How Liberals Make It Harder for Blacks to Succeed*. Encounter Books.

[30] 'Race consciousness helps cohere the political left, and black liberalism's main agenda is keeping race front and center in our national conversations…The last thing that organizations like the NAACP want is for America to get "beyond" race.' Ibid., pp. 12, 13.

[31] *Intellectuals and Race*, p. 113.

A civilised society of course protects its most vulnerable members and does not simply leave them to sink or swim. But the presumption that this can only be achieved through state interventions, safe spaces, special favours and wealth redistribution follows uncritically from the expectations that have grown to surround the function of government. It is almost as if, having constructed large and powerful governments with control of increasing sectors of private life, more functions must be found for them to fulfil in a bid to improve not only matters such as education and health but also the self-esteem and psychic well-being of entire races. Thus social policy and legislative interventions are often designed to address problems associated with socio-economic vulnerability, identifying those most at risk. Government intervention is prescribed, substituting individual decision-making with collective processes. As principles of social justice increasingly emphasise victimhood and vulnerability the proportion of those not able to make decisions on their own account continues to grow, extending to increasingly mundane aspects of daily life. For example, the 'Rhodes must fall' movement considers it to be 'violence' for black people to have to walk past a statute of Cecil Rhodes, so that some form of safeguarding measures are needed to enable them, at a very basic level, to go about their daily lives. Policy initiatives designed to promote equality are thus dominated by themes of vulnerability, inadvertently encouraging the perception that expressions of fear and vulnerability constitute the only secure path to progress.

This is not to deny the reality of socio-economic vulnerability. Various constraints certainly limit the scope of individual agency over the course of our lives, and it could be argued that it is important to acknowledge the harsh reality that racial discrimination is in many situations a fact of life. Harm caused to innocent victims is the hallmark of unfairness, and nobody would willingly choose to endure unfair circumstances if they had a choice. Thus the imperative to eradicate injustice directs our attention to situations in which victims are constrained by their race and unable to make free choices that might ameliorate their material conditions. For all intents and purposes they are trapped. The language of compulsion, lack of agency and the absence of free will is characteristic of many types of socio-economic disadvantage, for example when it is said that people are *forced* to work long hours in gruelling occupations for a low wage, or *forced* to consume an inadequate diet. This compulsive force is attributed to a 'systemic' or 'institutional' construct such as historical legacies of oppression. Such constraints are said to compel victims to choose the lesser of two or more evils which feels like no real choice at all. Be that as it may, human agency and individual control over improving one's own life circumstances do not require that all the vicissitudes and constraints of life must be eradicated. This is not to say that reality is entirely constructed by individual human agency. On the contrary, reality is what it is and life constraints are endemic. The point is that the ability and will to choose one's own path in life is no less a choice because it operates under material constraints. A good example of such a choice is working for a living, which many workers regard as something they are 'forced' to do in order to earn an income because they must work or starve. Yet it is nevertheless meaningful to describe a worker as exercising their free will in choosing to work, even though it is by no means a welcome choice to forego more leisure time or other enjoyable pursuits. That an important element of choice pertains in this situation remains true even in cases where the worker 'signs on the dotted line' accepting default terms and conditions of work put forward by the employer with no opportunity to negotiate special provisions. To give a different example, we might still choose to take out a loan from a bank, even though the terms and conditions of the loan are dictated by the bank giving us no 'choice' regarding whether or when to repay the loan or the rate of interest to be levied. We might therefore grant that the poor man finds it harder, even exponentially harder, to succeed in life than the wealthy man, without accepting that the poor man has 'no choice' about any of his life outcomes and needs the state to step up and make all his decisions if his life is to improve.

It is true that there is no universal agreement on the meaning and scope of free will and choice. The nihilist believes free will to be an illusion, while other philosophers argue that even in the most constrained material conditions human beings still retain their free will and ability to make meaningful choices.[32] That philosophical debate lies beyond

[32] 'Everything can be taken from a man but one thing: the last of the human freedoms—to choose one's attitude in any given set of circumstances, to choose one's own way', Frankl, V. E.

the scope of this discussion, but in evaluating the benefits of economic freedom for racial minorities it is not necessary to resolve that debate. It is necessary only to evaluate the life outcomes of those who *do* venture forth under the conviction that all human beings have free will and are able to make choices, compared to the life outcomes of those who believe that their lives are entirely beyond their control and are instead determined by external systems such as historical legacies, prevailing socio-economic conditions, the racists, the patriarchy, and that eternal bogeyman, The Man. In conducting such a comparative study it emerges that those who believe in free will experience better life outcomes:

> In modern capitalist societies, especially in the West, choice is generally regarded as positive and desirable…The belief in free will enables the person to view life as filled with choices, to regard ordinary actions as choices, thereby driving higher motivation for facing choice, resulting in lower difficulty in tackling decisions, and finally higher satisfaction in making decisions.[33]

This suggests that those who regard their choices as falling for the most part within their own agency are often happier and more successful than those who embrace the ethos of vulnerability and psychic unsafety, feeling constrained by the wealth of others and 'forced' by circumstances to live lesser lives compared to others. The advantages of free will and choice prevail even in circumstances where the comparison is made between people who are all operating under the same socio-economic constraints.[34]

(2004). *Man's Search for Meaning: The Classic Tribute to Hope from the Holocaust* (p. 75). Rider (Original work published 1946).

[33] 'Thus, at the workplace, people who believe in free will would perceive work life as filled with choices—that working for a company or an institution is a choice rather than an uncontrolled or deterministic obligation and that the work done for the company or institution involves a high degree of choice with little coercion or predetermination.' Feldman, G., Farh, J.-L., & Wong, K. F. E. (2018). Agency Beliefs Over Time and Across Cultures: Free Will Beliefs Predict Higher Job Satisfaction. *Personality and Social Psychology Bulletin, 44*, 304.

[34] Ibid.

The argument here is that vulnerability ought not to be regarded as the most significant attribute of the human condition, nor ought individual autonomy, independence and self-responsibility to be dismissed as fallacies simply because some people need support in order fully to act responsibly. Policies and principles designed to protect vulnerable people are not appropriate as a presumptive general foundation or justification for wholescale legislative interventions. The desire for individual autonomy is the foundational rule, albeit one with exceptions, because human beings are free agents even in the presence of vulnerable people in need of protection. The rule, not the exceptions, should identify the baseline for policy-making. When vulnerability or disadvantage confer the primary basis of entitlement to state largesse, this tends only to expand the social welfare role of the state and to displace individual agency, compounding the problem it is designed to solve. In addition to continually identifying new groups of victims, the social justice discourse attempts increasingly to shield these victims from any criticism. This immunity from criticism paradoxically puts 'victims' in a very powerful position that pays no regard to the effects on other members of society. Yet in any interaction, all the participants are important—it is myopic to protect one party on grounds that they are 'vulnerable' while overlooking the impact and implications for other participants. There are of course many circumstances in which a person may be incapable of evaluating and meeting their own needs, or too vulnerable to enter freely into voluntary exchange, but these are better regarded as exceptional circumstances than as the most appropriate baseline for public policy.

The role of government in safeguarding vulnerable people in this context is a matter not only for theoretical analysis but also for empirical inquiry. It is customary in Western societies to suppose that immigrants or ethnic minorities are more vulnerable than members of majority races.[35] The theory is that in virtue of their minority status together with a historical legacy of racial oppression their lives are inherently constrained. Yet there are many sources of vulnerability; people of all races, classes and backgrounds may be in a vulnerable position for one

[35] 'Being new, different and vulnerable, minorities are liable to deliberate or unintended discrimination. ...Even when immigrants are not discriminated against, they suffer from obvious economic, political and cultural disadvantages': Modood, T., et al., *Ethnic Minorities in Britain.*

reason or another. Nor is it necessarily correct to suppose that where vulnerability *does* overlap with race or ethnicity the causes of the vulnerability necessarily arise from discrimination. Therefore to the extent that state intervention in regulating interpersonal affairs is offered it should be offered to all, without regard to race or creed, or not at all. The sources of vulnerability must also be closely scrutinised to evaluate objectively the scale of the threat. Polls in the United Kingdom today suggest that most people regard racist behaviour as unreasonable, and as both morally and socially unacceptable, which suggests, objectively, that the vast majority of people will not knowingly engage in racist conduct. Even when it occurs, it tends to be hidden, to be disputed, and to be denied by the perpetrator who may honestly not be aware of the effects of their behaviour on others. This suggests, objectively, that even where it occurs the element of hostility and malice will be lacking—the racist incident will be ambiguous, open to interpretation and inadvertent. This implies a minimal level of objective danger, even in cases where the subjective level of outrage or despair may be significant. It is remarkable then that the fear of racism today is much more urgent than it was in the Jim Crow era. This threat indeed seems to grow over time, fuelled and magnified by the culture of fear described by Furedi.[36] While racial insults and bullying are to be abhorred, it is facile to assume that 'if minorities are subjected to insulting stereotypes, made butts of offensive jokes and remarks or viewed with suspicion, they lack a sense of self-worth and self-esteem'.[37] There are many ways to derive and promote self-worth, self-esteem and self-confidence, and resilience and self-reliance and the pursuit of meaningful goals are part of that. It is simplistic and wrong to frame self-esteem as a matter of eradicating offensive jokes and stereotypes. The perception that success in life depends on the quality of racial interactions and that legislative controls are indispensable in keeping one race safe from the hostility of another is now endemic. It implies that until the state can guarantee that no ethnic minority person will encounter an offensive joke their self-worth and self-esteem are unattainable. Ultimately, it is the need to engage with other human beings, and

[36] Furedi, F. (2018). *How Fear Works: Culture of Fear in the Twenty-First Century*. Bloomsbury.
[37] Ibid., p. x.

to participate in life itself on the same terms as other human beings, from which state seeks to offer protection. This protection comes at great cost.

The greatest cost concerns restrictions on individual liberty. It has been noted that in a safety-first culture the exigencies of social justice are said to override freedom due to the importance of protecting the weak. Restrictions on individual liberty are then said to be relatively unimportant, no more than a small price to pay to safeguard the vulnerable. If safety overrides liberty when there is a pressing social problem to be resolved then autonomy and the freedom to make decisions about all aspects of economic life are treated as irrelevant in contexts where particular groups are suffering from 'inequality'. The very question of how to balance freedom with anti-racist edicts implicitly characterises freedom as some sort of barrier to be overcome in order to protect vulnerable victims of racism. Freedom and racism are depicted as opponents in a battle for ascendance in which the only way to tackle racism is to sacrifice freedom. Freedom is in that context treated by progressives with a curious form of asymmetry—freedom to live and work is *insufficient* if some people are 'suffering' from inequality, but freedom to live and work ought to be regarded as sufficient if people are suffering from encroachments upon individual liberties such as free speech. Thus progressives who desire to achieve equality through legislative mandates highlight their commitment to liberty in order to argue that the poor cannot be free until wealth is equalised, but consider the ideal of liberty to be nothing more than a convenient façade when that ideal is defended by opponents of socialism. Opponents of socialism are said to hide behind liberty purely in order to oppose fairness and exploit the vulnerable, so that free speech defenders are said to be no more than apologists for hate-speech.[38] Their own encroachments upon individual liberty are not regarded as sinister or totalitarian by progressive activists because the motives behind them are said to be pure and good, designed to make the world a better place.[39] This asymmetric freedom is one which only

---

[38] See for example Titley, G. (2020). *Is Free Speech Racist?* Polity Press arguing that 'free speech has been adopted as a primary mechanism for validating, amplifying, and reanimating racist ideas and racializing claims.'

[39] Thus Dworkin remarks that 'a more equal society is a better society even if its citizens prefer inequality': *Taking Rights Seriously*, p. 239.

socialist visions of freedom count, and the commitment to 'anti-racism' is now central to the socialist edifice in so far as it is a useful ideological platform in justifying regulatory intervention.

3.3 Discrimination and Causation

This part of the discussion reviews the evidence that inequality is not caused by discrimination. One key error in evaluating the fortunes of racial minorities in free markets lies in the presumption that market participation, if it is truly free and fair, ought to produce equal outcomes. Unequal outcomes are then presumed to be evidence that there must be discrimination going on to explain the inequality, as no other explanation for unequal outcomes appears to present itself.[40] Public debates often presume that the link between discrimination and income or wealth differentials is self-evident, meaning that other causal factors tend scarcely to command any attention. Part of this is simply linguistic imprecision, as found by 2021 UK Commission Report on Race and Ethnic Disparities:

> In the call for evidence, the Commission noted a tendency to conflate discrimination and disparities; whilst they sometimes co-exist they often do not. The Commission believes this is symptomatic of a wider, repeated use and misapplication of the term 'racism' to account for every observed disparity. This matters because the more things are explained as a result of racial bias, the more it appears that society is set against ethnic minorities, which in turn can discourage ethnic minority individuals from pursuing their goals. If more precise language does not become a feature of our national conversation on race, we can expect to see tensions increase across communities – despite determined action by government and civil society to reduce discrimination.[41]

[40] 'Since egalitarians begin with the a priori axiom that all people, and hence all groups of peoples, are uniform and equal, it then follows for them that any and all group differences in status, prestige, or authority in society must be the result of unjust "oppression" and irrational "discrimination"'. Rothbard, p. 10.

[41] Commission on Race and Ethnic Disparities Report.

Race or ethnicity may correlate with many disparities, but this does not prove either that they are the cause of those disparities or that those disparities are caused by discrimination. The only potential role that may be served by tracking group outcomes based on identity characteristics such as race is where group or community status is a potential indicator of specific welfare parameters (such as genetic links to health outcomes) or captures some important trends that may be helpful in targeting resources for example in fields such as education where particular strategies may be in indicated to assist specific groups. But beyond that it is important not to overlook the multidimensional nature of ethnicity or to treat as stable racial categories that are, at best, fluid. For example 'black' identity includes 'ethnic groups with different cultures, religions, migration histories and geographical and socio-economic locations' all of which may influence life outcomes in different ways.[42] Variable patterns of disparate outcomes appear within groups of ethnic minorities who face the same level of discrimination but achieve variable outcomes due, for example, to variable levels of education.[43]

The result of overlooking these complexities is that there is little reliable evidence establishing a clear link between inequality and its various causes. Many studies of 'racism' are designed simply to detail anti-racist events and activities: how perceived racism makes putative victims feel, what we can do to support the anti-racism drives and make people feel better. To highlight these activities, the evidence of discrimination relies heavily on subjective reports of lived experiences, testimony from people who feel affected by racism. They tell us what happened to them, and how upset they felt. The policeman was rude to them, and used excessive force in the arrest. Reports substantiating racial discrimination tend to derive the conclusions about discrimination from statistical disparities and underrepresentation in the workplace and subjective reports of racist incidents where little is known about the context of the incidents

[42] Modood, T., et al., *Ethnic Minorities in Britain*, p. 227; see discussion of the methodological challenges of tracking data by race, pp. 226–228.

[43] 'The migrants come to Britain very differently qualified to each other. In most groups the second generation had made significant progress, but there is a continuing division between the ethnic minority groups. For some, educational qualifications are a success story, but there are clear points of concern'. Ibid., p. 4.

reported or the credibility of the source: Such reports underpin a recent influential study of 'systemic racism' in UK higher education sector which announced the university system to be intrinsically racist because 24% of all ethnic minority students and 9% of white students surveyed had experienced racial harassment.[44] Unhappy events had occurred, of which examples were given. Students left crying in the classroom because nobody wanted to be their friend or sit next to them. The report took no account of contextual factors such as the gravity of the 'harassment' experienced, the cultural background of the students or their performance at university generally, which may have yielded further insight into their fuller experience of university life. Without this information, it is difficult to draw reliable conclusions about the extent to which racism is 'systemic' rather than sporadic. Tracking reports of discrimination by itself falls short of establishing the causal connection to economic inequality.

When inequality is presumed to be an automatic outcome of discrimination, robust evidence of discrimination is seldom sought or required. If we presume that discrimination, by itself, causes socio-economic equality, then it might seem to follow that a failure to observe explicit discrimination is probably because the existing discrimination is invisible or so nuanced as to be impossible to detect. If we begin from a starting presumption that the existence of inequality is evidence of discrimination then whether discrimination is visible or not becomes irrelevant. The presumption is that failure in life endeavours amounts to evidence of discrimination, even if that discrimination is not directly observable; the explanation for the non-observance is interpreted as an indicator that the discrimination was too subtle to detect.[45] The presumption is that if

[44] Equality and Human Rights Commission. (2019). *Racial Harassment Inquiry: Survey of Universities* (Research Report No. 131). https://www.equalityhumanrights.com/en/publication-download/racial-harassment-inquiry-survey-universities.

[45] See for example '"It's not the exact words of racism. It's the implication and the reaction to it. To not want to address that because she is a Black woman and to try to dismiss it or to make it seem less than what it is, that's what makes it racist," Underwood said, clarifying the existence of racism although no 'exact words of racism' had been said': D'Zurilla, C. (2021, March 12). Piers Morgan Blames Bullies for Sharon Osbourne's Apology—And Says He Deserves One. *LA Times*. https://www.latimes.com/entertainment-arts/tv/story/2021-03-12/piers-morgan-sharon-osbourne-meghan-racism-apology.

there were no racism, there would be no inequality; if inequality persists there can only be one explanation: that racism lurks behind it as the key causal factor. The drive to eradicate discrimination is thus driven by an automatic conflation of what is observed and the causal factors behind it. We assume that observing inequality is the only 'evidence' of discrimination required to justify legislative interventions.

Attempts to test the causal links between discrimination and inequality tend to be regarded with suspicion, treated as an attempt to deny that discrimination 'exists' or an attempt to question whether the alleged discriminatory words or conduct in fact occurred or if they did, whether they were morally wrong. We can all agree that the behaviour reported by anti-racism activists is often very bad behaviour: insulting other people, shunning them, and make them cry. But the key regulatory issue here concerns the causal connections between discrimination and unequal socio-economic outcomes. A linear causal connection between discrimination and inequality is treated as self-evident in the dominant scholarly discourse due to a general lack of attention to robustly testing causal relationships between discriminatory practices and socio-economic outcomes. Even if we stipulate that inequality creates pressing moral problems, it still remains to evaluate the causes of inequality. Failure to appreciate that correlation is not proof of causality creates immense confusion, with protagonists often speaking at cross purposes as measures to tackle inequality are conflated with antidiscrimination policies. Thus Williams writes:

> To observe racial discrimination is one thing. Quite another is to ask whether it is an insurmountable barrier to socioeconomic advancement. If a given level of discrimination is not insurmountable, then spending resources to eliminate every vestige of it would be wasted, because those resources might be more productively used elsewhere to promote the same kind of advancement.[46]

There is an important distinction between discrimination, which entails choosing one thing in preference to another, and inequality, which

[46] Williams, W. E. (2011). *Race and Economics: How Much Can Be Blamed on Discrimination?* (p. 11). Hoover Institution Press.

reflects a reality in which things are not equal. We might observe, for example, that white men on average earn more than black men suggesting a racial gap or disparity in earnings. But without knowing the causes, reasons or context for that disparity it would be meaningless automatically to describe that disparity as discriminatory or unjust. Thus inequality falls to be treated as analytically distinct from discrimination or injustice, even in situations where the operation of these constructs exhibits a degree of overlap. Nor can discrimination be presumed to be automatically unjust. Justice is an abstraction whose demands depend on the context. There are infinite factors, traits or characteristics that may make progress difficult for an individual in a particular context, that are nothing to do with injustice. There is no evidence to suggest that the characteristics selected by antidiscrimination legislation for greater protection have greater impact on the life of an individual or community than other factors, particularly when broader socio-economic factors are taken into account. For example, being born in a home where there is long-term multigenerational unemployment has a greater influence on employment outcomes than race, ethnicity or even educational attainment. The causal connections between discrimination and income or wealth inequality are therefore not well established.

3.4 Causes of Inequality

Various studies have identified multiple causes of inequality. Inequality, like most complex social phenomena, has several contributing factors: education, ethnic origins, cultural attitudes, demographics, geography, history, among others. None of these factors is, by itself, deterministic and it is difficult to ascertain the relative weight of each factor given wide contextual variations. For example Higgs shows that in the aftermath of emancipation in the United States, patterns of black migration from the southern states were influenced not only by racism and the desire to escape from segregation but also by economic considerations such as better work opportunities and higher wages.[47] Higgs found that several other factors played an important causal role in influencing the fortunes of former slaves following emancipation, including geographical location and various labour market conditions such as job opportunities, demand for labour, and ease of migration in search of higher wages. Higgs also identified the influence of other economic factors such as income, availability of credit, land ownership, skills and training. Higgs emphasises that the explanation for inequality does not lie entirely in these economic factors, but also in 'intangible mental states and processes' including factors such as ambition or resilience and multiple other factors that may be philosophical or cultural. Thus personal characteristics such as 'motivation, attitudes and ambition' also have an important impact albeit one that is less easily quantified. Thus we know that history and economic conditions play a role in explaining socio-economic outcomes, but it is not clear what weight attaches to these factors compared to other factors such as geography or family background. Similarly it would be difficult directly to contrast the significance of discrimination compared to educational attainment. It is difficult accurately to assign a percentage of causal blame to all the factors that influence our life outcomes. The numerical weighting, the respective percentage weight attributable to discrimination as distinct from other factors, is to an extent unknowable.[48]

It is significant that all the causal factors identified by Higgs are seen to play a role in shaping the life outcomes of black Americans in the specific period studied, which covers the chaotic years following emancipation from slavery in 1865. This was a time when discrimination as we

[47] Higgs surveys the evidence that 'agricultural opportunities' played a role in influencing migration patterns: 'Clearly the black population was moving from state to state, from region to region, in search of superior economic opportunities.' At p. 28. Higgs, R. (1977). *Competition and Coercion: Blacks in the American Economy, 1865–1914.* Cambridge University Press.

[48] Higgs observes of the years following emancipation: 'Apparently, many possessed great resilience in the face of discouragement and difficulty, for many realized notable gains despite the discriminatory constraints. Equally evident were…those who had lost virtually all hope for a better future. And perhaps the largest group, as usual, comprised those in the middle, discouraged and frustrated but still trying. To know the relative magnitudes of these three groups would be to understand more deeply the economic history of black Americans. Because it is unlikely that anyone can know such magnitudes, our understanding must necessarily remain incomplete' Higgs, *Competition and Coercion*, p. 129.

understand it today, which usually means calling people the wrong name, looking at them the wrong way, or failing to acknowledge them when they walk into the room, would be the least of a black person's worries. Racial hostility in that era was expressed through 'downright murder, savage beatings, merciless whippings, hunting men with trained bloodhounds, through all the lesser degrees of cruelty and crime' including 'beatings, hangings, shootings, torturings, and drownings of blacks in a revolting variety'.[49] Former slaves were now free to work for a contractually agreed wage, but work contracts were enforced by an overseer 'brandishing a pistol or whipping the laborers' and employers often did not bother to pay black workers the agreed wage even after the work was duly performed.[50] Enforcing contractual promises in court was out of the question, as such a claim would be regarded by most judges as preposterous. Studying this immediate post-emancipation period is instructive because it enables a clear focus not on whether discrimination *exists*, but on the extent to which discrimination hampered the economic progress of black people. In conditions where discrimination meant being deprived of wages at the very least, and at worst torture and death, it would not be surprising if black people recused themselves from a hostile labour market; indeed it was widely supposed at the time that black workers would no longer show up to work if they were not compelled to work by the bonds of slavery. Yet rates of black employment in the era studied by Higgs were very high, in fact often higher than those of whites.[51] We must ask: is it plausible, in modern liberal democracies, where racism is expressed through nuanced and subtle microaggressions or the wrong 'tone of voice', where employment contracts are reinforced by a robust framework of employment rights

[49] Higgs, *Competition and Coercion*, p. 39.

[50] 'many complained that the employers failed to abide by the terms of their contracts: wages were not paid in full, poor-quality rations were supplied, and extra work was demanded without extra pay.' Higgs, *Competition and Coercion*, p. 45.

[51] 'The census of 1890, the first to make racial distinctions in the returns pertaining to occupations, revealed that of the black population 10 years of age and over, 79 percent of the males and 36 percent of the females were gainfully employed. The figures were probably underestimates, many family workers on farms being left out...Considering both sexes together, 58 percent of the blacks and 47 percent of the whites were gainfully occupied': Higgs, *Competition and Coercion*, pp. 40–41.

reinforced by antidiscrimination law that favours all those with 'protected characteristics' for compensation payments, that black unemployment could be more strongly influenced by racism today than it was in the nineteenth century Deep South?

High rates of black wage-labour in the post-emancipation era were of course not driven by 'social justice' sentimentality—of which there was none—but by the simple fact that demand for labour exceeded supply in the agricultural sector where most black people were employed.[52] While unscrupulous employers could easily cheat illiterate labourers out of their wages, and often did, honesty often proved itself to be the better policy as workers cheated out of their wages were not likely to return in the next season. Thus 'landlords who dealt fairly with their tenants gained a local reputation that made their plantations preferred places of employment' which was a worthwhile competitive advantage in times of labour shortage.[53] Fair treatment of black labourers was in the self-interest of white employers.[54] While this did not and could not by itself eradicate cheating or guarantee pleasant experiences for everyone, 'competition did moderate the extent to which the blacks were cheated'.[55] Moreover, the vulnerability to being exploited was not purely determined by race, but was shared by poor whites who often suffered similar labour market disadvantages including lack of education and susceptibility to fraud. A similar tale may be told of servants in England, subjected to floggings and whippings by masters of their own race. The tale of life in the workhouse or in the factories or mines is also instructive for those who attempt to

[52] Higgs, *Competition and Coercion*, p. 49: 'As a Tennessee man put it: "I believe there is no disposition on the part of our citizens to impose illiberal terms on those they employ; and I know they have not the ability to do so, as the demand for labor is so much in excess of the supply as to give all the advantage to the employe"'. Thus in share agreements 'competition for labor operated as the driving force in raising the share of the crop paid to black tenants'. Higgs also addresses fears that share agreements were unwanted by blacks, with evidence that these were demanded by both black and white tenants (at 45).

[53] Higgs, *Competition and Coercion*, p. 54. Higgs cites a Georgia planter in 1875: 'Whoever pays his black laborers regularly and honestly can get as many as he wants at all times, and they will work faithfully.'

[54] Higgs cites an Alabama planter in 1883 'the planter is disposed to protect his negro labourer, or his negro tenant, because it is in his interest to do so': ibid.

[55] Ibid.

understand difficult working conditions primarily as an outcome of racial discrimination.

This is not to say that race is irrelevant in understanding disadvantage. In relation to wages, Higgs's study shows that blacks generally earned a lower wage than whites for the same work. But the evidence of racial discrimination is complicated by variability in skills and training, attendance rates, union membership, and records showing equal wage rates between races in many industries. Thus wages often varied by race, but it is less clear the extent to which race was the primary causal explanation for unequal wages.[56] It is not straightforward accurately to ascertain the weight to be attached to each causal factor: if a black labourer who is less skilled is paid less than a white labourer, how much of that is explained by race and how much by the relative skills? Even without ascribing the precise proportion of blame to each factor, the existence of alternative explanations for wage variations matters for policy purposes because it signifies a clear distinction between a market where progress is possible and one where no reasonable progress can be expected. The distinction between the ability to make progress *despite* racism, and the inability to make progress *because* of racism, is crucial. At the individual level, in framing the decision-making of any individual black person, this distinction becomes dispositive—it is the difference between a world where it is worth putting in the effort to advance one's position, and one where any effort would be futile.

Similarly, Higgs shows that while racial discrimination imposed obstacles to land acquisition by freed slaves, making it more difficult for them to save the purchase price and more likely that they would be cheated in commercial transactions, it was not impossible for those with money to buy land: 'Though some whites objected to black landownership and attempted to prevent it, such attempts generally failed. Land was simply too abundant to be monopolized by the whites, many of whom did not share their neighbor's objections to land acquisition by blacks and stood to gain by a sale'.[57] Discrimination is costly, and not all those with

---

[56] Ibid., p. 87, discussion 'doubting that every racial wage difference represented racial discrimination'.

[57] Ibid., p. 52.

a taste for discrimination would be prepared to pay the price by foregoing a sale to prevent the land from falling into black hands.[58] There was also an observable degree of good old fashioned common sense, friendship and kindness. Apart from white landowners selling to black buyers simply because they needed the money, 'not uncommonly, blacks acquired land by virtue of the assistance of friendly whites'.[59] There was little scope for blacks to enforce contractual claims through a legal system hostile to them, but sufficient incentive for some white employers to honour the terms of their bargains and thus to allow progress however slow it may have been.[60] Ultimately, the evidence suggests that 'where individual actions were the decisive force, economic competition and racial discrimination often conflicted, with discrimination the loser'.[61] Higgs shows the same principles operating in the housing market, where racial discrimination was reflected in restrictive covenants creating a legally binding promise not to sell or rent the property to black families. Although courts would be perfectly happy to enforce discriminatory covenants, the restrictions were increasingly under pressure from market forces. It would only take one white person willing to breach their covenant for the edifice eventually to crumble.[62]

[58] Ibid., p. 54: 'The general absence of racial discrimination from the farm labor and land rental markets probably reflects the operation of competitive forces that made the practice of such discrimination too costly for the planters to bear.'

[59] Ibid., p. 52.

[60] 'To be sure, the progress was limited but, considering the circumstances surrounding their enslavement and emancipation, one might well marvel that the freedmen did so well.' Ibid., p. 61.

[61] Ibid., p. 60.

[62] The example from Harlem is typical of the trend: 'The basic cause of the collapse of all organized efforts to exclude Negroes from Harlem was the inability of any group to gain total and unified support of all white property owners in the neighbourhood. Without such support it was impossible to organize a successful neighbourhood-wide restrictive movement....The minority of Harlem landlords who adhered to their original restrictive covenants suffered serious economic consequences. Many were unable to find white people willing to rent their apartments. To encourage white tenants already in them to remain, some were forced to reduce rents drastically....The opponents of Negro settlement faced the dilemma of maintaining a "White Only" policy and probably losing everything, or renting to Negroes at higher prices and surviving. Most chose what seemed to them the lesser of two evils'. Ofosky, *Harlem*, cited in Higgs, *Competition and Coercion*, p. 116.

This historical analysis continues to retain its explanatory force. Hence Williams observes that it is a mistake to presume that socio-economic inequality today results from racial discrimination or injustice:

> Despite frequent assertions to the contrary, many of the seemingly intractable problems encountered by a significant number of black Americans do not result from racial discrimination. This is not to say discrimination does not exist. Nor is it to say discrimination has no adverse effects. For policy purposes, however, the issue is not whether or not racial discrimination exists but the extent to which it explains what we see today.[63]

Williams draws this conclusion from studying patterns of racial and ethnic minority progress in different jurisdictions, where despite a generalised experience of discrimination many ethnic minorities exhibit notable success. The automatic conflation of inequality with racial discrimination also fails to account for the existence of racial groups who achieve success despite having been historically oppressed for centuries. Williams's findings are also corroborated by evidence in the UK, where a recent government commission inquiry into race and ethnic disparities found that the greatest single influence on life outcomes is linked not to race or discrimination but to family circumstances, a finding reflected in other inequality studies.[64] The Commission reports:

> Put simply we no longer see a Britain where the system is deliberately rigged against ethnic minorities. The impediments and disparities do exist, they are varied, and ironically very few of them are directly to do with racism. Too often 'racism' is the catch-all explanation, and can be simply implicitly accepted rather than explicitly examined… our

[63] Williams, *Race and Economics*, p. 9.

[64] 'In many areas of investigation, including educational failure and crime, we were led upstream to family breakdown as one of the main reasons for poor outcomes. Family is also the foundation stone of success for many ethnic minorities': Commission on Race and Ethnic Disparities, p. 7.

> enquiries have also underlined to us that the roots of advantage and disadvantage for different groups are complex, and often as much to do with social class, "family" culture and geography as ethnicity.[65]

The Commission found the same causal complexity that emerges from Higgs's analysis: 'our enquiries have also underlined to us that the roots of advantage and disadvantage for different groups are complex, and often as much to do with social class, 'family' culture and geography as ethnicity'.[66] The Commission highlighted that whether discrimination *exists* will not supply a complete or even helpful explanation for why one race may, as a group, be wealthier than another. Comparative studies between different groups reveal an element of subjectivity in perceptions of discrimination and the ease of making progress in British society:

> There is also the question of the relative success of different groups. Those groups, particularly Indian and Chinese ethnic groups, who have the most success in British society tend to see fewer obstacles and less prejudice. And those groups that do less well, Black people and Pakistani and Bangladeshi Muslims, tend to see and experience more of both, though Black African people are considerably more positive than Black Caribbean people.[67]

Taking the example of income distribution, similar questions arise. Are income disparities between groups attributable purely (or primarily) to race discrimination? What weight ought to be attached to alternative explanatory factors such as skills, experience or training? If there is insufficient evidence to assign a specific weight to each explanatory factor, what implications may be drawn from the mere existence of other explanatory factors? We might acknowledge the existence of racial discrimination, while also acknowledging differences in educational attainment and other unquantifiable factors such as ambition and motivation that may also influence income disparities.

---

[65] Ibid., p. 8.

[66] Ibid., p. 10.

[67] Ibid., p. 45.

One of the most debated issues in understanding the causes of inequality is whether ethnic minority progress is attributable to open markets or attributable to equality legislation. If the progress outlined in this chapter is attributable to legislation that would seem to suggest that more legislation would yield even further progress. It is often feared that without an increasingly intrusive legislative framework of equality and non-discrimination there will be no further progress for racial minorities. As Sowell points out, this fear is rooted in a discourse which fails to understand the complexity underlying the causes of inequality, instead conflating discrimination, inequality, and injustice. This terminological confusion is in large part driven by a 'long tradition of intellectuals who more or less automatically transform differences into inequities and inequities into the evils or shortcomings of society'.[68] Failure correctly to identify the causes of inequality not only creates terminological confusion in the social justice debates but also raises two further problems. First, the claim that racism causes inequality causes racial minorities to feel that economic progress will be impossible for them to achieve until every last racist sentiment is eradicated from the earth—hopes which rest on a pipe dream. People of all races are well represented among the poor, but for poor racial minorities class identity adds further layers of complexity to racial identity so that feeling trapped in a socio-economic underclass is perceived to be causally connected to immutable racial identity. Poor white people may in principle work their way out of poverty but poor black people, so the narrative goes, are trapped by race discrimination. Against this reality it appears that personal effort is pointless, and that new 'equity' favours from the government are the only hope for emerging out of poverty. The result of embracing these assumptions is to distract attention from other potential causes of the gaps in attainment, foreclosing any attempt to address them and thereby turning a situation that was full of hope into a truly hopeless dead end.

Based on the studies discussed in this chapter, it is clear that legislation cannot claim to have played a significant role. For example, the historical record in the UK, long before the introduction of human rights

[68] Sowell, *Intellectuals and Race*, p. 109.

and equality legislation, shows that open markets and common law freedoms enabled and facilitated the social and economic progress of many minority communities—minority status is not simply a function of race but applies to any group that finds itself marginalised for any reason. Ancient liberties, such as are expressed in *Magna Carta*, played a key role in the evolution of modern British society. Examples include the common law duty of anyone offering service to members of the public, such as an innkeeper, to serve all comers.[69] Similarly the common law did not recognise the institution of slavery.[70] In the modern context the data corroborates a striking reduction in racist and other exclusionary attitudes. The evidence reviewed in this chapter suggests that even in difficult circumstances, competitive markets have created new opportunities and facilitated a remarkable degree of progress. That being the case, would legislation be more effective in speeding up the rate of progress? Markets work as a path to personal progress, but they admittedly do not always canter at a fast clip and many would prefer to see progress hastened through legislative 'equity' schemes.

[69] *Lane v Cotton* (1701) 88 ER 1458, 1464–65 (KB) 'where-ever any subject takes upon himself a public trust for the benefit of the rest of his fellow-subjects, he is eo ipso bound to serve the subject in all the things that are within the reach and comprehension of such an office, under the pain of an action against him'. Examples being 'a postmaster refusing a letter, inn keeper refusing a guest or blacksmith refusing to shoe a horse': Singer, J. (1996). No Right to Exclude: Public Accommodations and Private Property. *Northwestern University Law Review, 90*(4), 1283, p. 1306.

[70] As illustrated by Lord Mansfield in *Somerset v Stuart*, 'The state of slavery is of such a nature that it is incapable of being introduced on any reasons, moral or political, but only by positive law, which preserves its force long after the reasons, occasions, and time itself from whence it was created, is erased from memory. It is so odious, that nothing can be suffered to support it, but positive law. Whatever inconveniences, therefore, may follow from the decision, I cannot say this case is allowed or approved by the law of England; and therefore the black must be discharged' (1772) 98 ER 499, 510. Cited in Van Cleve, G. (2006). Somerset's Case and Its Antecedents in Imperial Perspective. *Law and History Review, 24*(3), 601–645.

4

The Scope of Equality Legislation

The argument so far has maintained that inequality is not presumptive evidence of injustice. The legislative treatment of racial equality within the value structure of liberalism therefore demands more careful scrutiny. This chapter examines in more detail the idea of 'equity' in the context of employment. Employment claims which arise in the law of contract are protected by principles of fairness and due process rooted in the classical ideal of formal equality. Equality legislation in the context of employment may give the impression of a reasonable and balanced approach to fairness befitting the Rawlsian overlapping consensus, but in reality it serves as a platform for equalisation measures that paradoxically undermine the very principles of equality it purports to endorse. Having started out as a legal framework conferring a right to *equal treatment* in employment, the law comes full circle back to mandating *unequal treatment* as a means of equalising racial outcomes in matters such as hiring and promotion. This contradictory outcome results from the internal inconsistency in the legal implementation of egalitarian ideals, which holds that it would be unfair to treat people equally if they are in fact unequal, and instead people should be equalised by treating them

W. Njoya, *Economic Freedom and Social Justice*, Palgrave Studies in Classical Liberalism,
https://doi.org/10.1007/978-3-030-84852-1_4

unequally with special favours for those said to need extra help.[1] The chapter argues that when the nature of legal rights is properly understood it becomes clear that there is no 'right' not to be discriminated against or 'right' to have the government smooth the course of one's life in the expected manner through protection from the risks that must be faced by all people in the course of market participation. The premise of the argument is that personal identity characteristics do not give certain groups a greater claim to legal protections than other groups.

To argue that lack of equality or diversity is not 'unjust' for purposes of legal intervention does not call into question the worthiness of equality and diversity as a matter of private moral or social preference. The concern of this book is with the validity of mandatory legislative schemes. There are of course many reasons why an employer may wish to promote racial diversity in employment, for example to encourage social cohesion, to draw upon a wider range of experiences and cultures or simply to express a moral or social commitment to racial equality. This does not transform diversity from a valuable goal into a principle that should be treated as central to a theory of justice, and thereby as an appropriate goal for state intervention into voluntary transactions. Within the private sphere freedom of contract envisages employers making hiring decisions purely to promote diversity, should they so desire. It does not follow, however, that this requires the goal of diversity to underpin the legal framework.[2] Nor does it follow from the promotion of diversity that racial identity should be relevant to decision-making in employment, or in regulating work relationships. For example, a Pew Research Centre survey in the United States in 2019 suggested that workers place a high value on racial and ethnic diversity in the workplace, and most reasonable workers would shun an employer known to be discriminatory, but they do not necessarily think race or ethnicity should be relevant in core decision-making relating to hiring, pay or

[1] 'The ark of the egalitarian covenant is becoming the symbol of inegalitarian wickedness. This change of front reflects neither dishonesty nor outstanding stupidity on the part of egalitarians, but the internal inconsistency of their ideal, absolute Equality': Lucas, J. R. (1965). Against Equality. *Philosophy, 40*, 296, 306.

[2] Kukathas, C. (2003). *The Liberal Archipelago: A Theory of Diversity and Freedom.* OUP.

promotion.[3] People may desire greatly to work with those of other races, or at least agree that race is irrelevant in the workplace, but this survey shows that they do not want decisions such as selection for promotion to be based on race.

Formal equality in employment would require treating people equally for example by setting required qualifications for a job to be applied equally to all candidates in the context of hiring or promotion, and as noted earlier this is a principle which satisfies the basic demands of fairness. Even such a requirement of formal equality would be, in itself, an encroachment upon freedom of contract because an employer should in principle be free to hire an unqualified person if he so chooses, in cases where he wishes to for whatever reason: maybe he wants to give the less qualified person a break, or maybe the less qualified person has a great sense of humour which improves workplace morale, and in the realm of private employers there should be no law prohibiting such exercise of the employer's decision-making prerogatives. The idea that an employer *must* hire the person best qualified may be a rational principle, and presumably this is what most employers attempt in practice to do because if they made their hiring decisions on arbitrary and whimsical grounds they would soon go bankrupt, but it is unjustified as a mandatory legal principle granting the courts oversight as to whether the employer indeed selected the 'best' candidate.

We shall see that a general duty to give reasons for one's decisions is alien to the common law of contract. For example there is no law that compels one to purchase the most cost-effective goods on sale, and everyone is free to overspend if they so choose without being required to give reasons for their idiosyncratic choices. However equality legislation justifies its interference with freedom of contract by presenting it as a minimal measure introduced in the interests of fairness that only requires a level playing field, a basic floor of rights or 'equalopportunities' as it is often phrased (although as we have seen life opportunities are neither equal nor capable of being legislatively equalised). But in fact,

[3] Pew Research Centre. (2019). *Americans See Advantages and Challenges in Country's Growing Racial and Ethnic Diversity*. Retrieved from https://www.pewsocialtrends.org/2019/05/08/americans-see-advantages-and-challenges-in-countrys-growing-racial-and-ethnic-diversity/.

the law goes much further than a minimum floor of rights in its operation. When read in light of substantive equality principles such as disparate impact, positive action and harassment, it becomes clear that the legislation requires treating people *as if* they were equal when they are not—for example, treating applicants *as if* they were equally qualified when they are not. The idea of equal opportunities is ultimately designed to create equal opportunities for both the qualified and the unqualified, on grounds that the unqualified are disadvantaged for no fault of their own. The presumption is that absent unfairness, we would all enjoy equal opportunities, and the role of law is to eradicate unfairness by ensuring that all our opportunities are equal. Thus for example the duty to promote substantive equality includes duties to encourage participation by underrepresented groups including the use of special programmes, targets and quotas. In this way, while the classical ideal of equality requires fair rules of the game and the absence of arbitrary barriers to participation, the policy framework of equity requires schemes designed to construct the superficial appearance of equality in employment.

4.1 Non-Discrimination in Employment

The employment relationship is based on a voluntary wage-work exchange that has been founded, since the demise of master and servant status-based relations, on the law of contract. But owing to the importance of employment in personal, civic and political life, the law makes a range of incursions into contractual freedom, freedom of association, freedom of conscience and the right to privacy in the context of employment. This is accomplished in three main ways: by closely governing the freedom to hire and fire and the terms of the engagement, by providing that in making these decisions the employer must not discriminate on grounds of race or other protected grounds and by monitoring workplace interactions including the expression of private opinions outside the workplace extending, in recent times, to social media platforms.

The law generally distinguishes between direct and indirect discrimination. Prohibiting direct discrimination, which most closely approximates the ideal of formal equality, means subjecting a person to less favourable treatment than others because of his race (disparate treatment). Indirect discrimination means formally treating everybody equally in situations where a detrimental impact falls more on one race than others (disparate impact). The legislative test for discrimination is based on comparison, and is thus concerned not with how favourably one is treated, but how one is treated compared (in reality or hypothetically) to those of a different race.[4] In a reversal of the usual probative burden the victim of indirect discrimination need not prove the existence of racial barriers, which are often said to be 'hidden' and thus 'not easy to anticipate or to spot' much less to prove.[5] Thus the legislation side-steps the burden of proof which, in other legal contexts, is upheld as essential to procedural justice. As discussed in context of the causes of inequality, the law presumes that hidden discriminatory barriers exist based on the fact that the results are unequal. The goal of bringing about equal results or outcomes between members of protected groups and those who do not share their protected characteristics necessarily relies upon statistical disparities.[6]

> No speck of evidence is required from those who implicitly assume that employee composition would be similar to population composition, in the absence of discrimination…Statistics alone are sufficient to establish the 'disparate impact' case that employers must rebut.[7]

[4] *Chief Constable of West Yorkshire v Vento* [2001] IRLR 124: 'a series of incidents occurred when fellow police officers criticised her conduct, her personal life and her character in an unwarranted, aggressive and demoralising manner. The treatment was found to be less favourable than a hypothetical male officer would have received in the same circumstances'.

[5] 'The prohibition of indirect discrimination thus aims to achieve equality of results in the absence of such justification. It is dealing with hidden barriers which are not easy to anticipate or to spot': *Essop v Home Office (UK Border Agency) [2015] EWCA Civ 609; [2015] I.C.R. 1063*, par. 25.

[6] 'It is commonplace for the disparate impact, or particular disadvantage, to be established on the basis of statistical evidence… Statistical evidence is designed to show correlations between particular variables and particular outcomes and to assess the significance of those correlations. But a correlation is not the same as a causal link': *Essop v Home Office*, par. 28.

[7] Sowell, *Intellectuals and Race*, p. 134.

Under the principle of 'disproportionate group disadvantage' an individual member of a disadvantaged group can bring a claim derived from the disadvantage suffered by members of their group. The group disadvantage raises a presumption which is treated as evidence of indirect discrimination (i.e. evidence of disparate impact) unless the employer is able to prove the contrary.[8] The equality legislation therefore does not require an inquiry into reasons for disadvantage.[9]

The same implications arise in the context of harassment since, unlike discrimination which focuses on specific detriment (e.g. detriment suffered from not being hired because of race, or being fired because of race) harassment is to a large degree a matter for interpretation that depends primarily on the subjective perception of the victim. The idea that it is unlawful to make people feel humiliated by reason of their race involves subjective evaluations that have major implications for the scope of individual freedom in day to day interactions especially in light of the fraught nature of human communication and miscommunication. For example in the UK the Equality Act provides that a person (A) harasses another (B) if A engages in unwanted conduct related to a relevant protected characteristic, which has the purpose or effect of violating B's dignity, or creating an intimidating, hostile, degrading, humiliating or offensive environment for B. Relevant factors in deciding whether conduct amounts to harassment include the perception of the victim, the other circumstances of the case and whether it is reasonable for the conduct to have the effect alleged by the victim.

This legislative framework has major implications for economic freedom. The first threat to the scope of individual discretion in making

---

[8] 'Where persons who considered themselves wronged by the non-application to them of the principle of equal treatment established facts from which it might be presumed that there had been direct or indirect discrimination, it was for the respondent to prove that there had been no breach of the principle of equal treatment': *Essop v Home Office.*

[9] 'There is no requirement in the Equality Act 2010 that the claimant show why the [test or requirement] puts one group sharing a particular protected characteristic at a particular disadvantage when compared with others. It is enough that it does. Sometimes, perhaps usually, the reason will be obvious: women are on average shorter than men, so a tall minimum height requirement will disadvantage women whereas a short maximum will disadvantage men. But sometimes it will not be obvious: there is no generally accepted explanation for why women have on average achieved lower grades as chess players than men, but a requirement to hold a high chess grade will put them at a disadvantage': *Essop v Home Office.*

decisions in employment arises from the fact that equality legislation becomes increasingly intrusive over time, encroaching upon new areas of concern, recognising new identity groups that require to be protected and spreading out from the workplace to other related interactions. The law began by prohibiting discrimination in narrowly defined circumstances, but over time has gradually expanded to cover almost any conceivable circumstances. Thus privacy rights and freedom of speech have also come under pressure in the employment context, as the exercise of these freedoms increasingly places employees at risk of losing their jobs and livelihoods. This is not due simply to the phenomenon of regulation-creep, although that plays a role, but is to be expected given the moral goals of the legislation. If the goal is to protect the vulnerable we would expect the reach of the law to expand as more and more people self-classify as vulnerable. The expansive scope of the law is therefore widely perceived as a welcome development because it offers increasing protection from unfair treatment and ideally, in egalitarian terms, everyone should be safeguarded from unfairness. Thus Lady Hale observes with approval that, 'The whole trend of equality legislation since it began in the 1970s has been to reinforce the protection given to the principle of equal treatment'.[10] But this level of protection is achieved only by sacrificing the ambit of individual discretion and judgement.

Nor is this intrusiveness an incidental feature that can be tweaked or constrained with a few procedural safeguards, as is imagined by those who call for equality legislation to be 'amended' to make it less oppressive. Its oppressiveness is an embedded design feature necessary to help the law to achieve its stated goals and without which the law would be entirely unenforceable. For example, one cause of general concern for those critical of the law is the fact that while legal culpability generally treats intention or state of mind as a relevant factor, in equality law neither intention nor motive are relevant in ascertaining liability for discrimination. The employer's motive or intention is irrelevant in establishing liability, although in some cases a lack of intention to harass may help to construct a defence that the victim's perception of being harassed was unreasonable. Nor need the employer, or the perpetrator

[10] *Essop v Home Office.*

in cases of vicarious liability, be aware that their conduct is discriminatory or is perceived as harassment. The need to maintain and expand the scope of the antidiscrimination principle obviates the need to show discriminatory intention.

Therefore the law focuses on the unequal outcomes, not the motives giving rise to inequality. This is the logically unavoidable result of prioritising equality. As soon as the quest for equality goes beyond formal equality before the law, the focus is naturally directed towards equalising outcomes and the employer's intention or conduct becomes increasingly immaterial.[11] If motive or intention were generally required as an element of discrimination claims an employer could easily avoid liability simply by showing, in the example offered by the courts, that he had treated people differently because of their race for motives of 'customer preference, or to save money, or even to avoid controversy'.[12] In other words the typical sorts of things that motivate business decisions, that are nothing directly to do with race, are superseded by the antidiscrimination principle. Thus treating a person less favourably because of his race incurs liability, even if the employer was motivated by concern for the employee or a desire to help, for example if the employer chooses not to hire an applicant because of his race out of concern that he 'would not fit in, or that other employees might make the applicant's life a misery'.[13]

It is but a short step from declaring intention or motive to be irrelevant to endorsing claims that discriminatory intention may well be present unconsciously or subconsciously. The presence of unconscious or subconscious bias is not necessary to satisfy the legal test, though the lack of hostile intention may be a mitigating factor in assessing the level of compensation payable. Suffice it that racial bias *appears* to exist, for example because of disproportionate representation of disadvantaged groups. The appearance of bias in itself supplies the potential explanation for disproportionate representation. Further, following the logic driving

[11] 'The intention or motive of the defendant to discriminate, though it may be relevant so far as remedies are concerned…is not a necessary condition of liability; it is perfectly possible to envisage cases where the defendant had no such motive, and yet did in fact discriminate': Lord Goff in *Birmingham City Council v Equal Opportunities Commission* [1989] AC 1155, 1194.

[12] *Birmingham v EOC*, ibid.

[13] Lord Nicholls in *Nagarajan v London Regional Transport* [2000] 1 AC 501, 510.

this legislation, the burden of proof must shift from the victim to the defendant as often as possible—the employer who has no black people among his senior staff must prove that this is *not* due to discrimination. If black people were required to establish that their absence was reflective of discrimination on the employer's part, the law would be rendered into no more than a statement of unenforceable ideals. Thus in the UK the Equality Act provides that 'if there are facts from which the court could decide, in the absence of any other explanation, that a person (A) contravened the provision concerned, the court must hold that the contravention occurred' unless 'A shows that A did not contravene the provision'.[14] An employer may also be vicariously liable for discrimination by one of its employees or a related party.

The evidence required to prove discrimination is necessarily circumstantial. Ideally there would be evidence of racial motivation in the paper trail. But in most cases rational people will respond to the legislation by designing their decision-making processes in such a way as to document that no unlawful questions were asked, and no unlawful characteristics taken into account. Anyone who has participated in a decision-making panel, such as an appointments committee, will be aware of how much care and attention is devoted to ensuring that the record is litigation-proof or at least unlikely to invite discrimination complaints. Rather than being eradicated, any discriminatory intention that might be present simply goes underground. Courts alive to the danger of people tailoring the record to mask discrimination double down by becoming increasingly astute to scrutinise carefully other forms of indirect and circumstantial evidence of unlawful conduct, to the extent that statistical disparities in practice give rise to something approaching strict liability for discrimination. As courts shift their attention to indirect and circumstantial forms of evidence statistical disparities assume even greater significance. This is because while it is difficult to prove people's motives it is easy to show, for example, the number of black people on corporate boards of directors and how that number compares to the racial demographics of society. The onus then shifts to the company to provide a plausible explanation to displace the inference of discrimination. The case becomes

[14] S. 136.

even more complex when, as they often do, people have mixed lawful and unlawful motives for their decision. An employer might say, 'she doesn't have the right qualifications (lawful) and she is black (unlawful)'. The costs of policing the reasons and motivations for decisions, disentangling lawful from unlawful strands of thought processes, are high: the costs of keeping a carefully tailored paper trail when discrimination goes underground, the costs of people making the wrong match because they unwittingly end up trapped in deals where the lack of suitability was not disclosed for fear of being accused of discrimination, the costs of artificially introducing quotas and targets to avoid troublesome statistical disparities, including the much maligned 'token' appointments, the costs of over-promoting people to jobs they patently cannot perform in order to signal equal opportunities only to end up unwittingly setting them up for failure and the inevitable costs of litigation and compensation.

This trend seems likely to continue. In the quest for total equality, no amount of progress in ameliorating racial disparities will satisfy the hunger for more. So long as unequal outcomes persist in a world of difference and diversity, any evidence of inequality will suffice to justify calls for further interventions. As Epstein cautions:

> The process has no logical stopping point. With the move from disparate treatment to disparate impact, the levels of external control quickly become intrusive...By a process of degree the legal system thus backs itself into a corner. It will never allow any objections on the workability or economic consequences of discrimination law to lead to a re-examination of the basic rule. That initial decision is engraved in stone for reasons that are said to be moral are indeed unexamined...On balance the antidiscrimination laws are a major social and intellectual mistake.[15]

A legal framework is now established in which the usual safeguards of due process are lacking. This approach is sometimes defended by arguing that an innocent employer is able to offer a defence of justification in cases of disparate impact. No justification is permissible in cases of *direct* discrimination, but in cases of *indirect* discrimination the employer may seek to establish that the disparate impact is justified by reference to the

---

[15] Epstein, *Forbidden Grounds*, pp. 445, 446.

goals sought to be achieved and the impact on disadvantaged groups: a test of proportionality. The law also attempts to strike a reasonable balance by providing that even where discrimination is established the detriment suffered by the victim must be viewed objectively and not be merely trivial or such as would be unlikely to be viewed as detriment by reasonable people: a 'test of materiality'.[16] For these reasons one might suppose, with the greatest of optimism, that the legislation has adequate safeguards. But as will be seen in the discussion that follows, the safeguards said to be incorporated in the legislative framework pale into insignificance when viewed in light of other mechanisms of the equality framework.

4.2 Affirmative Action, Quotas and Targets

Engineering equal employment outcomes is increasingly achieved through statistical measures such as racial quotas or proportional wage regulation. Targets matter. In the UK, universities report record numbers of ethnic minority students.[17] Proud of this progress, they are so pleased to have met and exceeded their racial targets that the wider implications seem to be immaterial.[18] Subjecting a person to less favourable treatment because of their race is unlawful, but treating a person *more* favourably because of his race is encouraged, despite the fact that this necessarily entails treating other races less favourably than the favoured race. For example the Equality Act 2010 creates a 'public sector equality duty' under which public bodies must take action to eliminate discrimination,

[16] *Shamoon v RUC* [2013] ICR 337 at 349G–373B.

[17] 'Record numbers of ethnic minority students were accepted at Cambridge University this academic year, its annual admissions statistics show. Nearly three in ten (29.3 per cent) British students admitted in 2020 were from black, Asian and minority ethnic backgrounds — up from 27.8 per cent the previous year. In the general UK population about 13.8 per cent of people are from a minority ethnic background': https://www.thetimes.co.uk/article/cambridge-takes-record-numbers-of-ethnic-minority-and-state-pupils-fsrtx8cf9.

[18] Announcing that 'What these statistics show is that we are meeting, or even exceeding, our benchmark targets': Cambridge University: Record number of BAME admissions in 2020 (May 19, 2020). https://www.bbc.co.uk/news/uk-england-cambridgeshire-57156553.

advance equality and 'foster good relations'.[19] This includes taking steps to 'remove or minimise disadvantages', 'tackle prejudice' and 'promote understanding'. Private persons performing public duties must also 'have regard' to these duties.[20] In practice this means they must be prepared to show the steps they have taken to have regard to these duties. Secondary legislation establishes specific duties to publish annual information on employees with protected characteristics and specify measurable objectives that need to be achieved to further the equality duties.[21] The legislation allows 'positive action' to promote these duties, while insisting that it does not permit discrimination regardless of intention, whether detrimental or benign.[22] The person being positively favoured must be at least as qualified as those against whom he is preferred, and the positive action in hiring or promotion must not be a general policy to favour a particular race.[23] This means that explicit quotas would in themselves amount to unlawful discrimination against those for whom special quotas are not implemented, but in practice it is difficult to see how compliance with the law can be achieved without the implicit quotas which often offer the only realistic way to avoid the statistical disparities which in turn amount to evidence of indirect discrimination.

This explains why several jurisdictions now prescribe quotas for ethnic minorities on corporate boards of directors.[24] They are concerned that many boards of directors do not have ethnic minority members: in the UK in 2020 '150 companies out of 256 (59%) did not have at least one

---

[19] S. 149: (1) A public authority must, in the exercise of its functions, have due regard to the need to (a) eliminate discrimination, harassment, victimisation and any other conduct that is prohibited by or under this Act; (b) advance equality of opportunity between persons who share a relevant protected characteristic and persons who do not share it; (c) foster good relations between persons who share a relevant protected characteristic and persons who do not share it.

[20] S. 149 (2) A person who is not a public authority but who exercises public functions must, in the exercise of those functions, have due regard to the matters mentioned in subsection (1).

[21] The Equality Act 2010 (Specific Duties) Regulations 2011. https://www.equalityhumanrights.com/sites/default/files/psed_essential_guide_-_guidance_for_english_public_bodies.pdf.

[22] S. 149 (6) 'Compliance with the duties in this section may involve treating some persons more favourably than others; but that is not to be taken as permitting conduct that would otherwise be prohibited by or under this Act'.

[23] S. 159 (4)(b) Equality Act.

[24] 'An individual who self-identifies as Black, African American, Hispanic, Latino, Asian, Pacific Islander, Native American, Native Hawaiian, or Alaska Native, or who self-identifies as gay, lesbian, bisexual, or transgender' (California Assembly Bill 979).

director of colour on their Boards'.[25] The aim of diversifying corporate boards of directors is, of course, to make everyone feel welcome, included and valued: 'Let us create boards and organisations where everyone feels respected and heard, where everyone belongs and thrives. This will invite greater diversity and not only improve board and corporate performance but also unleash our full potential as human beings'.[26] The UK's Corporate Governance Code therefore requires quotas for women and ethnic minorities on boards of directors. The fact that quotas and positive discrimination are generally prohibited by equality legislation did not prevent the Parker Review of ethnic diversity on UK boards from proposing that FTSE 100 companies should appoint at least one ethnic minority member by 2021 (and by 2024 for all FTSE 250 companies).[27] This is a voluntary target operating on a 'comply or explain' basis, which the sector is keen to embrace to avoid the need for more intrusive mandatory legislation. It is widely accepted that in order to meet these targets positive discrimination may be necessary, although, curiously, the Financial Reporting Council observes that while 'first steps towards inclusion are uncomfortable' they do not expect inclusion to reduce the quality of the board: 'I derive comfort from the evidence that suggests boards do not see demographic diversity or targets as a threat to the quality of directors'.[28] Revealing words, given that confidence in new corporate hires is not usually expressed in the form of reassurance that they will not pose a threat. Perhaps these self-comforting words from the corporate sector are an appropriate expression of make-believe confidence to go along with the make-believe equality they are introducing. The threat of which they pretend not to be afraid is that this is only the beginning, a mere first step towards cosmic egalitarian goals.

---

[25] Parker, Sir John. (2020). *Ethnic Diversity: Enriching Business Leadership: An Update Report from The Parker Review*. https://assets.ey.com/content/dam/ey-sites/ey-com/en_uk/news/2020/02/ey-parker-review-2020-report-final.pdf.

[26] Ibid.

[27] Ibid.

[28] Financial Reporting Council. (2021, July). *Board Diversity and Effectiveness in FTSE 350 Companies*. https://www.frc.org.uk/getattachment/3cc05eae-2024-45d8-b14c-abb2ac7497aa/FRC-Board-Diversity-and-Effectiveness-in-FTSE-350-Companies.pdf, p. 5.

These developments illustrate why equality law, with its antecedents in notions of formal equality, has come to be viewed as an impediment to the ambitions driving equalisation programmes. Even though the attempt in California to repeal the principle of equality before the law proved unsuccessful on a first attempt,[29] it is clear from the example of minority quotas on boards of directors that formal repeal of the law may not be necessary to enable further pursuit of egalitarian goals. Affirmative action, positive action and soft-law 'comply or explain' guidance have already, in practice, superseded the principle of formal equality. Thus 'equity' has continued its advance, having long outpaced the framework of equality law by which it made its first inroads.

4.3 Is There a 'Right' Not to Be Discriminated Against?

Equality law aims to secure equal opportunities for all. The legal framework is tied to the concept of discrimination. Two issues arise: first, the legitimacy of linking the right to improve one's life chances to the specific personal identity traits (the 'protected characteristics' or 'forbidden grounds') on which discrimination claims turn. Second, the hazard of creating an incentive structure under which the most reliable and predictable way to avoid the appearance of discrimination is to set up quota systems to hedge against the risk of exhibiting statistical disparities.[30] The only way for a corporation to signal that it is not discriminatory is to include members of all the protected classes on its board of directors, a strategy which may well be conducive to social

[29] California Proposition 16 proposed to amend the California constitution by repealing the principle of non-discrimination, in order to permit discrimination for those thought to need positive discrimination.

[30] Epstein, *Forbidden Grounds*, p. 234. Arguments supporting this incentive structure exhibit the 'systematic incentive' to overstate the degree of discrimination that has taken place; to dwell at length on the idea of unconscious discrimination; to attribute the discrimination that did exist [historically] to the marketplace and not to invidious forms of state action; to assert that prior remedial programs have been woefully inadequate to undo the corrosive effects of past discrimination; to claim that the pervasive dominance of racist or sexist attitudes in the larger society justifies the affirmative action programs undertaken by courageous private firms and government agencies: Epstein, *Forbidden Grounds*, p. 417.

harmony and yield many marketing advantages but seems to have little connection with the idea of equality as a 'right'. This part of the discussion considers the conceptual nature of the rights created by the legal framework. People are accustomed to designating their wishes, desires and dreams for social and economic change as 'rights', but the legal framework must be able to define the nature of a right as something other than simply a hope or expectation or vision. The aim here is not to ascertain the general nature of rights in a broader philosophical sense, but to outline the nature of non-discrimination rights. The discussion will focus on how these rights are depicted in the context of employment law.

There is an important distinction in the employment law discourse between civil liberties and fundamental human rights. Fundamental human rights, such as the right to life or the right to liberty, are vested in us because we are human not because they are granted by legislation. Legislation may help to protect these rights, but any legislation that purported to deny fundamental rights such as the right to life or liberty would lack legitimacy in a liberal society. Civil liberties, by contrast, relate to rights created by legislation and granted in respect of our interactions with other people, such as the right to vote or the right to enforce contracts. Civil liberties thus depend on some form of social contract or legal prescription. Everybody has a fundamental human right to work, but not to be given a specific job; the human right to own property, but not to purchase a specific house. The right to buy a home or to earn a wage in one's chosen profession are civil rights which recognise that it is unfair and inimical to the good ordering of society to exclude people from economic participation. It is easy to understand that these are not fundamental human rights by recalling that such rights in many liberal jurisdictions are often reserved by immigration laws to its own citizens. Human rights, which vest naturally in all human beings, do not depend on rights of citizenship.

The declaration that 'all men are created equal' reflects a universal truth concerning the nature of human rights which is complete in itself, and does not require the superimposition of a further set of associated rights. For example freedom of association confers the right to exercise free choice over our interactions, but subject to the right of others to do the same. For example we have the right to make friends with anyone we choose, but not the right to force anyone to make friends with us. The right to interact with anyone we choose does not override the other person's right not to interact with us. Rights as classically defined entail the freedom to act—the freedom to own property, to work or produce things, to enter into contracts. In that light, it is clear that there is no free-standing 'right' not to be discriminated against or to compel others to show us the respect we feel that we deserve, if they do not share our estimation of the value we offer them.[31] The principle of non-discrimination enshrined in Title III of the EU Charter of Fundamental rights declares that 'everyone is equal before the law' and prohibits discrimination based on specified grounds including race.[32] In that sense the non-discrimination principle entails a civil right to the extent that it asserts a freedom to enjoy one's substantive rights without being constrained in the assertion of those rights on the grounds only of race, for example freedom to buy property (property rights) or enter into contracts (contractual rights) irrespective of race. In that sense non-discrimination is not a free-standing right in itself, but an enabling right protecting the enjoyment of one's vested rights without discrimination. Indeed it is framed this way in the European Convention of Human Rights, which provides in Article 14 that.

> The enjoyment of the rights and freedoms set forth in [the] Convention shall be secured without discrimination on any ground such as sex, race, colour, language, religion, political or other opinion, national or social origin, association with a national minority, property, birth or other status.

[31] The Equality and Human Rights Commission advises: "The protection against discrimination in the Human Rights Act is not 'free-standing'. To rely on this right, you must show that discrimination has affected your enjoyment of one or more of the other rights in the Act. However, you do not need to prove that this other human right has actually been breached." https://www.equalityhumanrights.com/en/human-rights-act/article-14-protection-discrimination. Accessed 12 May 2021.

[32] Charter of Fundamental Rights of the European Union 2012/C 326/02.

A claim based on breach of Article 14 must identify the substantive right, e.g. the right to life or liberty, that is alleged to be in issue.[33] With that analytical distinction in mind, it is necessary to evaluate the nature of equality rights on two levels: as a fundamental human right and as a civil right attached to the enjoyment of other rights. The argument advanced here is that anti-discrimination rights are not fundamental human rights, but civil rights designed to enhance the protection of fundamental human rights. Some examples might help to explain the importance of this analytical distinction. Laws against murder defend the underlying, or prior, right to life; laws against theft defend the right to one's own property. We have an inherent and inalienable natural right to life and liberty regardless of what the contemporary criminal laws might state. But no prior right is defended by equality law. There is no inalienable right 'not to be discriminated against' or to be treated a particular way by other people in private transactions because it would infringe upon the rights of those people to make their own choices in such transactions. A buyer may wish to buy something, but the seller has no duty to sell it in the absence of a contractual claim. Nobody has an inherent or natural human 'right' to be given a particular job or house or any other material good. Unless it amounts to a breach of contract, choosing to prefer one person over another does not breach any prior rights. In the absence of a monopoly, where only one seller exists in a market, it does not breach any rights to prefer one buyer over another. If there are no real choices and thus discrimination could prevent people from having access to material goods, the problem that needs to be resolved is that of the monopoly (or near monopoly). The monopoly problem is also relevant in understanding the distinction between public and private life; in public life most people have obligations to pay taxes to fund public services to which they are therefore entitled, and often have no option to

[33] 'Article 14 only complements the other substantive provisions of the Convention and the Protocols. It has no independent existence since it has effect solely in relation to "the enjoyment of the rights and freedoms" safeguarded by those provisions. Although the application of Article 14 does not presuppose a *breach* of those provisions – and to that extent it is autonomous – there can be no room for its application unless *the facts at issue fall within the ambit* of one or more of the latter' (emphasis added)—a substantive right must be in issue, though it need not be proved to have been breached: *Sommerfeld v Germany* (31,871/96) [2003] ECHR 341 (8 July 2003).

go elsewhere without incurring inordinate costs, so the principle of non-discrimination may become relevant. Thus there may be a 'right' for a taxpayer to have access to public services that would supply the rationale for the antidiscrimination principle in health and education, for example, but its application to the personal employment relationship, especially in the context of private employers, is less straightforward.

Specific legislation which purports to grant statutory antidiscrimination rights, of which employment law offers the clearest examples, therefore rests on unsound philosophical foundations. Employment legislation generally avoids the need to offer ethical justifications by purporting to treat equality as a procedural entitlement in deciding questions of fair treatment at work. In the UK unfair dismissal legislation provides that if the reason for dismissal is a protected ground, the dismissal is automatically unfair and no explanation or justification is admissible in defence. But as detailed in the discussion above, to describe antidiscrimination as a right implies something more than procedural fairness and sets up expectations of an independent, free-standing claim-right or entitlement. The discourse of human rights implies something more fundamental, more significant, than a quest for fair treatment. Designation of a claim as a right, in making arguments about fairness, presupposes the identification of a prior right which is to be defended by treating the person fairly.

Like the distinction between 'opportunity' and 'outcome' the distinction between a right and the *enjoyment* of that right tends in practice to be overlooked. In practice the non-discrimination principle is treated as an independent right conceptualised as a free-standing claim or demand concerning the behaviour of other people, for example a demand to regulate the language other people are permitted to use in cases where no substantive right is in issue. This tension between antidiscrimination principles and fundamental freedoms has been publicly debated in the context of free speech, in relation to the freedom to express views that others consider to be offensive because of their race or other identity traits protected by discrimination law. It is customary in that context to respond to complaints by arguing that there is no 'right' not to be offended. Particular instances of offending others may be socially harmful, for example where it involves a breach of the peace or incitement to violence—both of which are criminal offences. Hence the classic example of shouting 'fire!' in a crowded theatre in the absence of an actual fire: there is no freedom to put life and limb at risk by wantonly triggering a stampede. But these context-specific principles do not justify general limits on free speech; a right not to be offended would amount to such a general limit on free speech.

A free society is characterised by tolerating difference of opinion and dissent from the prevailing moral or social consensus. The meaning of toleration 'requires little more than indifference'; it does not require respect, admiration, endorsement, engagement or empathy with different opinions.[34] Moreover, 'it certainly does not require taking the tolerated individuals or groups seriously; and it is perfectly consistent with a contempt for everything for which they stand, as well as with an unwillingness to engage them in rational dialogue, or even to understand them. Tolerators need not sit down with the tolerated; but they will stand them'.[35] The law does not prescribe what is 'offensive' or 'intolerable' because what offends me may be perfectly benign to you, and in a free society there will be a diverse range of moral opinions and standards. One may voluntarily go further than toleration and choose to understand or embrace different views, in order to promote and celebrate diversity, but this would not be an appropriate basis for conferring legitimacy on coercive legislation.

Thus social and moral priorities, where they form the basis of legislative restrictions on fundamental freedoms, must be applied without imposing general limits on the underlying right. A key issue that arises is how to implement these ideas in daily decision-making processes. As often stated in employment law reasonableness is a spectrum or a band that does not lend itself to straightforward 'reasonable or not' bright line distinctions. Some employers might think it reasonable to dismiss summarily a good worker who is caught stealing a small amount of money; others might think it reasonable to give that worker a warning and second chance; others still might turn a blind eye if the worker is that

[34] Kukathas, *The Liberal Archipelago*, p. 23.

[35] Ibid.

good and the amount involved is that small; or there might be multiple other responses, such as taking that worker off the tills. These are just examples to illustrate that in practice there is always a wide range of decisions that differ but are all nevertheless reasonable: known in the case law as the 'range of reasonable responses'. It is here that law comes up against the knowledge problem that all regulation faces. The people involved in the interaction are best placed to decide what is reasonable in the circumstances. As we shall argue in the next chapter, knowledge problems are best resolved by allowing the widest possible scope for private decision-making. The point to make here, drawing lessons from the free speech debates, is that the tolerance of racial diversity and other emanations of diversity in a free society does not give rise to a duty positively to embrace diversity in the employment context or to a right to have ones diverse characteristics treated with 'respect, admiration, endorsement, engagement or empathy' by all who cross our path in life. It may be what we would all desire, but there is an important analytical and philosophical distinction between desires and legal rights. That distinction defends the scope of individual liberty.

4.4 The Distinction Between Public and Private Life

Since its emergence in the 1960s, the antidiscrimination principle has extended far beyond its initial application to education, health and housing, to encompass all aspects of public life and increasingly intrude into the private sphere. The goals of social justice constructed around equality have 'sought to mold the whole of society – down to the most intimate private acts – around the ideology of anti-racism'.[36] Anti-racism ideology has such compelling moral power that it increasingly reaches into the realm of private interactions with scarcely pause for reflection on the implications for privacy and individual liberty. There is a growing social expectation that the right to be treated equally

[36] Caldwell, *The Age of Entitlement*, p. 10.

applies to all contexts, including the most private of interpersonal relations. The sphere of private life has increasingly been diminished as the state exercises ever greater control over any decisions with potential to cause harm to others, regardless of whether they arise in the public or private sphere. The civil rights era in the United States marked the end of a clear distinction between public and private life, as the idea gained traction that 'it was impossible to defeat the quasi-caste system faced by African Americans without some interference with the private sector'.[37] This interference started out with relatively limited incursions into private decision-making, but over time the public–private divide has been eroded almost into extinction.[38] Private institutions open to the public, or having an impact on public life, are now almost invariably deemed to be quasi-public and thus subject to the same legal duties as public bodies. Any defence based on being a private institution is increasingly unlikely to succeed. For instance the civil rights legislation originally applied to educational institutions receiving public funding, but now privately funded institutions are subject to the same laws because they are open to members of the public. The law in Scotland now extends the public order offence of 'stirring up hatred' into private dwellings such as the home, an extension defended by the Scottish government on grounds that distinguishing speech made in the home from public speech would be an 'entirely artificial distinction'.[39]

> Are we saying that, as a society, we are comfortable with no criminal sanction being applied to people because [hate speech] is being done within

---

[37] Bernstein, D. E. (2003). *You Can't Say That! The Growing Threat to Civil Liberties from Antidiscrimination Laws* (p. 5). Cato Institute.

[38] 'The question of civil rights was perceived first and foremost as a moral issue, as a question of simple justice, which admitted only one categorical answer: any form of discrimination on the basis of race is morally wrong and ought to be illegal. It was the practice of discrimination that mattered. What was wholly irrelevant was its source, public or private' Epstein, *Forbidden Grounds*, p. 93.

[39] 'Tory attempts to reintroduce a "dwelling defence" failed this month, with Yousaf insisting such a defence would draw an "entirely artificial distinction" that would allow threatening and abusive bigotry simply because it was inside the home': Jayanetti, C. (2021, February 26). How Scotland's Hate Crime Bill Ignited a Freedom of Speech Row. *Prospect*. https://www.prospectmagazine.co.uk/politics/scotland-snp-hate-crime-bill-trans-rights.

> the confines of their dwelling whereas if they stepped out into the street outside of their house then that would be an offence?[40]

The incredulity with which that question is framed implies that there can be no serious objection to hate speech based only on the fact that it occurs in the private sphere. The question is asking whether there is any moral distinction between performing acts in a private dwelling and performing them in the public space. The reasoning there is that if people say hateful things about others, that is in principle harmful, and the harmful features of hate speech ought not to be treated differently depending on whether the words are uttered within or outside the privacy of the home. It is no longer deemed to be self-evident that there is an essential difference between speaking at the dinner table in one's own home and speaking in a public place; the distinction between private and public has altogether lost political significance. Thus 'public order' offences extend to the private realm where there is no 'public' present to be triggered into disorder; the illogic of piggy-backing onto public order offences to regulate speech within the home is disregarded in imposing liability because the sanction is directed squarely at the moral wrongfulness of the speech, regardless of context. And after all, as was argued in the case of Scotland, words uttered in the home may be overheard by children who may repeat them in public, so by these steps in reasoning the private dwelling should not be exempt from public order regulation. Even if there are no children present, what if the words are overheard by a passer-by through an open window? Or surreptitiously recorded by the rogue robot embedded in the smartphone? The possibilities for harm are endless, even in the most private of private dwellings.

This inexorable tendency to expand the scope of equality claims is inherent in the logic of the legislation, and is inimical to liberty.[41] Within

---

40 Hate Crime and Public Order (Scotland) Act 2021.

41 'There is no natural limit to the scope of antidiscrimination laws, because the concept of antidiscrimination is almost infinitely malleable. Almost any economic behavior, and much other behavior, can be defined as discrimination. Whom people employ, befriend, marry, and love are all products of one sort of discrimination or another, including discrimination based on education level, discrimination based on family connection, discrimination based on looks, and discrimination based on personality…there is no consensus as to what constitutes "real" discrimination, nor, not surprisingly, does there appear to be any principled definition that

the private sphere each decision-maker is free to speak and free to choose at will. Public decisions, being funded by the public and not conducive to opt-outs, must be subject to public accountability. But private decisions owe no similar duty of accountability to give reasons for one's personal choices or preferences. In the private sphere of human interaction, each individual is free to discriminate based on race or any other identity characteristic when choosing for example whom to marry, or with whom to start a business, or in making decisions on matters such as one's hobbies or friendships or career choices. The principle of self-ownership suggests that in the private sphere each individual should retain his decision-making prerogative subject to not infringing upon the rights of others or committing acts of aggression against them.

> A liberal society stands or falls by the distinction between the political (or the state) and society, or by the distinction between the public and the private. In the liberal society there is necessarily a private sphere with which the state's legislation must not interfere…the prohibition against every 'discrimination' would mean the abolition of the private sphere, the denial of the difference between the state and society, in a word, the destruction of liberal society.[42]

Individual freedom is of crucial importance in the private sphere, and the distinction between public and private life is crucial for social order. As Furedi argues, 'The erosion of the symbolic boundary between these two domains has had a profound bearing on how people conduct their informal and intimate relationships'.[43] There are compelling reasons to defend the private space as essential to human integrity and happiness. The boundary between public and private, between the domain of state regulation and our personal lives, is rooted in antiquity and predates modern law. This boundary is essential in ordering human interaction and exchange. As Furedi explains:

legislatures have followed': Bernstein, D. E. (2018). The Boundaries of Antidiscrimination Laws. In M. Todd Henderson (Ed.), *The Cambridge Handbook of Classical Liberal Thought*. CUP. Also available at https://papers.ssrn.com/sol3/papers.cfm?abstract_id=3286092.

[42] Caldwell, *The Age of Entitlement*, p. 15, quoting Leo Strauss.

[43] Furedi, F. (2020). *Why Borders Matter: Why Humanity Must Relearn the Art of Drawing Boundaries* (p. 70). Routledge.

> The distinction between the public and private spheres underpinned the growing trend towards the liberalisation of political and social life. By the middle of the 19th century, it was widely recognised that people's freedom to act in accordance with their conscience and cultivate their capacity for moral autonomy required a space that was genuinely private. The very idea of tolerance had as its premise the conviction that individual conscience and private belief should not be subject to the laws directed at the regulation of public behaviour and views.[44]

The private sphere is necessary for individual autonomy, for the personal sense of agency and control over one's life and how much of that life to make public, and ultimately to be able to develop a healthy sense of self-knowledge and self-esteem as a uniquely individual member of society. Furedi further explains:

> The separation of the public and private spheres has been essential for the emergence of the modern individual. The aspiration for autonomy and identity cannot be entirely resolved in the public sphere. The private sphere not only provides a potential space for reflection but also for the development of personality. Intimate relationships require privacy if they are not to disintegrate under the pressure of public scrutiny. Whatever problems might exist in the private sphere, it is the prerequisite for the exercise of freedom.[45]

Thus the regulatory question in a liberal society is not simply how to choose between different conceptualisations of equality, but also where to draw the line in delineating the scope of public decisions to which equality law applies. The grey areas arise at the boundaries of public and private. Part of the pressure to erode the public–private divide comes from the desire to prevent powerful private bodies, such as large private corporations, from exercising quasi-state functions. The fear is that large powerful corporations should not be free to treat individuals unfairly and arbitrarily by invoking the excuse that being private they owe no duties of transparency or accountability. The desire to hold private bodies

---

[44] Ibid., p. 71.

[45] Ibid., p. 85.

exercising quasi-public functions to account then extends to holding all private individuals accountable in the same way. Nobody objects because nobody wishes big powerful institutions to behave with impunity merely because they are privately owned.

Furedi takes a principled view of the importance of the private sphere, and he is critical of the ways in which the sanctity of the private space has come under assault from the public demands for transparency and accountability. He describes the growing fear that the private sphere has potential to cause harm, in contexts where the highest priority in liberal societies is to keep citizens safe from harm. The fear driving the assault on the private sphere is that allowing free discretion within the private space would enable people to keep 'secrets'. Secrets pose an amorphous risk of harm both to the person keeping harmful secrets, who may be vulnerable, and to society at large which will be threatened by secret dangers. It is often said by those who encourage intrusive regulations that we should simply not keep any secrets, because then we will have nothing to hide and should be very happy to have our private affairs exposed to public scrutiny. It is feared that permitting a zone of private space beyond the reach of government intrusion would also tend to 'undermine the authority of the state' in a time when growing numbers support authoritarian state control because it makes them feel safer.[46] What if there is a terrorist lurking behind those closed doors? It is safer if the state can see what goes on within private dwellings. Furedi also explains how the erosion of the private space has proceeded apace with the 'disillusionment with family life' as an autonomous sphere of life.[47] Keeping thoughts or lifestyles or family affairs private is increasingly regarded as pathological: 'in a world where the uninhibited display of emotion is frequently applauded by cultural influencers, privacy and intimacy are often targets of mistrust'.[48] Thus 'the view that the private sphere is an intensely dangerous place, particularly for women and children,

46 Ibid., p. 72.

47 Ibid.

48 Ibid., p. 74.

has acquired the status of an incontrovertible truth in media commentary and academic literature'.[49] The notion of the 'private' life is now all but extinct, as complaints about unlawful harassment call for judicial oversight over whom people associate with, how they order their social interactions and what they say on Twitter.

This explains the debates surrounding the contract of employment, which is regarded as a private relationship with such important public implications that it should be regulated as part of the public sphere. While there are some exceptions for very small employers (with fewer than, say, five employees) in general the equality provisions do not depend on the size of the undertaking. One could argue that the employment relationship is not experienced in private; unlike the intimate circle of family or friends, employment relationships resemble in many respects an open interaction with strangers at arms' length. But even in the context of employment and market interactions individual autonomy and personal preference in making decisions is key. For example, one employer might measure value by reference to a worker's output, while another might measure it by reference to a worker's community spirit. The choice as to which of these measures would be preferable in all circumstances ought not to be a matter for public decision-making nor need such decisions be ideologically driven. One employer might consider, for example following theories of enlightened shareholder value, that prioritising community spirit above productivity paradoxically yields higher productivity and profitability.[50] The idea is that the enlightened shareholder prefers to invest in companies that value shared community ideals, so that the pursuit of shareholder value will indirectly guide the company in the direction of community priorities such as signalling a commitment to anti-racism. How best to measure value is a matter for each employer or institution to decide, rather than for centralised regulation to dictate the measure of value that ought to apply to all. Under private decision-making anyone who wishes to favour any groups with characteristics that they regard as disadvantaged, would be entirely free to do so. Those who genuinely feel a sense of private guilt

---

[49] Ibid., p. 81.

[50] Kay, J. (2011). *Obliquity: Why Our Goals Are Best Achieved Indirectly*. Profile Books.

for the sins of their ancestors would be free to do whatever they think appropriate to expiate their guilt, to pay out all their profits in reparations for historical grievances should they wish. Moreover, it raises decision-making and governance costs when deep conflicts of interest between members make it more difficult to agree among themselves, so the cost–benefit analysis of diversity programmes would only work effectively as a voluntary decision. The point is that this would remain a matter for private decision-making, in consultation with investors where necessary, rather than falling to be decided through public rules governing all employers.

The public realm is governed by democratic rule by the majority, where it is agreed that the majority view will be reflected in governance, but it is not legitimate for the majority to impose their view on matters that ought to be privately decided. The sphere of private decision-making extends not only to questions such as whom to marry or the selection of one's holiday companions, but also to questions of individual economic liberty such as the selection of business partners or choices surrounding those with whom one wishes to enter into contracts including contracts of service. If members of a family, or a group of friends who share the same religion, band together to start a business, there is no reason why their staff should proportionately reflect all the identity groups of society as a whole, given especially that anybody is free to start their own business and hire whomever they please.

4.5 Discrimination in the Private Sphere

In the common law tradition the employment relationship is based on a contractual relationship between employer and employee, rooted in the contract at will. The law of contract falls squarely in the private realm and permits one freely to enter into any contract for good reason, bad reason or no reason at all, subject in some jurisdictions to implied duties of good faith. Equality legislation intervenes in cases where employment decisions are based on 'protected characteristics' or 'forbidden grounds'. It is no business of the ordinary law of contract should you prefer to hire someone based solely on, for example, the fact that you went to the same school, but under equality law it is unlawful to hire someone based solely on the colour of their skin. We presumably deem individual preferences based on ties of friendship to be morally acceptable, but preferences based on race to be morally wrong and socially harmful. The reasons lie partly in historical suffering and partly in the immutability of race—we can choose (to a degree) which school to attend but we do not generally choose our race. For many people racial identity lies at the core of their personal identity; presumably nobody identifies as closely with their school in quite the same way as they identify with their race and thus would not suffer psychic harm if they were denigrated for their school as they might if they were denigrated for their race.

But this is a rather simplistic way of understanding the regulatory issue for two key reasons. First, defining legal rights by reference to personal characteristics such as race or sex seeks to protect minority groups by imposing costs on others; exercising this type of control over individual preferences in private decision-making is not costless. Further, by violating the principle of equality before the law in order to confer special protection on certain groups equality schemes incite inter-group resentment and hostility. Everybody who is not protected wants to know why they were left out. This is neither an effective nor a sustainable way to govern private interactions. In seeking to uphold one moral tenet, namely the duty not to cause harm, it violates another moral tenet that no one should seek to advance their own position by imposing costs on others without their consent and without offering any benefit in return. As Epstein writes, this regulatory strategy involves a 'mental conjuring trick' of creating new 'rights' and imagining that some abstract entity will bear the correlative duty, thus absolving us of the obligation to count the cost to liberty of such rights:

> If we do not recognise—explicitly and publicly—the duties associated with rights, there will be an inherent tendency to ignore the associated costs. We will have the happy illusion that the constraints of scarcity do not really matter—that we will be able to magnify those rights without

limitation while nobody need pay the cost either directly or indirectly. That is, of course, a fantasy.[51]

Second, the expectation that the membership of private associations should reflect the same proportion of race or sex as the wider population is questionable. Common sense dictates that statistical disparities between races are not problematic, in themselves. As Walter Williams points out, nobody seems unduly concerned about the underrepresentation of black people at ice hockey games, dressage events or wine tastings, nor are there campaigns for the government to 'do something' or to pass new guidelines to engineer a 'pleasing racial mix' in all these activities ensuring that the number of black participants reflects the proportion of black people in society generally.[52] Further, as Williams notes, no account is taken of the diversity of racial demographics from one location to the next. He gives the example of states in the United States where the total black population might be less than 1%, while being over 50% in another state. Similarly in the UK, where London for example is over 40% ethnic minority. Would 'underrepresentation' rules vary from one location to the next? Would ethnic minorities be bussed around from one district to the next to ensure a 'pleasing racial mix' in all locations?

Williams's argument is that the test should be whether black people, indeed all people, are free to participate in any activity they wish because they are not excluded by any law from doing so, not whether the actual participants in that activity reflect the proportion of different races in society. Applying statistical analysis to the characteristics of members of a private group and requiring that the numbers be engineered to reflect the demographics is thus an unjustified encroachment on freedom of association. Williams further highlights a more pressing issue concerning the underlying redistributive goals of the antidiscrimination discourse. His point may be illustrated by reference to the example of corporate governance. Clearly, it makes no more sense to expect all corporate boards of directors to reflect specified racial demographics than it would to expect the same demographics at the opera house. Tellingly, therefore, the

[51] Epstein, R. A. (2002). *Equal Opportunity or More Opportunity: The Good Thing About Discrimination* (p. 3). Civitas. Retrieved from http://www.civitas.org.uk/pdf/cs18.pdf.

[52] *Race and Economics*, pp. 111–113.

reason for focusing on certain events (corporate boards of directors) while remaining unconcerned about others (the opera) seems to arise from the potential for wealth redistribution between groups. Egalitarians are wholly unconcerned about racial demographics unless they suspect that there may be potential for wealth and income redistributions. Thus they set their sights on corporate governance while ignoring the opera house: the opera house has no redistributable financial reserves. One might have thought Williams's examples of sporting and classical musical events to be much more obviously public spaces than the corporate boardroom, but these particular public spaces escape the attention of the egalitarians as they are unlikely prospects for wealth transfers. Public spaces which operate on a shoestring budget propped up by charitable contributions are of no interest to 'equality' artists; of much more interest is the corporate boardroom because that is where decisions on executive pay are made. This lack of principle behind the statistical disparities commonly highlighted in the equality discourse explains the importance of questioning the ethical and moral basis of extending equality principles and redistributive schemes to the private sphere.

Discrimination in the private sphere, regardless of whether it is unlawful, is regarded by most reasonable people as morally abhorrent. Racists are ostracised and shunned. But the issue here is not whether their conduct is admirable, but whether it should be unlawful. Legal obligations are not synonymous or coterminous with civilised behaviour or polite social norms, in the sense that breach of social obligations ought not to incur legal liability. Classical liberalism prioritises voluntary association and deems legal coercion to be appropriate only in clearly defined and limited circumstances. Thus a goal may be worthy, and indeed emblematic of the ideal society, without it following that legal mandates are required to give it effect. Difficult questions arise concerning the role of legislation in signalling aspirational standards and nudging behaviour that promotes society's moral values. The prospect of forging a better and fairer society through legislative engineering is attractive. But because legislation is backed by the force of the state the issue here is not simply whether a stated social or moral ideal is worth pursuing, but whether it is appropriate to mandate its observance through legal sanctions. Ideal behaviour that everyone should exhibit in a fair and just society, including decisions that we imagine everyone would freely take if they gave careful thought to the matter, do not necessarily justify resorting to force to bring them into effect. Persuasion, rather than coercion, is preferable. Thus we tolerate views we may privately consider to be abhorrent, because we do not suppose that our moral values give us license to impose our superior preferences on others and invoke state sanctions to that effect. This means that within the private realm preferring to deal with one person rather than another based on their race or culture may be socially unacceptable but it does not automatically follow that it should give rise to legal liability. As a general principle legal liability attaches to causing physical or economic harm to another person or, in cases where there is a duty of care, causing psychological harm to someone to whom a duty of care is owed. But there is no legal duty to be polite to other people or to choose to treat them 'equally' in private transactions based on close interpersonal ties.

Discrimination in public life which results in depriving people of access to public space or public services based only on their personal characteristics is squarely within the realm of public policy. We would not expect a public park to put up 'Whites Only' signs as was typical of the apartheid regimes. The public shares equally the duty to fund public services through taxes, and is therefore equally entitled to have access to public resources. Regulating race discrimination may have an important role to play in this context, including pursuing priorities identified through democratic processes. But the choice of when to be other-regarding and when to prioritise private interests should usually, and as often as possible, be an individual matter rather than decided collectively through the democratic process. It is not controversial to argue that public decisions about, say, the upkeep of roads and bridges should be determined through collective decision-making processes and funded by taxes. The difficult issue is where the boundary lies between private decision-making and matters which are best centrally determined and backed by law. Moreover, as Epstein cautions, even in the regulation of public life, caution is required to ascertain the demands of equal treatment and prevent the moral ideal of equality being used as cover to promote partisan ideologies.[53] There is more to be considered in addition to the question of public morals—the ethical foundations of the interventions must be considered, as well as the implications for individual liberty.

4.6 Fairness in Employment

Many people support equality measures in employment out of a concern for fairness. This part of the discussion identifies the core elements of an alternative approach to fairness in employment, constructed around classical ideals of equality and justice and grounded in principles of procedural fairness. Employment relations in market societies are governed primarily by the principles of contractual freedom and freedom of association, underpinned by property rights and private ownership of the means of production. State intervention in the employment relationship creates a framework of statutory rights designed to protect the importance of employment as a source of income for the majority of workers. Legislation provides for employers' decisions to be scrutinised to ensure that they do not treat workers unfairly. The substantive equality provisions are part of a broader protective framework within which legislative rules and regulations play a significant role in supplying the content of employment agreements and ascertaining the parties' rights and obligations. The rationale underlying the statutory framework is the need to redress the unequal bargaining power between employer and employee, for example by guaranteeing for workers greater control over the performance of work and safeguarding their expectations of income security. Yet that rationale captures only one aspect of the reality of employment. Workers are not invariably in a weaker bargaining position than their employer, nor do they look to employment only for financial security and 'the job'. Against income and job security they balance their desire

[53] It is important therefore 'to distinguish between those cases in which explicit racial or sexual preferences represent a policy for the public good and not the outgrowth of private factional pressures' Epstein, *Forbidden Grounds*, p. 413.

for meaningful work, flexibility surrounding family and other life interests that make demands on their time, social interaction with colleagues and collaborators, amenable working conditions, and a whole host of other values that lie beyond the ability of a regulator to prescribe on a one size fits all basis. Individual preferences vary widely, and one person's idea of intolerable working conditions may be another person's idea of a lucky career break. Freedom of choice, and freedom to strike a bargain with those for whom the exchange has value, provide the best means of recognising this diversity. The example of employment suggests that the ideals of freedom must override the narratives of market exploitation which are relied on to justify legal regulation of employment. The fear driving the regulations is that without legislative protections offering basic guarantees of income and work, workers will be left at the mercy of changing market conditions which might destroy them. But no prosperous society was ever founded on fear, and in a vibrant economy when some types of jobs are destroyed new types of jobs are created.

This is where procedural fairness plays a role in defending contractual rights and expectations while permitting flexibility required by both parties to the employment exchange. The principle of fairness depends on due process. The common law of contract has developed to recognise implied terms of fair treatment which provide an important procedural protection for both sides of the employment relationship. The employee has an implied duty of loyalty to the employer and the employer has an implied duty to treat the employee fairly; hence the principle is defined in English law as a duty of mutual trust and confidence. Principles of fair treatment accord with the classical ideals of equality and justice, as they require law to be based on general rules of fair process rather than aim to engineer equal results.[54] Procedural fairness runs as a golden thread throughout the law. The presumption of innocence, and the maxim that he who asserts must prove, are key tenets of procedural fairness.[55]

[54] 'Equal treatment...has nothing to do with the question of whether the application of such general rules in a particular situation may lead to results which are more favourable to some groups than to others: justice is not concerned with the results of the various transactions but only with whether the transactions themselves are fair.' Hayek, *Law Legislation and Liberty*, p. 141.

[55] 'Ei incumbit probatio qui dicit, non qui negat'—the burden of proof lies on he who asserts, not he who denies. The presumption of innocence has been described as the 'golden thread'

Outside the implied term of mutual trust and confidence, procedural fairness at common law does not however encompass a duty for an employer to justify his policies or decisions, nor a general duty to give reasons. Such a duty may of course be observed as a principle of good industrial relations and basic common courtesy, but without the threat of legal liability for breach. A duty to give reasons is well founded in the public realm where the circumstances merit, but is usually regarded as an exception to the general common law position. The tradition of the common law has instead been to defend the freedom of contract and freedom of conscience. Thus the common law does not generally impose on private decision-makers a duty to give reasons for their decisions. In the employment context, at common law the employer may hire or fire without giving reasons, and may do so 'for good reason, bad reason or no reason at all' subject (in some jurisdictions) to giving reasonable notice of dismissal. In public law, where there is a duty of accountability to the public, in many circumstances it may be unreasonable or irrational for a decision-maker not to give reasons for a decision affecting the life and livelihoods of members of the public and in this context the common law often, justifiably, imposes a duty to give reasons. The police, for example, are often charged with a duty to offer an explanation for exercising discretionary stop and search powers and under public pressure not to stop a suspect without justifiable cause (not merely because 'something didn't look right'). Nevertheless the rationale for not generally requiring reasons in private decision-making is clear: a legal duty to give reasons is incompatible with individual autonomy, freedom of choice and the prerogatives of ownership.

A social duty may well arise in sheer courtesy, as may a moral duty in the context of certain relationships, to give reasons for decisions. Most people would give reasons for turning down an invitation, for example, rather than simply announce their non-acceptance. Convention requires that it should be a plausibly good reason, unlike Academy Award winner Anthony Hopkins who failed to show up to receive his awards as he

of the English common law to be upheld in all cases 'no matter what the charge or where the trial': *Woolmington v DPP* [1935] UKHL 1 (23 May 1935).

was elsewhere engaged.[56] Whether the duty to give reasons should be enforceable in law, and subjected to judicial scrutiny as to the cogency of the reasons offered, is a different matter. Legislation may, and frequently does, introduce a duty to give reasons where it is deemed socially or economically expedient. For example in the UK the Employment Rights Act 1996 requires an employer to give a 'substantial' reason for dismissal to allow a tribunal to evaluate whether the reason for dismissal was justified or fair. Under the Equality Act 2010 a justification is required for every act or omission that, although in itself non-discriminatory, puts people with protected characteristics at a disadvantage compared to others: the presumption is that observers have a legitimate interest in evaluating the moral conduct of their fellow citizens, and for this purpose the reason or explanation for the conduct must be offered.

The duty to explain one's decisions or conduct extends to an increasingly intrusive set of questions. Why did you not look your colleague in the eye? Why did you not smile? If you smiled, was your smile genuine or was it an in-between smile? Giving reasons or explanations can be intrusive, complex, costly and time-consuming. The desire to avoid having to give reasons is itself a key driver of the pressure to avoid statistical disparities that might call for an explanation. For example it is simply easier to pay men and women the same wage than to try and explain the differences in the value they offer to the employer. Thus the duty to explain statistical disparities directly gives rise, in practice, to a duty to promote equal outcomes because that is simpler than attempting to offer reasons for any discrepancy. Examples of this can be seen in the BBC's equal pay litigation where they attempted, unsuccessfully, to explain why a more popular male presenter was paid more than his less popular female colleague. There was no ready answer to the question why they were not paid the same wage for doing the same job. Thus the legislative

56 'It takes the shine off things when you sense they weren't interested or somehow had better things to be doing. In Hopkins's case, at least according to his Twitter feed, this appeared to be going on a ramble in the Welsh countryside.' Robey, T. (2021, April 11). Anthony Hopkins and Frances McDormand's Bafta No-Shows Ended the Night on a Sour Note. *The Telegraph*. https://www.telegraph.co.uk/films/0/anthony-hopkins-frances-mcdormands-bafta-no-shows-ended-night/.

protections which superimpose an additional layer of rights onto the employment contract all drive towards the same egalitarian goals.

The advantage of fair process over moral edicts is that procedural rights permit greater scope for individual decision-making, which in turn creates greater scope for individual liberty. Fair process is rooted in principles of normative proceduralism which hold that 'there is no external criterion for what constitutes a just outcome, other than conformity with the procedure itself'.[57] Fairness is in turn reflected in objective standards of reasonableness, and a decision which takes irrelevant factors such as race into account is likely also to be unreasonable. A test of reasonableness is inherently context-specific which makes the legal protection offered by a reasonableness test sufficiently robust and in some cases even stronger protection than that offered by the legislative framework.[58] Procedural fairness therefore offers a standard that evolves to suit changing times and contexts. Procedural fairness does not by itself produce equal outcomes, nor would we expect it to do so where merit or effort are unequal.[59] Longer-term sustainable progress based on principles of procedural fairness would be preferable to the immediate and short-term appearance of superficial equality produced by equality mandates. Securing support for procedural standards is therefore a considerable political challenge—long-term effects do not generally commend themselves to a political environment that favours quick results.[60] Procedural fairness is regarded by egalitarians as insufficient, as they consider unequal outcomes to be viscerally aggravating. The slogans to which fair process give rise, such as 'harsh but fair' or 'lawful but

[57] Tebble, *Epistemic Liberalism*, p. 36.

[58] Conduct may be unreasonable without being discriminatory: 'In addition, the tribunal has made findings of discrimination where no proper evidential basis for it exists; and it has inferred in some cases that unfair and unreasonable treatment alone is evidence of discrimination.' Rozenberg, J. (2003, August 1). Law Society Chiefs Are Cleared of 'Ludicrous' Sex and Race Bias Claim. *The Telegraph*. https://www.telegraph.co.uk/news/uknews/1437697/Law-Society-chiefs-are-cleared-of-ludicrous-sex-and-race-bias-claim.html.

[59] 'We must face the fact that the preservation of individual freedom is incompatible with a full satisfaction of our views of distributive justice': Hayek, F. A. (1958). Individualism: True and False. In *Individualism and Economic Order* (p. 22).

[60] 'By calling for the renunciation of the pursuit of special interests, it even demands sacrifices, though, of course, only provisional ones, involving the giving up of a relatively small advantage in order to attain a greater one.' Mises, *Liberalism*, p. 123.

awful', do not tend to animate demonstrations and social movements. Placards demanding that 'Rhodes must go' invite more widespread attention in the public arena than the Oxford Chancellor's calls for a 'sensible discussion' on 'fundamental issues which touch on Black Lives Matter, like education, like public housing, like public health'.[61] It is surely more exciting to watch activists topple a statue and cast it into the harbour than to debate the finer points of early years education. Moral arguments are more accessible, and have a more immediate appeal, than intricate questions of fair process. Social justice activism is driven by a desire for immediate or speedy equalisation of outcomes without regard to authenticity and sustainability. Hence those seeking advantages for their own racial group at the expense of others are often heard to say that they have run out of patience.

Yet in the longer term focusing on enhancing capabilities in a context that is fair to all without special preferences for some yields deeper and more lasting progress through peaceful cooperation. This is why upholding the principles of formal equality before the law is central to liberty and classical liberal theories of justice. Fairness rooted in principles of normative proceduralism upholds justice by guaranteeing a right to fair process where outcomes are evaluated by reference to a standard of reasonableness that applies equally to all. Fair process has stood the test of time as a core component of justice. Fair process demands that we abandon the racialisation of society. No race has a greater claim to reasonable or fair treatment than any other, and comparisons between races are meaningless as a way of determining whether decisions are reasonable or unreasonable. Fairness in that context expands the scope of individual freedom and each person's capacity and potential to make something of his life. It may be feared that general standards of reasonableness and fairness would not be sufficient to meet the demands of justice for racial minorities. Two responses may be offered. First, such fears may have been valid when the first race legislation was introduced, but public opinion surrounding standards of reasonableness has evolved since then. Most people now regard racist behaviour as morally and socially unacceptable.

[61] Way, F. (2020, June 10). Oxford University Chancellor Comments on Cecil Rhodes Statue. *Oxford Mail*. https://www.oxfordmail.co.uk/news/18508464.oxford-university-chancellor-comments-cecil-rhodes-statue/.

It is time to move on. It is mistaken to defend equality legislation by reference to how people behaved in the distant past. Law must keep up with changes in society. It is also feared that extra protection is necessary to forestall reversion to segregation, forgetting that the key driver of segregation in the American South or apartheid South Africa was the racialised legislation itself, which implemented mandatory segregation backed by the force of the state.[62] Paradoxically, then, it is the presence of coercive legislation that continues to racialise public discourse when most people have long ago moved beyond that if indeed ever they paid it any attention. For example the law now requires public bodies to classify and track racial outcomes, which only serves to highlight race as a divisive attribute.

Second, it is realistic in concluding a study of racial diversity to acknowledge that racists will always walk among us. This is no reason to subject everyone to race-relations regulation for their own protection. There will always be some people who behave irrationally, defeating their own best interests for example by choosing not to hire a qualified person simply due to their race, or by only befriending those of their own race, or in extreme cases by bearing ill will towards those who are different from them. But purging society of every last racist has countervailing implications for liberty and social cohesion. Regarding the fact that many people look to legislation to keep them safe from being discriminated against and may feel afraid that without such legislation intolerable racial hatred is likely to be unleashed upon them, it must be considered that the narrative of fear is endemic in modern society and it does not serve us well to fuel it further. Fear of racism is undoubtedly part of that. Yet paradoxically the more legislation we introduce to make people feel safe from ill-treatment, the more fearful they become. Recent events attest to that, where social justice activists who demand 'safe spaces' now claim that racist thoughts and words should be criminalised even in people's homes to make everyone safer.[63] As Furedi argues, 'fear itself has become politicized to a point where debate is rarely about whether or not we

---

[62] Epstein, *Forbidden Grounds*.

[63] On the extension of hate crime laws see the Law Commissions proposals published at https://www.lawcom.gov.uk/project/hate-crime/.

should be fearful, but about who or what we should fear'.[64] The message that society is 'institutionally racist' teaches us to fear that those who are different from us are a threat, and emphasises that restrictive legislation is needed to safeguard ethnic minorities from being harmed by their fellow citizens. There is an alternative to this hopeless and destructive narrative of fear, and that is to highlight the freedom and opportunity that abounds.[65]

[64] Furedi, *How Fear Works*.

[65] Ridley, M. (2011). *The Rational Optimist: How Prosperity Evolves*. Fourth Estate.

5

Free Markets and Economic Progress

This book has so far argued against the notion that past unfairness towards marginalised races is best corrected by institutionalising preferential treatment for marginalised groups, thereby creating new forms of unfairness against those unable to claim marginalised status. Instead, where market participation plays the dominant role in shaping socio-economic outcomes society as a whole benefits from encouraging cooperation through voluntary exchange. As Walter Williams argues, 'free-market resource allocation, as opposed to allocation on political grounds, is in the interests of minorities and/or less-preferred individuals'.[1] Williams shows that long-term sustainable progress for racial minorities has historically been determined by market participation and good old-fashioned hard slog, not through lobbying for political power, favours and special welfare programmes. Open markets predicated upon economic freedom are based on objective determinants such as price,

[1] Williams, W. E. (2011). *Race and Economics: How Much Can Be Blamed on Discrimination?* (p. 1). Hoover Institution Press.

W. Njoya, *Economic Freedom and Social Justice*, Palgrave Studies in Classical Liberalism,
https://doi.org/10.1007/978-3-030-84852-1_5

supply and demand, rather than being dished out by political wheeler-dealers to their favoured groups. The wheel of political fortune rises and falls, and its gains can never be more than fleeting. Previous chapters have observed that the quest to safeguard equality through mandatory legislation is rooted in fears that unregulated markets would only be hostile and exploitative towards vulnerable groups. It is often supposed by Rawlsian liberals that the economic gains made by racial minorities are attributable not to free markets or to their own efforts but to the various legal protections conjured by egalitarian dreams. The claim is that none of the social and economic gains of ethnic minorities would have occurred without equality legislation, from which it would follow that if the legal framework is continually strengthened and expanded we would expect to see less racism, more economic opportunities and greater prosperity with equally distributed wealth. The chapter shows that these left-liberal interpretations are unsupported by the facts. On the contrary, economic progress for racial minorities emerges in contexts where law permits the broadest possible scope for individual liberty.

The previous chapter has shown some of the ways in which special legislative protections against market competition, such as equality, wage and employment protections, impede the scope of contractual freedom thereby restricting individual liberty. Paradoxically, jurisdictions in which the law upholds individual liberty come closer to facilitating the creation of more equal outcomes than those which purport to engineer equal outcomes through wealth redistribution or by policing what people say and with whom they associate. The classical liberal approach upholds individual liberty, and therefore holds economic liberty key to delineating the boundaries of law and regulation. Economic freedom does not entail, as often supposed in public discourse, a simplistic 'money versus equality' trade-off. It requires an investigation of the freedoms that go towards making life meaningful and fulfilling and ensuring that these are not undermined by legislative interventions.

On that premise the critical question to be considered by this chapter is whether the non-discrimination principle appropriately falls within the scope of regulation in situations where it encroaches upon economic freedom. This is not to suggest that the problem merely concerns regulatory failures or misguided regulation. It has been argued so far that the problem consists in the ethical unworthiness of the goal itself. Substantive equality is conceptualised in a manner that undermines the classical ideal of justice based on formal equality before the law. In this discussion the aim in discussing the regulatory encroachment on economic freedom is not to evaluate the various methods of free market regulation nor to engage in the usual regulation versus deregulation debates—the intricacies of regulatory methods are scarcely worth our concern if the goals are fundamentally unjust. Instead the aim is to defend economic freedom against claims that regulation is needed to protect the interests of ethnic minorities. The central argument is that the interests of ethnic minorities are advanced through expanding economic freedom, not by restricting such freedom.

5.1 Relative Inequality and Rising Prosperity

One of the key contestations in the literature on economic inequality is whether to focus on levels of prosperity or whether instead to 'mind the gap' between the wealth outcomes of different races. Does it matter whether black people today are exponentially better off than they were in the past, if it turns out that white people are better off too and thus there is still a gap between racial outcomes? Free market societies tend over time to exhibit a rise in *absolute* levels of prosperity, including better outcomes for the poorest, but the *gap* between rich and poor rises and falls at different times depending on many exogenous factors that bear no connection with discrimination. Although the gap between the richest and poorest has risen in many contexts, in absolute terms more people are better off today than at any previous time in history. Following the industrial revolution absolute levels of wealth have risen for all classes of society, regardless of fluctuations in the wealth gap between poorest and richest. Thus social and economic progress has been achieved by many communities whose outcomes, while exponentially better than where they began, are not equal to others. The wealth gap is troubling to many, who monitor the gap closely by fixing their sights on comparisons. In doing so, they take their eye off progress and instead worry about disparities. They hunt relentlessly for disparities, scouring the tax havens for signs that wealth is not equally distributed. They suppose that rising prosperity is caused by legislation, thus more legislation is required to close the wealth gap.

The unprecedented scope of prosperity and opportunities for advancement in liberal market economies are, to an important extent, an outcome of social and economic evolution rooted in classical liberal principles. They are not the result of government legislative interventions as is often supposed.[2] For example Higgs's study of 'economic competition' as a key determinant of progress for black Americans in the immediate post-emancipation era casts doubt on the influence of oppression and discrimination as a historical determinant of life outcomes, with evidence of *higher* levels of market participation and economic success among black Americans in the first fifty years after emancipation when racial segregation and exploitation were undoubtedly rampant, than today when racism is widely regarded as morally reprehensible.[3] More recently, Williams measured the success of black Americans by reference to earnings, finding that 'compared with any other racial group [they] have come the greatest distance, over some of the highest hurdles, in a shorter period of time', an achievement which Williams shows through comparative data analysis to be largely attributable to living in a market economy. This has enabled the improvement of black American material conditions to exceed that of many nation states.[4] Williams shows that the same trends apply to many other countries around the world.

The egalitarian perspectives on relative inequality and prosperity are influenced by their moral precepts, which hold economic value to lack the priority of equality. They depict life as a trade-off between wealth and moral virtue, and therefore prioritise equality even if equalisation risks destroying economic value. Anthony Atkinson, for example, is so

---

[2] The defence of individualism 'rests largely on the contention that much for which the coercive action of the state is usually invoked can be done better by voluntary collaboration': Hayek, F. A. (1958). Individualism: True and False. In *Individualism and Economic Order*, p. 23.

[3] Higgs, *Coercion and Competition*.

[4] 'If one were to total black earnings and consider black Americans a separate nation, he would find that, in 2008, they earned $726 billion. That would make them the world's sixteenth-richest nation, just behind Turkey but ahead of Poland, Belgium, and Switzerland [table included, data sources worldbank.org and census.gov]' Williams, *Race & Economics*, pp. 5, 6.

concerned by inequality that he considers it better to have a smaller economic 'cake' more equally distributed than a larger cake with more unequal distribution.[5] According to that perspective people may have less money, but they will be 'better' people in a moral sense and thus happier, relatively untroubled by being somewhat poorer. In this 'the economy is like a giant cake' worldview, wealth distribution bears much greater moral significance than wealth production, the argument being that it is ultimately better to risk having no wealth than to have wealth which is unequally distributed. Nobody wants to be Mr. Scrooge, wealthy but morally vacant, and in the quest for moral redemption through egalitarianism the loss of wealth is deemed to be a price worth paying. As Gordon writes:

> A state of affairs in which everyone lives in poverty ranks morally superior to one in which a group of people in the society have risen to wealth. In the latter situation, the remainder of society stays poor and inequality has thus increased. Even though none is worse off in the changed circumstances and some have gained, our egalitarian dogma requires us to remain content with universal poverty. The benefits of the altered situation are bought at too high a price.[6]

Debates about redistribution thus proceed with no regard to the implications for wealth creation because the moral importance of egalitarian redistribution (making sure that everyone has the same access to resources) simply overrides the importance of productivity. The wealth gap is deemed to be intolerable because it is presumed to reflect an underlying unfairness, so that even though we may disagree on what exactly needs to be equalised we should aim at that form of equalisation that would yield more fair outcomes, with everyone having their 'fair share of social resources'.[7] The idea is that in the absence of unfairness, wealth would be more equally distributed.

---

[5] Atkinson, A.B. (2015). *Inequality: What Can Be Done?* Harvard University Press.

[6] Gordon, D. (2017). Don't Dream the Impossible. In *An Austro-Libertarian View vol II*, p. 147.

[7] See for example Dworkin, R. (1981). What Is Equality? *Philosophy & Public Affairs*, *10*(3) (Summer), 185.

A number of interrelated problems with that view may be highlighted. The first has been adverted to already, concerning the ethical basis of equality expectations. The second is the fact that the pursuit of more equality never reaches its goal, and never quite specifies how much equality, short of total equality, it intends to achieve. Third, the reality of human progress is that there will always be a gap between people whose activities yield different outcomes. To the extent that progress is inherent in human aspirations, there will always be some ahead of others. No progress is ever achieved everywhere all at once, and there will always be a gap or a time lag following every discovery with advancement at different rates in different places. Free markets facilitate progress for all without dictating that each individual must enjoy the benefits of progress at the same rate as others. Nor is wealth inequality a market failure, as free markets are not designed so as to ensure that all participants achieve the same results or enjoy the same level of success. As Tomasi explains, '[Adam] Smith did not imagine that this liberal program would solve all of humanity's problems, or that it would result in a social order with even rough equality of possession'.[8]

Many guilt-ridden and disillusioned liberals are troubled by this reality; they feel that economic freedom sticks in the craw when we live surrounded by 'the great left behind'.[9] They would argue that racial inequality is so morally problematic that economic progress is only worthwhile if we bring everyone along equally at the same rate and in the same time. But, as Angus Deaton argues, some degree of inequality of economic outcomes is inherent in the pursuit of human progress. We must take the long view towards sustainable progress. A robust defence of individual liberty seeks meaning and value in the ideals of liberty even in cases where wealth and power are unequal. Freedom has its value not simply in what one is presently able to achieve, but in the potential that one may achieve over a lifetime, or that groups may achieve from one generation to the next. In creating an environment

[8] *Free Market Fairness*, p. 9.

[9] Deaton, A. (2013). *The Great Escape: Health, Wealth, and the Origins of Inequality*. Princeton University Press.

conducive to individual liberties, societies that exhibit inequalities therefore tend over time paradoxically to come closer to the evolution of more equal outcomes than societies which choose to engineer equality through legislative mandates. A focus on relative inequality inevitably chases a moving target, where goals for group advancement are pegged on what other groups are achieving.[10] Thus the demands for increasing favours and privileges designed to close attainment gaps know no limits or bounds. Each group will always be jostling for what the next group has achieved and repositioning itself to protect its own gains against encroachment by other groups. As Mises observes, when political claims are based on special group advantage 'The demands they raise for each particular group are limitless. There is, in their eyes, only one limit to the quantity to be demanded: the resistance put up by the other side'.[11] This is a blueprint for divisive disputes, not social cohesion. As Mises cautions:

> Society cannot, in the long run, exist if it is divided into sharply defined groups, each intent on wresting special privileges for its own members, continually on the alert to see that it does not suffer any setback, and prepared, at any moment, to sacrifice the most important political institutions for the sake of winning some petty advantage.[12]

5.2 A Defence of Economic Freedom

Much has been said about economic freedom in constructing the argument so far, and this section examines in more detail the claims advanced by the ideal of economic freedom. The aim is to clarify a few misunderstandings about the nature of economic freedom which are frequently encountered in the social justice debates. In principle egalitarians may

---

[10] 'Envy is promoted against those collective names, not because of what they are, but because of the adjectives imparted on them by the resentment of ideologues: enterprising people are called "exploiters"; the best are called "privileged"; the bosses are called "authoritarian"; the happy ones are called "selfish"; and so on': De la Mora, *Egalitarian Envy*, p. 80.

[11] Mises, *Liberalism*, p. 131.

[12] Ibid., p. 136.

pay lip service to economic freedom but consider it irrelevant to, or would postpone its priority to, the pursuit of social justice. This leads social justice to be prioritised almost above all else as a foundation for the legal framework. Thus the defence of economic freedom offered in this book is not necessarily controversial as a general principle. The controversial issue to be addressed concerns a narrower set of questions arising from the interplay of economic freedom with social justice in contexts of racial diversity. This requires a closer inquiry into three distinct but interrelated issues: the degree of importance we should attach to economic freedom, whether we should sacrifice economic freedom in pursuit of other social goals such as equality, and whether economic freedom is only worth defending in situations where it also promotes equality.

It has been noted in the foregoing discussion that economic freedom is expressed in contractual freedom and freedom of association; the freedom to decide with whom to enter into contracts and how to organise productive activities.[13] These freedoms are supported by the private law of obligations, through the law of contract, property and tort (civil wrongs), which constitute the foundational legal principles governing private interactions. These freedoms are not treated within the law as absolute, nor does the ideal of individual liberty provide a complete justification for personal choice in all situations. On the contrary, justified abrogation from individual liberty is conceivable in specified situations where other rights supervene. Tensions may also arise between different freedoms, requiring the prioritisation of one over the other. An example may be seen in cases where religious freedom conflicts with the freedom to express one's sexuality.[14] Another example is the curtailment of freedom of conscience in the provision of public services, for example in cases involving medical or judicial personnel

[13] 'Freedom is not only an economic or a political concept, but also, and probably above all, a legal concept, as it necessarily involves a whole complex of legal consequences.' Leoni, B. (1961). *Freedom and the Law*. D. Van Nostrand Company.

[14] Corey argues in favour of a shift away from 'the politics of warring freedoms' towards 'the politics of liberal truce': Corey, D. D. (2020). Liberalism and the modern quest for freedom. In D. F. Hardwick & L. Marsh (Eds.), *Reclaiming Liberalism* (pp. 125–162). Palgrave Macmillan Studies in Classical Liberalism p. 126.

whose personal convictions conflict with offering professional services.[15] Thus classical liberalism in context of the legal framework does not uphold an absolute concept of individual liberty but recognises that the boundary between one person's freedom and the freedom of others may in some cases be difficult to delineate.

The scope of things people should be free to do in exercise of individual liberty has always been the subject of heated debate.[16] Each individual's ability to make his own choices about how to pursue his economic ends has raised some of the most controversial issues. As discussed in Chapter 2, Rawlsian liberalism does not accord priority to economic freedom in theories of justice. We noted also that despite its highly controversial terrain it could be said that in a superficial sense every society values economic freedom to a greater or lesser extent. Yet the social justice debates proceed without any reference to the implications for economic freedom or, where economic freedom is adverted to, there is a tendency to depict it as a distasteful exercise in trying to assign a dollar amount to the worth of a human life when in truth life is priceless.[17] The intrinsic value of freedom is called into question in debating responses to socio-economic inequality which is often depicted, by those who regard comparison as a key measure of progress, as a global crisis whose urgency takes priority over economic freedom.

The notion that inequality of life experiences renders freedom meaningless, and that comparative group advantages are more important than individual liberty, lies behind the intuitive appeal of egalitarianism. Equality is depicted as a higher ideal, a goal more worthy than mere freedom. The cost to freedom is thus deemed to be immaterial in demands for more equality. Freedom as the absence of constraint means

[15] McCrudden, C. (2018). Marriage Registrars, Same-Sex Relationships, and Religious Discrimination in the European Court of Human Rights. In S. Mancini & M. Rosenfeld (Eds.), *The Conscience Wars: Rethinking the Balance between Religion, Identity, and Equality*. Cambridge University Press.

[16] Corey, Liberalism and the Modern Quest for Freedom.

[17] Harford, T. (2020, April 3) observes that 'We spend money to save lives all the time—By building fire stations, imposing safety regulations and subsidising medical research. There is always a point at which we decide we have spent enough. We don't like to think about that, but better to think than to act thoughtlessly.' How do we value a statistical life? *Financial Times*. https://www.ft.com/content/e00120a2-74cd-11ea-ad98-044200cb277f.

that no man can enslave another and transform him by law into a chattel. This aspect of freedom is uncontroversial. But as Bruno Leoni highlights, this is not all that is meant in the popular demands for freedom; the claim is not merely to be free from constraint, but to be granted an extra layer of 'enough economic security' to enjoy one's freedom in the same way as others.[18] As Leoni explains:

> People often mean by 'freedom' (or 'liberty') both the absence of constraint and something else as well – for instance, as a distinguished American judge would have said, 'enough economic security to allow its possessor the enjoyment of a satisfactory life.'[19]

In many cases 'enough' is understood in a relative sense by comparison with what others enjoy—I will have enough to enjoy a satisfactory life when I have the same amount as everyone else. This means that the double-layered goal of freedom will not be achieved until everyone achieves equality, enjoying the same privileges and achieving the same life outcomes. The popular appeal of the quest for 'enough' is easy to understand. Equality of life circumstances seems at first glance to offer a compelling vision, which explains why socialism remains an attractive political ideology despite its historical failures. The promise that socialist dreams can be attained through legislation seems simple, straightforward and utterly beguiling. It promises to yield much faster gains for historically oppressed groups than can be achieved by relying on the slow unfolding of organic progress through market participation and the sweat of one's own brow. When economic inequalities correlate with race and ethnicity the case for legislation equalising the enjoyment of everyone's lifestyles seems doubly compelling.

---

[18] Leoni, *Freedom and the Law*, p. 6.

[19] Ibid., adding that 'The same people very often fail to realize the possible contradictions between these two different meanings of freedom and the unpleasant fact that you cannot adopt the latter without sacrificing to a certain extent the former, and vice versa.'

The language of freedom is accordingly turned towards promoting equality, as illustrated by demands for 'freedom from economic exploitation'[20] in order 'to free the economically disadvantaged from the greed and corruption of the economically privileged classes'.[21] A striking example of the concept of freedom as a justification for restrictions on contractual freedom is seen in wage regulation. Minimum wage legislation is often justified on grounds that it is designed to liberate the low-waged from living standards harmful to their well-being by raising their economic condition.[22] Similarly job security provisions which restrict the employer's (but not employee's) power to terminate the contract of employment are regarded as a defence of the worker's freedom emanating from his 'right to work'. These amorphous conceptualisations of the aims of freedom are particularly significant in the context of equality legislation which is said to offer freedom from discrimination. The legislation itself represents a form of liberation—freedom from historical disadvantage and other forms of oppression or servitude. In that context justice, freedom and liberty are associated with social goals, detached from individual rights and harnessed to the goals of the welfare state and the social engineering role of government.

Thus the recourse to the language of freedom in the collectivist context of social justice discourse serves as a strategy that erodes individual freedom.[23] Mutually exclusive goals are advanced under the banner of 'liberty' with debate then ensuing about which liberty is more important than the other, or how to balance conflicting liberties. If freedom is not to be a meaningless abstraction, a label that may be annexed to any claim, it is crucial to ascertain what we wish to be free *from* and the price to be

[20] Corey, Liberalism and the Modern Quest for Freedom, p. 143, drawing attention to how this idea influenced the development of socialism and Marxism.

[21] Ibid., pp. 144–145.

[22] For example the aim of the US Fair Labor Standards Act of 1938 (as amended) is 'to correct and as rapidly as practicable to eliminate' unfair working conditions defined as 'labor conditions detrimental to the maintenance of the minimum standard of living necessary for health, efficiency, and general well-being of workers' 29 USC Ch. 8 §202.

[23] '"Identity politics," for instance, bears something of the character of [freedom from discrimination based on moral prejudice]. It is an attempt to eliminate cultural intolerance and inequality for myriad "intersecting" minority groups on the assumption that these groups have been and continue to be oppressed by traditional attitudes and structures': Corey, Liberalism and the Modern Quest for Freedom, pp. 146–147.

paid to retain that freedom. This is not easily done. As Corey explains, the historical evolution of freedom has not exhibited a straightforward 'linear movement' in which new freedoms build on previous freedoms so that society becomes increasingly free; instead the spread of liberty has been 'a halting one with significant reversals' with new freedoms sometimes gaining ground at the expense of previously won freedoms as social and political priorities change.[24] The boundaries between one freedom and another are in constant flux, a notable example being the interaction between religious freedom and freedom of expression. Value judgements are necessary, to decide which freedoms are worth prioritising, and in what circumstances. It is in that context that we approach the question concerning the priority to be accorded to economic freedom. In promoting equality, where should we draw the line in encroaching upon personal liberties? A defence of economic freedom requires three crucial elements: to define what is, and is not, entailed in economic freedom; second, to identify situations where freedom appears to undermine social justice and third, bearing in mind that it does not automatically follow that freedom must be curtailed to remedy socio-economic inequality, to evaluate whether deprivation of economic freedom is a price worth paying to remedy the perceived harm caused by discrimination. In a modern liberal democracy, does justice demand that economic freedom should yield to racial equality?

In the Smithian tradition economic freedom is accorded priority, but not regarded as a moral absolute. Economic freedom may therefore be robustly defended without supposing that it must be defended at all costs. Writing in defence of spontaneous order and the competitive processes of free markets, Hayek observed that there was an appropriate role for state action, including social security and other functions of the welfare state, in circumstances where the price mechanism of the market would not adequately satisfy the public good. To acknowledge that economic freedom is not absolute is a helpful and productive starting point in entering this contested ideological arena, and in this sense classical liberalism offers a 'middle of the road' defence of liberty—it acknowledges the need for specified encroachments upon liberty unlike

[24] Ibid, p. 138.

more purist libertarianism, of which Ayn Rand's work may perhaps be the best example, which would defend individual liberty in a more absolute sense. Yet as highlighted earlier in discussing the meaning of individualism, even in an absolutist sense freedom entails the prioritisation of self-interest properly understood, not short-sighted and self-defeating hedonism of the type commonly derided. In addition to clarifying the relative nature of economic freedom, it is important to address a few related misconceptions about economic freedom and to distinguish economic freedom from the caricatures with which it is sometimes associated. The case for economic freedom suffers from its conflation with privilege, exploitation and causing wanton harm to others. Economic freedom is not synonymous with decadence, licentiousness or greed, nor does it invoke such notions of egotism or 'selfishness' as would involve negligently or recklessly causing harm to others in order to maximise profit. Self-interest is crucial to rational decision-making, but self-interest is not synonymous with self-obsession or disregard for the welfare of others. In making decisions one might (and would usually) consider their own best interests while being at the same time other-regarding in their world view. There is a strong correlation between being community-oriented, for example by giving to charity, while taking into account one's own interests for example by making investments that will maximise financial returns. Virtues rooted in strength of character, frugality and hard work are central to Adam Smith's moral philosophy and nobody would suppose such virtues to be 'selfish' purely because they are correlated with success in one's endeavours.

Another misconception is that liberty in economic life is defended purely to facilitate economic growth and wealth maximisation. But economic growth and prosperity are not ends in themselves. They are the means to attain two more important ends, namely to promote the social harmony that comes from progress, and also to safeguard the individual liberty that is essential to human flourishing. Freedom enhances the meaningfulness of life in all its different manifestations—individual, political and economic. Individual liberty is therefore a key component of economic freedom. It enhances human dignity and autonomy, and incentivises wider participation for marginalised minorities in economic progress as means of enabling them to thrive and to feel responsible for successes in which they can take pride, rather than living lives at the expense of others and suffering the loss of self-esteem that comes with state-dependence. The ability to define the terms on which we live our lives is key to our overall sense of well-being.[25] Self-actualisation and productive activity in turn promote human flourishing. In that indirect way, by expanding our ability to pursue our goals, prioritising economic liberty is the appropriate means to achieve precisely the outcomes which those concerned about racism desire, namely the eradication of deprivation and poverty.

It is often supposed that the value of economic freedom lies only in wealth creation for its own sake and entrenching more privileges for the rich, but its more enduring value lies in the idea of prosperity, of addressing the problems of deprivation and poverty through enhancing material progress. As Mises writes, liberalism defends free markets as a path to freedom from want and misery:

> That there is want and misery in the world is not, as the average newspaper reader, in his dullness, is only too prone to believe, an argument against liberalism. It is precisely want and misery that liberalism seeks to abolish, and it considers the means that it proposes the only suitable ones for the achievement of this end.[26]

To ascertain whether economic freedom in reality privileges only those who already enjoy social and economic advantage at the expense of the poor and racial minorities, the question is not simply whether particular groups suffer disadvantage but whether they suffer *more* disadvantage than they would in the absence of economic freedom, or whether in truth they suffer *less* discrimination in free societies. This is, in many respects, about *causation*—whether the freedom of some has caused the deprivation of others. It was seen in Chapter 3 that there is little evidence linking discrimination with inequality and economic progress. In addition to problems of causation we may question what counts as disadvantage. One could reasonably argue that the loss of one's own

[25] Pennington, M. (2017). Robust Political Economy and the Priority of Markets. *Social Philosophy and Policy*, *34*(1), 1–24.

[26] Mises, *Liberalism*, p. xxiv.

freedom, autonomy and self-actualisation is a grave disadvantage in itself, with major implications for self-esteem and quality of life. Freedom matters, even in the absence of enough money to match the lifestyle enjoyed by others. Thus progressive proposals for disadvantaged people to be supported by the government which focus narrowly on equalising material outcomes, without considering the implications for human dignity, merely displace one type of disadvantage with even worse disadvantages. Human dignity is not just about having equal material goods, but also entails self-worth and being the author of one's own life. That egalitarian activists never worry about the self-esteem implications of encouraging ethnic minorities to demand financial gifts and handouts through legislative mandates is enough to cast serious doubt on the moral and ethical basis of their 'socialjustice' schemes. Egalitarians denounce industrious people for being 'greedy' and 'selfish' if they wish to keep what they have earned, but do not regard it as greedy or selfish constantly to demand that more unearned money should be directed towards them by the state through wealth redistribution schemes.

Egalitarians might consider that a person in conditions of socio-economic vulnerability would struggle to be a 'responsible author of their own life' and thus be unlikely to prioritise economic freedom.[27] Vulnerable people might instead prioritise securing state provision of an income, education, housing, healthcare and other aspects of social welfare, as a prerequisite to exercising free choice. It may be supposed that victims of harsh socio-economic circumstances are not able to exercise autonomy or choice, and granting them agency over their lives is tantamount to blaming them for their predicament.[28] Thus some scholars have argued that notions of free will and choice are valuable only within the privileged echelons of society where people have 'real' choices as they have numerous opportunities to select alternative viable

---

[27] See for example Fowler, T. (2015). *Markets, Choice and Agency* 21(4) *Res Publica* 347 arguing that 'market solutions generate choices which are not valuable ones for the agent to have to make'.

[28] 'framing outcomes as a product of "choice" invites a critical judgment of the chooser and assigns her, and no one else, the responsibility for the consequences' which may be unfair in situations where 'they are under significant stress and no other reasonable alternative exists': Fineman, M. A., Mattsson, T., & Andersson, U. (Eds.). (2016). *Privatization, Vulnerability, and Social Responsibility: A Comparative Perspective*, p. 71.

paths in life. The very notion of choice is said to be meaningless for the underprivileged. The presumption is that they would care nothing for self-esteem or self-worth while they are starving. Feed them first, then they can attend to their self-esteem. The theoretical framework of legal realism lends credence to this perspective, by holding that 'the background rules of property and contract that structure the distribution of wealth and bargaining power' are instrumental in explaining life choices.[29] The effects of these ideological biases are clear in the legal framework of equality. It is supposed that redistribution is justified by inequality without further inquiry. For example in the context of discrimination in employment the courts are accustomed to observing, almost in passing as if the matter is self-evident, that employees lack any choice or control over whether and for whom to work or the terms and conditions of their work. The premise underlying the reasoning in employment disputes is that socio-economic vulnerability is altogether incompatible with contractual freedom and economic liberty.

It is certainly true that most people who are poor, who lack independent sources of wealth and rely on their labour for an income are vulnerable to the whims of their employer. But so too is the employer vulnerable to the workers' whims. All market participants are vulnerable to the whims of others. The way to improve matters for all parties is not by introducing special protections for certain groups and not for others, but to allow them oversight over their own bargains and free choice as to whom they deal with. As highlighted by Tomasi, economic liberties such as 'freedom of economic contract' and the 'freedoms of working' have enduring value not only for the privileged but also for the most vulnerable workers[30]:

> Economic liberties have intrinsic value: they carve out a sphere of protection that allows people to become responsible authors of their own lives. Economic liberties are instrumentally valuable too: the protection of such liberties helps generate a social world of variety and abundance.[31]

---

[29] Bagenstos, S. R. (2019, August 2). Consent, Coercion, and Employment Law, pp. 1, 2. Retrieved from https://ssrn.com/abstract=3431330 or http://dx.doi.org/10.2139/ssrn.3431330.

[30] *Free Market Fairness*, p. 43.

[31] Ibid., p. 29.

As Pennington argues, classical liberalism does not merely represent a quest for higher earnings or wealth maximisation, but also a way to improve our sense of well-being and the quality of interaction and exchange in our human relationships.[32] Economic liberty is itself a precondition of the very productivity that sustains material welfare and the prosperity in which all wish to participate. As Mises argues, productivity and prosperity are not incidental or independent outcomes that would arise in the same way in the absence of liberal foundations, so that we can destroy them without incurring any penalty, but are rooted in the institutions to which economic liberty gives rise. The wealth and abundance that sustain the welfare state are derived from the same freedoms that yield the inequalities of market systems. Nor can those inequalities be eradicated without destroying the very foundations of free market society. Individual agency and free will support the innate ability of each individual to have *some* influence on their life circumstances and outcomes. Freedom is not rendered meaningless by the presence of material constraints. Our freedom and ability to make choices, to exercise free will, to exercise individual agency or autonomy in ordering our own lives, to experience self-realisation or self-actualisation, is inherent in everyone's humanity and a necessary component of living a meaningful life. It is wrong to suppose that ethnic minorities care nothing for living a fully human life, and wish only to demand financial retribution against others. To be the author of one's own life is not a privilege reserved only for some races, nor does it depend on how much wealth one enjoys compared to others. Individual liberty remains an important aspect of what is valuable in the human experience, what it means to be human, constraints and challenges included. To say that one lacks free will or self-responsibility, because of their race or because of racial discrimination, is to deny an important facet of their own humanity. It amounts to a defeatist approach to life.

[32] Pennington, M. (2017). *Robust Political Economy: Classical Liberalism and the Future of Public Policy*. Edward Elgar.

5.3 Opportunity Through Free Markets

A preference for market ordering is not premised on the assumption that unregulated markets would produce equal outcomes for everyone. The defence of free markets rests on the more limited claim that voluntary transactions incidentally tend to produce more equal opportunity than regulation designed to enforce equality. The defence of economic freedom is therefore qualified rather than absolute. The argument is that economic success requires underlying market conditions in which individual liberty is prioritised, and individual liberty in turn sustains more prosperous material conditions. Markets are blind to personal identity, which seems to upset some people who do not like their personal characteristics being ignored by strangers, and thus feel that the law ought to compel everyone they meet to celebrate their race, their sex or whatever other identity they have chosen to embrace. Free markets will not meet those personal needs. What free markets do offer is an opportunity for everyone to pursue a fuller and more meaningful life experience through voluntary exchange with others. Free markets may be indifferent to racial justice, but this does not mean that economic freedom is irrelevant for racial minorities. On the contrary, racial minorities have tended to thrive most in free market societies.

When the nineteenth century civil rights legislation in the United States set out to protect the economic rights of black Americans that protection included not only freedom of contract and the right to own property but 'all productive forms of human activities; the same principle that protected the ability to buy and sell wheat also protected the ability of people to marry whom they chose'.[33] Thus the concept of economic freedom is not limited to questions of material or financial advancement, but understands quality of life in a broader sense. Life in the round is more meaningful when we are involved in relationships and transactions we value, based on free trade. This applies as well to the low waged as the high earners, as trade signifies an exchange between any two parties whether it be a simple wage-work exchange or a more sophisticated corporate endeavour. Liberty ultimately enhances

[33] Epstein, *Equal Opportunity or More Opportunity*, p. 2, referring to the Civil Rights Act 1866.

our entire life experience. This remains true not only in a special set of stylized circumstances or for those with great material wealth but in all states of the real world. History shows that paradoxically, the worst effects of discrimination tend to occur where legal interventions restrict individual liberties such as freedom of conscience, freedom of association and freedom of contract. Where people are not free they dare not stand in defence of the oppressed, for fear of reprisals. Open markets predicated upon those freedoms are the great equaliser as they are based on individual action, not group identity, and as Williams points out 'one person's dollar has the same power as anyone else's'.[34] The comparative quality of life in liberal market economies in itself suggests that free markets yield more sustainably equal societies than command and control economies because wealth is more widely dispersed.[35] The more widely wealth is dispersed, the more opportunity abounds for all members of society.

As Tomasi explains, basic rights which many adherents of social justice would prioritise are guaranteed in free markets not through special-interest protections but through 'market-based forms of social construction', in particular through strategies that evolve from freedom of choice, rather than through direct redistribution of wealth by centralised decision-makers to predetermined targets. The legislative framework reflects the second-order role of markets which 'protects persons and their property against direct forms of coercion such as theft and fraud, and which secures the freedom of persons to exit arrangements they deem relatively unsatisfactory. The primary form of coordination within such an order is one of consensual exchange and freedom of contract'.[36] In

---

[34] *Race & Economics*, p. 2.

[35] In a free society 'ownership of property, though not necessarily equal, is widely dispersed between an array of individuals and voluntary associations': Pennington, *Robust Political Economy*, p. 4.

[36] Pennington, Robust Political Economy and the Priority of Markets, p. 5; 'The role of nonmarket/non-contractual institutions at the second-order level is confined to the maintenance of a constitutional structure that secures property rights and enforces contracts, to the resolution of disputes when there is doubt over ownership claims or jurisdictional authority, and to a limited number of tasks where competition may not be possible as an organizing principle': p. 6.

facilitating the functioning of markets the focus is not on how one group compares to another, but on creating conditions for everyone to thrive.[37]

Markets do not function perfectly, as we are constantly reminded by those who wish to displace markets in favour of legislative design. Markets are not perfectly competitive, and there are no pure unregulated absolutely free markets anywhere. Markets certainly do not ensure perfect equality, nor would perfect equality be a realistic or even desirable goal to pursue.[38] The 'neoliberal' perspective is said to oppose state intervention by arguing that unregulated free markets always work perfectly with no monopolies, rigidities, externalities or transaction costs. It is fashionable in academic circles to lump together all classical liberal ideas as 'neoliberalism' in that sense or, even more specifically, 'Chicago-style' neoliberalism, in order to imply a preoccupation with stylized economic abstractions and mathematical modelling, a lack of interest in or relevance to the real world social problems that concern regulators, and dependence on the choices and preferences of the perfectly rational *homo economicus*. But the classical liberal preference for market ordering over centralised command and control does not rest on a thesis of optimality or perfect rationality. It rests instead on a thesis of institutional comparison which seeks to identify the rules and principles that work best in real world conditions, not those that would work best in an ideal world.[39] The Smithian analysis of free markets does not posit ideal conditions in which markets are perfectly competitive or decisions are always rational. It also rests, essentially, on the classical ideals of justice and the rule of law without which market societies cannot function.

[37] Tomasi, *Free Market Fairness*: 'business owners have wide freedom to hire or promote workers by whatever criteria they choose - even when such decisions may reasonably be said to be based on race, gender, religious beliefs, sexual orientation, or aesthetic judgements about a person's 'looks'. As a matter of ordinary justice, though, free market fairness affirms that the legal system can neither impose legal disabilities nor confer advantages on the basis of ascriptive, status-based characteristics': p. 241.

[38] Mises argues that liberalism cannot be criticised by arguing that 'what it created was only equality before the law, and not real equality' because 'all human power would be insufficient to make men really equal. Men are and will always remain unequal.' *Liberalism*, p. 10.

[39] 'The strongest argument for "free markets" is not that prices provide surrogates for perfect information, but the modest comparative institutions claim that they communicate relatively more information than a centrally directed alternative': Pennington, Robust Political Economy and the Priority of Markets, p. 9.

Neoliberalism may indeed be an idealized theory to the extent that it 'judges institutions against the requirements for a Pareto optimal equilibrium'.[40] Thus it is important to emphasise that defending free markets does not depend on a claim that markets work perfectly in ideal conditions.[41] Nor does the argument that free markets offer the most effective path to freedom and equality rest on a claim that there is no role for state regulation. The argument is, instead, that free markets ultimately yield more benefit than a planned economy. Even in situations where markets are said to fail, centralised direction of daily conduct typically yields worse, not better, outcomes. The argument is comparative: whether markets work *better than* prescription, not whether markets are perfectly free. The claim is that free societies which uphold individual liberty work better than command and control systems.[42] Free markets do not inherently or automatically produce perfect outcomes; they have potential to encourage both ideal as well as exploitative conditions for individual market participants. The argument is, then, that markets enhance distributive justice in a more sustainable and meaningful way than prescriptive legal rules. All organisational systems have weaknesses and failures; thus the issue is not whether classical liberalism allows the construction of a world with no social problems, but whether it resolves pressing social problems more effectively than the alternatives and whether it works better than other approaches in yielding the sought-after benefits without imposing unacceptable costs in the process. Far from arguing that classical liberalism is a philosophy with no drawbacks, the argument is that even with its drawbacks it yields better outcomes in real world conditions than progressive ideologies, for reasons rooted in the importance of freedom to human flourishing. It is often said that socialist ideals would work better than free markets if only we

[40] Ibid., p. 2: 'These include perfect information; perfect competition — where there are large numbers of buyers and sellers, none of whom can exert a significant effect on prices; zero transactions costs; costless mobility of resources; and the absence of externalities'.

[41] Pennington, Robust Political Economy and the Priority of Markets, p. 1.

[42] Particularly in 'minimizing the difficulties in building a system that reconciles individual liberty with the common good – more so than any alternative that could be put into its place': Epstein, R. A. Meeting the Fundamental Objections to Classical Liberalism. In M. T. Henderson (Ed.), *The Cambridge Handbook of Classical Liberal Thought* (p. 282). Cambridge University Press.

would take the trouble to implement them. There may be some value in idealist theorising in philosophical debate, constructing a vision of the ideal society.

Similarly, a defence of egalitarianism ought not to rely on an ideal vision, highlighting its worthy intentions and presuming that government interventions will always work precisely as intended in ideal conditions with no unintended effects. Governments do not have magic-fairy properties enabling them simply to wave a legislative wand, give the magic money-tree a little shake and proclaim 'let justice be done!' for wealth immediately to be fairly distributed without any costs or unintended effects.[43] The role of legislation is to be determined not by reference to how it would operate in an ideal world in which everyone agrees with the preferred egalitarian moral code, but how it would likely operate in real world circumstances where we disagree on the ideals of justice and morality. Pennington frames this as a 'robust political economy' approach, the regulatory question being 'which levels of coercive state authority can sustain social cooperation when agents are not fully rational, where they disagree about justice, and where they may not comply with various rules'.[44]

As public debate becomes increasingly polarised each ideological perspective regards the other as divisive, declares its own side to be in favour of unity and identifies its own supporters as the good people. To unravel the debate it is crucial to distinguish the ideal society proposed by each side from the actual society that results from its proposals. Symmetry of comparison is important, to avoid the Nirvana fallacy identified by Harold Demsetz: comparing capitalist free market *ideals* with the socialist *reality* of totalitarianism and decay, or comparing socialist *ideals* of equality with capitalist *reality* of corporate corruption. As Nozick writes:

[43] 'At the heart of the egalitarian left is the pathological belief that there is no structure of reality; that all the world is a tabula rasa that can be changed at any moment in any desired direction by the mere exercise of human will—in short, that reality can be instantly transformed by the mere wish or whim of human beings.' Rothbard, *Egalitarianism as a Revolt*, p. 17.

[44] Robust Political Economy and the Priority of Markets, p. 3.

> In comparing two ideals, we have to judge the first's actual situation against the second's, and the first's 'ideal situation' against the other's. It would be unfair to judge another actuality against your ideal – that is to judge how another ideal actually works out against how your ideal ideally does...Perhaps we live at a historical time when communism's 'ideal situation' has very great appeal to many around the world, while how capitalism actually works out, flaws included, is greatly better...It is quite difficult to resist the allure of the 'ideal situation,' to avoid hoping and believing that things will manage to work out better this next time.[45]

Contemporary social justice is in its very essence a form of ideal justice, whose ideals rest on unrealistic premises. We are exhorted to treat people as equal when they are not; in fact, we are asked to treat them as equal precisely *because* they are not, on the supposition that in an ideal world they would be equal. As Sowell argues, social justice theories take an ideal position by assuming in favour of government interventions omniscient knowledge, complete understanding of the demands of justice with no information gaps and omnipotence in bringing about just results without incurring any costs or producing any injustices or unintended consequences of its own. Moreover the costs of cosmic justice are often invisible and thus play no part in public debates.[46] Unlike the classical liberal who will check his premises to ensure that the argument works, the egalitarian idealist might readily accept that the quest for cosmic justice is unworkable but might nevertheless consider that embarking on a hopeless quest is morally superior to doing nothing to address inequality; and may proceed on the premise that doing something to try and help, however futile, may potentially produce more equality and fairness than we would have if we never aspired to a better world. At the very least it would have the psychic advantage of making the social activist feel better for trying to do something to improve the world. In theory anything could happen, the thinking goes, so it may not hurt to aim for utopia. It might also be argued that pursuing the goal of equality

[45] *The Examined Life*, pp. 283, 284.

[46] A concern also raised by Epstein: 'We can have "rights" that are extraordinarily costly for other individuals, and instead of treating them as infringements of ordinary liberties we treat them as the price that must be paid to enforce some outcome which is seen as self-evidently desirable': *Equal Opportunity or More Opportunity*, pp. 4, 5.

is a worthwhile journey in itself, regardless of whether the goal is achievable. Since it appears to be in any event a step in the right direction, many people reasonably suppose this to be a valuable pursuit regardless of the outcome, often expressed as 'we have to do something', or 'at least we tried'.

An idealist might reasonably suppose that unattainable ideals are sometimes nevertheless worth striving for in a purely aspirational sense: follow your dreams, aim for the sun and you might land on the moon. As Nozick acknowledges, 'it is inspiring to have an admirable ideal, even when we are falling short of it. It can be illuminating to see the world in its light, and we might even be willing to be in a slightly worse actual situation when that situation basks in the glow of a considerably better ideal one'.[47] In that sense ideals help us to aim in the right direction. As Pennington observes, 'without the guiding star of ideal theory we cannot identify measures that might improve on an imperfect status quo' and thus an ideal theory offers a standard against which to measure our progress: 'specifying ideal criteria facilitates institutional evaluation by determining how closely different arrangements approximate the ideals in question'.[48]

Aspirations also serve a social purpose in uniting citizens around a common goal, especially when those aspirations are framed around an institutional or national sense of pride such as belonging to a society in which everyone feels welcome and included. Signalling the right intentions is particularly important when moral judgements are based on evaluation of *intentions* rather than results or impacts. Thus much effort is invested in formulating policy statements promoting ideals of equality and inclusiveness. It may well be that such expressions of good intentions go a long way to helping everybody feel valued, which is an important component of social cohesion. Signals are not always unimportant. But reference must be made also to how people adapt their behaviour in response to those signals. Nozick in his discussion of 'the ideal and the actual' observes that 'a wise ideal will take account of the way it will get followed' and be evaluated not merely by reference to the

[47] Nozick, *The Examined Life*, p. 282.

[48] Robust Political Economy and the Priority of Markets, p. 2.

ideal statement of its principles but also how it operates in practice.[49] The capitalist ideal often provides cover for protectionism, government bailouts and cronyism. The socialist ideal for its part often collapses into rank hypocrisy of the governing elite who formulate rules designed to exercise control over every aspect of citizens' lives, leading to totalitarianism and 'brutal and autocratic rule, a state that sees no part of the society as private or immune to its actions'.[50]

The worldview that promotes the pursuit of worthy intentions without regard to outcomes may be rousing, but it overlooks an important point highlighted by Sowell: policy choices 'should be based on a clear understanding of the costs and dangers of the actual alternatives, not simply the heady feeling of exaltation produced by particular words or visions'.[51] The pursuit of unworkable egalitarian aspirations extracts a heavy price in the attempt and creates harmful externalities. The quest for cosmic justice presumes that creating more equal opportunities through benign reallocation of existing opportunities in a more socially just distribution, by taking from advantaged groups to redirect to disadvantaged groups, should hopefully ensure more equal outcomes. What actually transpires when equality is measured by reference to group advantage is that the progress of each race tends to be predicated on attaining dominance over other races. Forms of prejudice and hatred that would be utterly unacceptable if directed at those who belong to historically disadvantaged groups, tend then to be politically encouraged if directed at those from groups which were historically advantaged. Fairness is then interpreted predominantly through the lens of neo-Marxist power structures, so that the powerful are said not to deserve fair treatment even while the powerless demand it. The gateway to fair treatment therefore depends on evidence of belonging to a racial group defined as powerless, which is an assault on the very notion of fairness. The quest for cosmic justice is not a costless ideal. Much of value is bound to be lost in a process which entails the destruction of liberty. Rather than leading

[49] 'if time after time an ideal gets institutionalized and operates in the world a certain way, then *that* is what it comes to in the world' in *The Examined Life*, p. 279.

[50] Nozick, *The Examined Life*, 280.

[51] *Cosmic Justice*, p. 47.

to peace, love and harmony, the emphasis on comparative racial advantage and endless narratives of historical guilt and oppression are more likely to lead, as Sowell cautions, to create 'a more unequal and more embittered society'.[52]

5.4 Market Failures

We might agree that in practice the market works better than command and control systems in the absence of arbitrary or artificial barriers to market entry, but nevertheless question whether legislation would be more effective in eradicating those barriers than self-correcting market mechanisms.[53] Where some people or groups of people find themselves disadvantaged in their life fortunes it is customary to blame market failures. The idea of market failures refers to situations where, for example, a racist employer does not suffer from reputational effects that might cause workers to shun him, due for instance to operating in a market where many workers do not care one way or the other about racism. In theory, employers who exhibit irrational preferences will only go on for so long before they inevitably incur market sanctions, but in the meantime what harm could it do to introduce a bit of legislation to speed up their just deserts? It could be argued that the urgency becomes more pressing in a tight labour market where ethnic minority workers have no suitable alternative employment opportunities and it is not practicable for them simply to shun that employer and work elsewhere. In that situation the market fails to offer an alternative, and it could be argued that legal sanctions would be needed to inhibit the employer's desire to indulge his taste for discrimination. Where markets yield sub-optimal outcomes it might be hoped that legislative correction would be a quicker and more effective path to the desired outcome. Law would keep the workers safe in their workplace, if they had no alternative work. The progressive case is that

[52] Ibid., p. 74.

[53] 'To use Knight's and Johnson's terminology, democratic collective action should have "second-order" priority, either as a device for improving the performance of markets or in choosing to replace systems based on private contracting with alternative allocation procedures': Pennington, Robust Political Economy and the Priority of Markets, p. 7.

democratic processes and legislative mandates work better in identifying social priorities and resolving social problems than market participants who may neither know nor care about problems which do not directly affect them.

Richard Epstein disagrees, arguing that resolving market failures by intervening in employment contracts is not the appropriate function of legislation: 'the chief job of the state is to ensure that all persons enjoy the civil capacity to own property, to contract, to sue and be sued, and to give evidence'.[54] Beyond protecting the basic civil rights that allow full participation in the economy, Epstein considers further state involvement in regulating employment relationships difficult to justify, and he would not regard 'market failures' as sufficient justification because there is no reason to suppose that government interventions will produce better results than the alleged failure. Simon Deakin, by contrast, views antidiscrimination law not as antithetical to market freedoms but as supportive of markets.[55] Deakin argues that 'classic liberal rights are not sufficient to ensure effective economic participation. In themselves, they cannot prevent forms of inequality and social exclusion which diminish the scope of the market and threaten its existence. A market which benefits only a minority of society cannot ultimately be sustained'.[56] Deakin argues that 'formal' rights granting access to markets, such as property rights and rights to enter into and enforce contracts, are insufficient for 'effective' participation and thus require to be supplemented by 'substantive' rights 'by providing for substantive market access, going beyond the idea of formal market access which is found in private law'.[57] Deakin's argument is rooted in ideas similar to those defending 'substantiveequality' over 'formal equality', in that he sees substantive rights as an extra layer of rights to enhance the exercise of formal rights: 'such legislation, rather than denying the market, often works in conjunction with

---

[54] *Forbidden Grounds*, pp. 3–4; see also *Equal Opportunity or More Opportunity?*

[55] 'The non-discrimination principle supports the market…it operates in a close relationship to the market, rather than being fundamentally opposed to it': Ibid., pp. 41, 42.

[56] Ibid., pp. 41, 42.

[57] Ibid., p. 42.

market mechanisms, such as reputation and exit, to enhance economic welfare'.[58]

But much depends on what counts as 'effective' participation and on the empirical causes of participation that is not deemed to be effective in that sense. As seen in the discussion of the causes of inequality, there is no evidence that the causes of market exclusion are primarily linked to discrimination, so there can be no presumption that tackling discrimination would resolve barriers to market participation, nor that conferring a set of rights linked to equality would address the underlying problems. As Epstein observes, 'neither Deakin nor, as far as I can tell, anyone else, has supplied any definition of what counts as an effective right of market participation above and beyond the ability to hold property and enter into contracts'.[59] Without knowing the test of effectiveness the corrective legislation is operating in the dark in pursuit of the cosmic justice Sowell describes, an amorphous sense that markets ought to be 'fair' in yielding more equal outcomes. As Epstein puts it, 'In any large population, some portion of the population will fail in economic activities, no matter what legal régime is in place. It becomes, therefore, something of an impossibility for anyone to make operational a test for when participation is effective, for when people with full legal capacities have adequate social capacities'.[60] We have seen in previous chapters that it is wrong to presume that 'discrimination' is the reason for lack of effective participation, and also wrong to presume that if market outcomes are unequal this proves the participation to have fallen short of an unspecified 'effectiveness' standard. Thus when Deakin argues that 'a system of private law is compatible with the persistence of forms of inequality and exclusion which will ultimately undermine the market' it is not clear what would count as undermining the market unless it is to be supposed that the market is undermined by factors such as the mere existence of unemployment or inequality, not 'enough' equality, or subjective claims of feeling excluded, or feeling that one has to work harder than others to earn the same wage, or similar complaints typically cited as evidence of

---

[58] Ibid. See discussion in Sect. 2.1 of Chapter 2, on the shift from formal to substantive equality.

[59] Ibid., p. 58.

[60] Ibid., pp. 58, 59.

'racism'. Free markets surely can be a hard taskmaster, but it is not clear that the solutions ought to target protection to specified groups while leaving others to battle against harsh market forces as best they can. The Factories Acts for example protected children from working in factories; it would have been ethical to select certain children (say, by reference to gender) for protection while leaving the other children to get on with it.

If what is meant by undermining the market is more in the nature of a general argument that markets would be expected to yield superior outcomes with a little help from facilitative legislation, tweaks and nudges that would yield less inequality and greater levels of ethnic minority participation, that suggestion does not accord with the empirical evidence from studies such as Higgs's and Williams's. One could track the numbers of ethnic minority 'participation' by reference to, for example, public sector employment. Taking the example of doctors, 'About 40% of all doctors in the NHS in Wales are from black or ethnic minority backgrounds' despite black people being 0.6% of the Welsh population. It is unclear whether this significant overrepresentation would count as 'effective' participation, since some of these black doctors complain about feeling 'unwelcome' and 'having no formal place at the table'. Whatever the solution is to resolving the problem of racial minorities feeling unwelcome, it is unlikely to lie in legislative mandates and greater proportional representation.[61] Similarly, failures related to underperformance in education can hardly be remedied by affirmative action even as the admissions figures give the impression of progress in the numbers of ethnic minority admissions. The University of Cambridge reports that 'Nearly three in ten (29.3 per cent) British students admitted in 2020 were from black, Asian and minority ethnic backgrounds — up from 27.8 per cent the previous year. In the general UK population about 13.8 per cent of people are from a minority ethnic background'.[62] This overrepresentation again goes along with increasing complaints about microaggressions and feeling unwelcome,

[61] ''Some ethnic minority doctors in Wales feel unwelcome'. https://www.bbc.co.uk/news/uk-wales-57273961.

[62] Woolcock, N. Cambridge takes record numbers of ethnic minority and state pupils (May 19, 2021). https://www.thetimes.co.uk/article/cambridge-takes-record-numbers-of-ethnic-minority-and-state-pupils-fsrtx8cf9.

forcing the university to introduce new measures restricting free speech in a desperate bid to resolve the situation.[63] Thus boosting the numbers of participation through affirmative and positive action or quotas does not seem to resolve feelings of inequality. Indeed Deakin observes that 'This process [of expanding antidiscrimination law] has not consistently brought about the desired results; indeed, anti-discrimination legislation may not always be the best means of dealing with social exclusion'.[64] The numbers amount only to evidence of precisely the phenomenon referred to by Sowell as make-believe equality—the superficial appearance of equality achieved by packing institutions with ethnic minorities. This was described by Clarence Thomas as a cruel farce precisely because it convinces nobody, not even the beneficiaries of the special measures, that they are 'equal' especially because it is not even clear what equality means in this context. As Riley observes, these black perspectives on the harm caused by affirmative action have been consistently ignored for decades:

> In a 1970s essay, Sowell had anticipated [Clarence] Thomas's ordeal. 'The double standard of grades and degrees is an open secret on many campuses, and it is only a matter of time before it is an open secret among employers as well,' he predicted. 'The market can be ruthless in devaluing degrees that do not mean what they say. It should be apparent to anyone not blinded by his own nobility that *it also devalues the student in his own eyes.*'[65]

It may be said that going on the market with a devalued degree is not the worst thing that could happen, but it is less easy to dismiss the hubris entailed in wilfully devaluing ethnic minority students in

---

[63] 'We have thousands of students and staff from different backgrounds and countries. They are all entitled to feel welcome and valued. So we are providing a safe way to report concerns and help tackle bullying and harassment while raising awareness that small, often unintentional gestures can be upsetting. As is set out in our policy on freedom of speech, the university expects everyone to be tolerant of the opinions of others, while remaining courteous.' Professor Eilís Ferran Pro-Vice-Chancellor for Institutional and International Relations, University of Cambridge. https://www.telegraph.co.uk/opinion/2021/05/23/letters-surging-demand-gp-care-means-system-breaking-point/

[64] In *Equal Opportunity or More Opportunity*? p. 42.

[65] Riley, *Maverick*, pp. 69, 70 (emphasis added).

their own eyes. Yet the inequality ideologues are unconcerned about such effects. They simply double down by demanding further restrictions, stricter guidelines and more special rights for minorities, driven by the emotionalism discussed by Furedi—yet the more regulators give in to expressions of fear and psychic harm, the more unwelcome the fearful feel. It is a downward spiral. No responsible legislature sets out to create a perfect utopia—perfect equality is never explicitly stated to be the goal of equality law. Yet we hear always that there is 'not enough' equality although it is never specified precisely how much equality would ever be enough. As Epstein has argued, once the law sets off down the equalisation path there is no logical stopping point.

Further, as Epstein argues, corrective legislation is not only ineffective but also costly. In addition to containing no guarantees it imposes deleterious unintended effects of its own. Legislative intentions do not automatically translate into legislative effectiveness. Moreover, incentives matter in influencing human behaviour, and it often happens that legislative prescriptions change the incentives in unexpected ways or destroy them altogether.[66] Sowell offers the example of minimum wage regulation, which is intended to raise wages but may do so at the expense of job creation by reducing the incentive to hire more costly workers. Similarly antidiscrimination legislation intended to protect people from being fired based on protected grounds may end up reducing the incentives to hire protected persons in the first place. Thus even when markets fail to meet the anticipated standards of free competition and free operation of the price mechanism, it does not automatically follow that interventions would be free from even worse failures.[67] In evaluating the effectiveness of interventionist legislation it is therefore important to have sight not only of the laudatory motives and intentions behind it, but also of the associated costs. Discrimination is costly for both perpetrator and victim,

[66] 'The annual product of social labor...is not a natural or technological phenomenon independent of all social conditions, but entirely the result of our social institutions...were this incentive to be destroyed, productivity would be so greatly reduced that the portion that an equal distribution would allot to each individual would be far less than what even the poorest receives today.' Mises, *Liberalism,* p. 12.

[67] 'The issue must always be one of "failure" compared to some available "real-world" alternative, and not in comparison to an unattainable and unidentifiable ideal': Pennington, Robust Political Economy and the Priority of Markets, p. 8.

and antidiscrimination law seeks to reduce the costs incurred by victims such as the costs of taking longer to find work, the costs of taking work at a lower wage than would otherwise have been available or the psychic costs of feeling rejected and humiliated or watching others being rejected and humiliated. But from a regulatory perspective there are other costs to consider, including costs associated with administering and monitoring equality schemes including costs of training, litigation, enforcement and compensation. It could be argued in that context that the cost of self-correction through free markets, for example through the reputational costs suffered by a business which is known to discriminate, is lower than the cost of regulatory correction. Where firms are boycotted for making offensive comments this is a far heavier sanction than the individual threat of a lawsuit. Enforcing individual claims is certainly costly, but when regulation goes wrong then the mistakes and costs of regulatory failure are borne by society as a whole, unlike a private transaction going wrong which affects only the parties to the transaction (and, at most, their associates).

Legislation certainly plays a legitimate role in 'correcting' decisions that are deemed to be wrong or harmful, and in underpinning a core set of moral values to create the fundamental moral structure necessary to temper self-interest, such as respect for private property, enforcement of contractual bargains and protecting fundamental human freedoms such as free speech and freedom of association. This does not entail a binary either-or choice between markets or centralised regulation, but sheds light on the appropriate balance to be struck between facilitating competitive markets and mandatory regulation designed to promote equality. The law already exhibits a nuanced attempt to strike such a balance, for example in allowing certain forms of discrimination (such as indirect discrimination) to be justified by an employer to meet business needs such as flexibility or tailored market demands. Therefore the issue is not whether there is a role for legislative regulation in facilitating free markets, but whether that legislation falls within the legitimate scope of coercive state power and whether it is effective in achieving its stated goals, and whether it entails inordinate costs in its implications for individual liberty. At a superficial level we may suppose that these questions are settled by duly elected representatives institutionalising the majority view of the public interest through legislation. We all uphold the antidiscrimination principle for the simple reason that the law mandates that we do so. But this would be an overly simplistic way to understand the interplay between the democratic mandate and individual liberty. Justice requires something more than simply a position that most people would agree with because most people can be, and often are, wrong about many things. Democratic processes can have no valid mandate to abolish individual liberty. Democracy is not valid regardless of its moral outcomes; it is valid only in so far as it respects and protects fundamental human freedoms.

5.5 Moral Emotionalism and Legislative Mandates

> The commitment to 'social justice' has in fact become the chief outlet for moral emotion, the distinguishing attribute of the good man, and the recognized sign of the possession of a social conscience.
>
> –Hayek, *Law, Legislation & Liberty*, 230.

In the ideal of classical liberalism individuals manage themselves, their relations with other individuals, and their economic activities, to the greatest possible extent, rather than have their lives primarily managed through the authority of state power and legislative edicts. Where legislative intervention is necessary it does not merely express general ideals and goals to be pursued but also requires a *justification* for its impositions. Thus the state plays a more attenuated and less interventionist role limited to ensuring that there are no institutional features artificially favouring or disfavouring specific groups.

Some philosophical traditions regard the state as the main guarantor of individual liberty, charged with protecting individuals from the tyranny of the majority. The role of the state as protector assumes greater proportions in the culture of fear described in previous chapters. In the context of racial diversity it is feared that without protective legislation historical racial oppression would return like an unvanquished terminator because the majority or those in power would immediately embark on unfairly discriminating against others—it is supposed that only the law currently holds them in check from implementing their nefarious desire to ruin ethnic minorities. Protective legislation is also justified as an aspirational standard or guideline, to nudge people to behave better than they otherwise would have, in pursuit of the social ideal of equality and to build a better world. Protective legislation encourages us to be more kind and gentle, more warm and welcoming. It gives racial minorities the confidence to participate in market activity, earning higher wages and being more equal in terms of wealth, health, education and other prosperity markers. These arguments carry great political weight because they evoke a powerful moral vision that appeals to voters across the political spectrum. Such arguments offer practical solutions that can easily be implemented by governments anxious to do something (and be seen to be doing something) about social problems. New legislation can be passed, new equality commissions established, new officers appointed, more public funds allocated. Unlike tackling basic education and health needs which would require complex interventions whose impact would be difficult to measure in the short term, it is easy for governments to monitor the numbers of racial minorities admitted to universities, appointed to public offices or installed onto corporate boards of directors. Racially proportionate results are thus an attractive benchmark for favoured 'equity' schemes.

But this vision of the state as protector is historically questionable. As will be discussed below, in the context of racial diversity the state has historically been the main threat to individual liberty, often through the very measures designed to safeguard society. The appropriate role of legislation is not to manage race relations but 'to prevent unjust action'; not to favour one group over another or attempt 'to achieve particular results for specific persons or groups'.[68] It is self-defeating to attempt the prevention of unjust action by seeking unjust special privileges for

[68] Hayek, F. A. (2013). *Law, Legislation and Liberty: A New Statement of the Liberal Principles of Justice and Political Economy.* Routledge (Original work published 1973), *I*, 2.

favoured groups. Progressives argue that special privileges for disadvantaged groups are not unjust; on the contrary they are said to be just because they compensate for endemic disadvantage and bring the weak up to the level of the strong. But the claim that inequality between races is inherently 'unjust' is stipulated with little attempt to investigate the causes of inequality. To earn more by working harder may lead to a higher wage that is unequal to the wage earned by those who did not work as hard, but that is no injustice. Paying the same wage to those who merit it and those who do not—that would be unjust. Nor does it make any difference that the reason for favouring special interest groups is benign, being to reverse historical oppression, because history cannot be reversed. The legal framework must look forward.

Antidiscrimination legislation is primarily valued as a defining symbol of a society's moral virtue and evidence of being 'on the side of the angels against evil'.[69] The legal framework is overtly aspirational, springing from ideals construed as inclusive and emotionally intelligent, breaking new ground in envisioning a higher evolutionary ideal of human experience, a break from centuries past ridden with racial oppression, slavery and colonialism. These historical grievances play a central role in creating moral anxiety for those whose sense of collective or associative guilt compels them to do something to make right the wrongs of the past. The impossibility of going back in time to right the perceived wrongs of the past frustrates their cry for moral redemption, their regret for the actions of their ancestors and the moral overtones of guilt-and-punishment soon give way to expressions of shame and repentance. The signalling virtue of law is increasingly highly valued by a society unsure of its moral foundations.

Translating moral emotional into legislation poses challenges. It is essential to the rule of law that the ambit of legislation is clear, certain and predictable. While legislation plays a foundational role in the pursuit of justice, law cannot fairly enforce vague notions of 'justice' which are open to widely varying interpretations. For justice or fairness to be treated as the basis for legislative mandates, the goals must be

[69] Sowell, *Cosmic Justice*.

concrete and capable of precise definition. Injustice as a basis for law-making cannot simply denote any situation that incurs social or moral opprobrium or any unhappy circumstances that people would wish to escape.

Further, in a complex world legislative mandates must take account of all relevant considerations. For example, even the most restrictive employment legislation does not create absolute protection from dismissal but seeks only to control the circumstances and processes of dismissal to uphold basic principles of natural justice such as the right to be given reasons for dismissal and to be heard in one's own defence. The legislation does not simply forbid employers from dismissing employees. While an absolute ban might meet social expectations of justice in the intuitive sense that workers generally prefer not to get fired and dismissed workers would hardly ever feel that their dismissal was fair, regulation of dismissal raises broader implications for the workplace and ultimately comes up against the reality that no employer can be forced to run a business or to create jobs in the first place. Reality thus necessitates limits to our quest for social justice, which it would be unwise to ignore. Similarly, in the pursuit of racial equality close regard must be paid to other closely related questions. Does antidiscrimination legislation help or hinder social cohesion? All legislation entails hidden or unintended costs; does antidiscrimination law entail inadvertent burdens for its intended beneficiaries? Does forbidding discriminatory decisions or preferences work effectively in promoting equality? In outlawing discrimination should a clearer distinction be drawn between private interactions and public life?

The underlying ideological concerns that influence our understanding of these issues tend to remain obscure and unstated, only occasionally being explicitly identified or acknowledged. The courts in interpreting the law rightly remain blind to, or at least independent from, the varying political colours that tint legislation. A key concern in antidiscrimination legislation is the appropriate scope of distributive justice, and particularly the extent to which equality law is ultimately intended to redistribute of wealth and power. The rise of identity politics in recent decades, with inequalities linked to characteristics such as gender or race taking centre stage, has only served to heighten these concerns. The prevailing deontological understanding of race discrimination, as reflected for example in 'critical race theories', therefore pass without critical scrutiny. For example the American Medical Association defines critical race theory as 'Critical race theory born out of both legal studies and education scholarship is a framework that centers experiential knowledge, challenges dominant ideology, and mobilizes interdisciplinary action and research in order to uncover inequalities related to race and racism and other intersectional identities and/or experiences' and states that

> We must adopt collaborative and participatory approaches and ensure that we use the theories (intersectionality, critical race theory, etc.), tools and approaches that allow us to consistently identify, elevate and work with marginalized groups in any spaces.[70]

It is clear from this definition, with its desire to 'challenge dominant ideology' that an ideological position is being adopted. This reflects an ideological commitment to pursuing the right aspirational goals regardless of whether it yields beneficial results—with the ultimate goal of achieving 'equity', defined as giving preference to marginalised communities, as a good thing to do *in itself*. The moral ideology of equality is less concerned with what actually works in improving life outcomes and more focused on the intentions and moral goals of the legislation. The result is a substitution of reason with moral emotion. The policy priority has shifted from civil, political and personal freedoms towards promoting subjective moral ideals.

The question of coercion arises when some people aver that they are selflessly willing, voluntarily, to sacrifice their freedom to enhance equality, while others declare themselves determined to defend every last personal freedom. If they will not willingly give up their liberties and embrace critical race theory, somebody will have to force them to do so and this is where the law comes in. The rationale for mandating moral edicts framed as social justice measures is that for a sacrifice of personal

[70] American Medical Association. (2021). Organizational strategic plan to embed racial justice and advance health equity, 2021–2023. Retrieved June 26, 2021, from https://www.ama-assn.org/system/files/2021-05/ama-equity-strategic-plan.pdf, p. 38.

freedom to have its intended impact it must be universal. It is not enough for a few upstanding moral citizens to embrace the new morality; everyone else must be forced to join in the sacrifice. For example, billionaires who profess to want to pay extra voluntary taxes argue that paying extra taxes would only make a difference if *every* billionaire contributes and therefore this worthy goal must be mandatory and legally enforced. Those who profess a desire to pay more will not do so voluntarily; instead they lobby for laws mandating compulsory billionaire taxes. The rationale is that if a social or ideological goal is worth pursuing, it must be mandated to ensure that dissenters do not undermine the pursuit of worthy goals. Mises explains this coercive inclination as a function of the purpose of law:

> A small number of anti-social individuals, i.e., persons who are not willing or able to make the temporary sacrifices that society demands of them, could make all society impossible. Without the application of compulsion and coercion against the enemies of society, there could not be any life in society… One must be in a position to compel the person who will not respect the lives, health, personal freedom, or private property of others to acquiesce in the rules of life in society.[71]

Thus it is not supposed that society can function without rules, or that rules should be optional. Legislation by its very nature has an inbuilt coercive nature, to the extent that it reflects the majority position ascertained through specified procedures such as elections and referenda but is binding also on the minority. The issue concerns drawing a distinction between rules that are legitimate, for which coercion is justified (such as the defence of life, liberty and property), and rules that lack legitimacy (such as the desire that all should declare allegiance to partisan critical race theories). Democratic decision-making on such disputed issues is of course necessary as it would be impossible for a society to function on the basis of unanimity, and social cohesion would soon give way to chaos if legislation only bound those who happen to agree with the

71 Mises, *Liberalism*, p. 16.

law. Dissenters could then treat the legislative framework as a smorgasbord of suggestions from which they could pick and choose according to their private preferences, and the rule of law would break down. Majority rule through democracy, with all its pitfalls, remains the best system of government yet devised. But the danger immediately arises that the tyranny of the majority may soon follow. How to justify the coercive effect of law is thus a complex problem that has occupied political philosophers for millennia; how to derive fair and just rules without oppressing minority groups. A central function of the rule of law is to defend the individual against the tyranny of the majority, and the citizen from the tyranny of the state. A legal system accords with morality to the extent that it is ultimately based on voluntary consent, including consent to decision-making and law-making processes. As Leoni argued, 'only a limited measure of success can be attained through the extension of legislation and the threat of coercion that supports it'.[72] Coercion should therefore be limited to a core set of rights and functions—'the protection of property, liberty and peace'.[73] Limiting the reach of the state does not reflect a negative 'aversion in principle against any activity on the part of the state'[74] but a positive commitment to individual liberty which is necessarily encroached upon by state prescription.

Thus we see a contest between two moral visions in the equality discourse: one based on a dominant role for government in wealth redistribution, and the other based in individual virtues and economic liberty with a limited role for state intervention. The question whether discrimination is moral in the context of making private decisions is conceptually distinct from whether it ought to be policed by the state. For example, the moral and cultural presumptions underlying the 'protectedcharacteristics' in equality law, such as the protection of race and religion, reflect the idea that for many people these are core elements of their individual identity which they prioritise highly in relation to their other personal attributes and consider to be the most fundamental characteristic of their identity. Yet this prioritisation is not universal.

[72] Leoni, *Freedom and the Law*, p. 17.

[73] Mises, *Liberalism*, p. 17.

[74] Ibid., p. 18.

Many people, for example, regard their career or their hobbies or their talents or even which football team they support as much more constitutive of their identity than their race or religion. By getting the law involved in prioritising a specific conceptualisation of personal identity, such as what it means to be black or what it means to be white, matters which preoccupy the adherents of critical race theory, the law imposes one particular conception of the principles that ought to govern one's life onto other people who might reasonably disagree even though they share the same characteristics—it is not mandatory for black people to agree on what it means to be black, nor should the law get involved in attempting to unravel racial identities. The fact that some people consider racial identity to be a good way of expressing their moral emotionalism on the public stage does not make it a suitable matter for legislative intervention, not even under the umbrella of 'equality'.

The real world of decision-making exhibits phenomenal diversity. This means that decisions that raise allegations of 'discrimination' are not purely governed by the types of moral considerations that would make evaluation of the decision purely a moral issue. In many instances routine decisions largely involve making private choices between competing personal preferences. Many spheres of social and economic life are governed by informal norms and best-guess decisions in transacting with others, where many people rely more on trust and lessons from past experience than on formal contracts. Nor do people tend to expect, or demand, enforcement of their legal 'rights' in dealing with others unless the relationship has already broken down irretrievably and they are engaged in hostilities, so that introducing rights into contexts of interpersonal disagreement may only exacerbate the hostilities. In this context, making decisions about whom to interact with across race or gender lines is not purely a moral question, but also reflects a rational attempt to make those decisions that are most likely to have a successful outcome in conducting one's day to day affairs. We would expect personal experience to influence decision-making, to a greater or lesser extent depending on the time frame in question, the issues at stake, the available information and other variable factors that typically influence decisions. Framing this as a purely moral issue oversimplifies what is in fact a more complex issue about human interaction. For example, in some contexts it may be rational to discriminate in favour of a group of one's preference. In these situations moral issues are no doubt important, but cannot be legally predetermined or prescribed by simple rules and expectations that apply to all cases.[75] Nor is finding the choices of others offensive or distasteful a basis for regulating behaviour in public life; even more so in private life.

As Sowell has argued, the expectation that legislation is a tool capable of equalising life outcomes is a mirage.[76] Legislation has no more power to eradicate discrimination or to create socio-economic equality than it does to eradicate poverty or illness or any other unhappy vagaries of life or to construct meaningful lives for citizens. Resolving these questions is not a straightforward matter of voting yea or nay to economic freedom or racial equality. Everybody wants freedom and equality, together with prosperity, peace, love, universal harmony and other social ideals and values that we all desire. We should all like to wave the magic-fairy legislative wand and create a new world that is more fair and just.[77] As Sowell counsels, we may indulge in dreams of cosmic justice and encourage our legislators to intervene in the unfairness of life, to reallocate ability and luck to where it is most deserved so that everyone marches in step to the beat of the same drum and nobody gets ahead of others, but all attempts in history to do so have failed dismally. Governments simply do not have the knowledge required to implement cosmic justice. History warns that such attempts always end in totalitarianism.

> Thus, the Fabian of yesteryear becomes inexorably the totalitarian of tomorrow, and ultimately the victim of his own creation. Horrified by

[75] 'Sound judgments about whether a given legal rule is good or bad cannot begin with an untested moral assumption that simply calls some preferences out of bounds before the discussion begins. All have to be taken into account, and when that is done, a powerful case exists for allowing persons to sort themselves voluntarily by inclination and taste. There are forms of discrimination that outsiders may find offensive, but which are rational nonetheless': Epstein, *Forbidden Grounds*, p. 76.

[76] See Sowell, *Cosmic Justice*, chapter 2: 'The Mirage of Equality'.

[77] '[The legislator] regrets people's poverty. Don't we all. Would that everyone in the world would be a millionaire many times over! But legislation can't achieve that, and, if it could, she could rightly be denounced for being stingy. Why not mandate a wage of $1000 an hour, if that's all there is to it?' Rockwell Jr, L.H. (2006, September 10). The Political Hoax Exposed. *Mises Institute*. https://mises.org/library/political-hoax-exposed.

> some evils and excesses in a free society (which will always be imperfect) he turns hopefully to the blueprint of a controlled society which promises a heaven on earth in the very near future. But since the individual must always be imperfect this side of paradise, his society must always be imperfect, and the more absolutely it is controlled by single committees or groups of imperfect men with unlimited power, the more imperfect it is likely to be.[78]

The quest for perfection is in any event far in excess of what each person needs to live life to their fullest potential.Epstein's analysis shows that it is not necessary for 100% of people in society to be potential trading partners for every single person, or for 100% of employers to be willing to hire every job applicant. The important question for each trader or job applicant is not the percentage of firms willing to deal with them, or the percentage of employers willing to hire them, since in the end one can only enter into one employment relationship or a finite number of trading relationships, and each person has preferences regarding their ideal or desirable employer or business associates: no individual would regard every business in the market place as equally suitable for their needs. Sellers do not have a right to be given 'equalopportunities' by buyers; buyers are free to discriminate on any basis they wish, whether rational or irrational. Resources are therefore misdirected if channelled into policing the preferences of every market participant and ensuring that they would all give every person in their society an 'equalopportunity'. The critical empirical issue is whether a person who encounters discrimination from one firm would in practice have a realistic possibility of finding a different opportunity with another firm, in the absence of laws mandating equal opportunities. That opportunity does not have to be 'equal' to another person's opportunity. It has only to be sufficient for the job seeker to find the job they desire. To complain that someone else had a 'better' job opportunity or an 'easier' path to success is impossible to verify and unlikely to yield any useful information for purposes of the legislative framework in a free society.

[78] Schuyler, G. (1939). Cited in Reed, L.W. (2021, May 22). George Schuyler: Journalist, Individualist, and Courageous Contrarian. *Foundation for Economic Education*. https://fee.org/articles/george-schuyler-journalist-individualist-and-courageous-contrarian/.

Epstein argues that 'in a world of free access to open markets, systematic discrimination, even by a large majority, offers little peril to the isolated minority': the isolated minority always finds sufficient people wishing to do business with them.[79] Owing to discrimination their opportunities may not be the numerical equivalent of the opportunities of others who do not face the same discrimination, but this is entirely irrelevant to their outcomes. The critical point is that both the person with 98% availability of opportunities and the person with only 40% availability of opportunities have enough people with whom to transact. Thus the relevant issue is not the potential total number of available opportunities, but the actual number of opportunities needed to achieve one's goals. Epstein thus highlights the analytical distinction between the imperative to use law to prohibit, for example, the use of force, which we prohibit even though we know that most people will not resort to force, and legal prohibition of discrimination in and of itself which we should not prohibit simply because we know that some people do discriminate against others. That is the classical liberal position on the role of the limited state. Legislative coercion is not justified simply in order to try and make the world a better place based on nothing more than a pipe dream. Failure to realize the gains from trade with a particular person is of course disappointing, and costly, but this is best resolved not by resorting to law to force that particular person to trade, but by trading with someone else. Move on to the next opportunity. Simply put, law backed by the coercive force of the state is not the right approach to deal with individual disappointments, setbacks or slights.

5.6 Inequality Through Law

In twenty-first century western liberal democracies, even in the absence of laws prohibiting an establishment from displaying the once-endemic discriminatory signs excluding black people, no reputable establishment would choose to do so: it would lose customers and there would be nothing to gain by it. Defenders of equality legislation argue that without

[79] *Forbidden Grounds*, p. 32.

such prohibitions business establishments up and down the land would immediately put signs up barring non-white patrons from entering. They imagine that the majority of people are barely constrained by the law from the evil discrimination they wish to unleash on everyone who is different from them in some way. This is unlikely to be practically feasible in the context of a global economy. The cases highlighted in the news to prove that racism is endemic always have a back-story, typically involving crime and crime control, that go a long way to explaining what might otherwise appear to be 'random' acts of discrimination.

That presumption concerning the need for law to serve a protective function in case people choose to be mean to each other is also unsupported by historical experience. For example apartheid and Jim Crow legislation empowered state authorities to implement and enforce segregation, even in contexts where people of different races were happy enough to mix in their families, neighbourhoods and work environments.[80] In the UK, where racial segregation was not legally mandated, the degree of segregation was much more attenuated.[81] The evil of inequality in free markets lies only in a system constrained by law in such a way that nobody can escape the strictures of their race, as for example in the Jim Crow era where segregated train carriages not only excluded black people from white carriages, but also excluded white people from black carriages. The fear that without equality mandates society would revert to the Jim Crow era is mistaken, because Jim Crow was not merely a pattern of behaviour preferred by a majority but an institutional system based on 'laws that *required* segregation, discrimination, unequal taxes and biased enforcement of the law'.[82] The Jim Crow system was sustained by legislation and defended by the broader institutional framework of the legal system and state action (or inaction where the state had a duty to act) rather than simply in organic hateful attitudes of ordinary citizens. Even under Jim Crow, 'most people' did not run riot wearing white sheets and wreaking racial havoc: those who

---

[80] See for example the evidence that many people, black and white, were opposed to the Jim Crow laws discussed in Epstein, *Forbidden Grounds*.

[81] Modood, T. et al., *Ethnic Minorities in Britain;* see discussion of 'neighbourhoods and housing', pp. 5, 6.

[82] *Forbidden Grounds*, p. 96.

did were able to exercise dominance because they were backed by the legal and political system. It must be remembered that Jim Crow legislation mandated discrimination by forbidding people from offering equal opportunities across race lines, and there would have been no need for these restrictions if in fact 'most people' were already racist enough never to offer those opportunities to blacks in the first place. To a large extent the legislation served the purpose of preventing rogue white liberals from undermining or even perhaps dismantling the integrity of segregation by departing from racist norms.

Apart from the moral issues surrounding racism, there were those who would hire black labour if that proved to be cost effective. Epstein cites examples of 'the coal companies, which, when forced to compete strenuously in a regional labor market, assiduously courted black labor',[83] or the railways which were opposed to segregation simply because it was more expensive to provide separate carriages for black and white passengers and also costly to enforce compliance with the segregation rules.[84] Each train operator had no discretion over whether or not to segregate its own carriages nor flexibility to make ad hoc adjustments in response to demand. Not all train operators were interested in paying the extra costs (in time, money, effort and manpower) of enforcing segregation in their carriages, and it is no wonder that many businesses regarded segregation laws as 'a costly nuisance'.[85] It is evident that in an open economy there will always be sufficient people with good reasons to buck the trend even if the majority may have a taste for racism. Jim Crow thus represented a state-enforced legislative framework of discrimination, and Epstein rightly questions 'whether Jim Crow would have survived if southern whites had voluntarily relinquished their control over the ballot, the police force, the courts, and the other instruments of state domination' which kept segregation in place.[86]

The evidence gives cause to conclude that progress through voluntary exchange offers a more sustainable alternative than progress through

[83] Ibid.

[84] Ibid., p. 102.

[85] Bernstein, D.E. *You Can't Say That!*, p. 5.

[86] *Forbidden Grounds*, p. 97.

policy interventions favouring special interest groups. Markets are open to exchange and cooperation between all members of society. Liberalism, and the free trade on which it is based, promotes the welfare of all in society. The free market ideal creates greater scope for decisions to be made by private individuals and firms rather than by multiple and increasingly complex layers of centralised legislation regulating private transactions.[87] Unfair or irrational discrimination—discriminating when there is no rational justification for doing so—is the exception rather than the norm in modern society, and becoming increasingly rare over time as moral values and social outlooks continue to evolve in a global context. It is true that there will always be some people who wish to indulge their racial tastes. But although the current legal framework is implicitly based on a presumption that most people will behave in discriminatory ways unless prevented by law from doing so, the opposite presumption is closer to reality: most people will behave rationally most of the time. That is the nature of life. This reality allows us to avoid attaching undue gravity to exceptional cases. It is not a matter of life and death that someone, somewhere on the internet, has made a discriminatory joke that some people find offensive. Where discrimination crosses the line into a legal wrong, whether civil or criminal, there are ample laws to deal with the situation. But the fact of discrimination itself, whatever may be its moral value (a matter we explore in more detail below) need not by itself constitute a legal wrong.

5.7 Rational Discrimination

> Yes, I'd give the Devil benefit of law, for my own safety's sake!
> Thomas More, *Man For All Seasons*

---

[87] 'Opening the gates of prosperity to ever more people around the world, economic freedom has made our globe a profoundly better place. More people are living better lives than ever before. Clearly, this monumental reduction in global poverty is an achievement that should inspire celebration of the free-market system, deeper understanding of its dynamics, and greater commitment to its promotion': Heritage Foundation. (2019). The Power of Economic Freedom. *Index of economic freedom.* Retrieved from https://www.heritage.org/index/pdf/2019/book/chapter4.pdf.

If freedom of contract and freedom of association are upheld, some people might use that freedom to discriminate against others. If we uphold free speech, some people might take the opportunity to say things that make other people feel bad. They might tell offensive jokes on purpose, just to hurt others. Freedom of expression and freedom of conscience are rights for all, not only for those who speak with civility, courtesy and sensitivity to the feelings of others. A defence of fundamental freedoms must account explicitly for those who depart from accepted social and moral codes, to avoid the danger that such departures will come to be viewed as justifications for devaluing individual liberty. The price of freedom is the acceptance that not everyone uses that freedom to make moral choices with which we agree: 'Liberal society necessarily makes possible, permits, and even fosters what is called by many people "discrimination"'.[88] Hence it is sometimes seen that the defence of liberty is left to the wicked, who see clearly that freedom serves their preferences, with the unfortunate result that those who view themselves as fighting on the side of the angels are forced to oppose freedom. Caldwell wryly observes that in the US civil rights debates it tended to be Southerners and other segregationists raising concerns about individual liberty and property rights: progressives preferred to stay silent when the risk to liberty became clear, as it seemed that liberty would favour the position of those who were opposed to their equality schemes.[89]

It has been no part of our discussion to assert that discrimination does not exist, or that people do not cause racial offence to others in exercise of their freedoms. The aim is, instead, to consider the appropriate role of legal interventions. In this part we argue that from a regulatory perspective, discrimination may or may not fall within the scope of rational decision-making. All decisions should be rational and intelligent. But human nature means that they are not always so. As Mises explains, 'Liberalism does not say that men always act intelligently, but rather that they ought, in their own rightly understood interest, always to act intelligently'.[90] Market participants are not always rational; as Hayek observes,

[88] Caldwell, *Age of Entitlement*, p. 15, quoting Leo Strauss.

[89] Ibid., p. 18.

[90] *Liberalism*, p. xxi.

'individual reason is very limited and imperfect'. Human behaviour is often far from rational, clear or predictable and individuals often lack a complete understanding of their own motivations and preferences. Thus trying to understand society from the standpoint of individual interactions may not seem very promising. It may seem more promising to imagine society in its ideal form, and then attempt to nudge or guide or coax individuals—coerce them where necessary—to fit within the social ideal. In the context of antidiscrimination it is presumed that irrational people will always tend to be hostile to those of a different race, therefore law is needed to guide their behaviour towards mutual respect and social cohesion. Thus antidiscrimination law is treated as a type of regulation needed to produce the desired behaviour, and other important questions are overlooked, such as how individuals go about pursuing ends they have reason to value.

Most people would agree that it is not usually rational to take into account race or other protected grounds when making choices. Some people would go further and say that one should desist from taking race into account even when it might be rational to do so. Perhaps the police should stop and search elderly white ladies even when they know that the person they are looking for was a young white man. It would at least help to show that they are not stereotyping anyone, and there may be some value in that. The issue is not what would or would not be rational, but who should decide and specifically, whether discrimination should always be unlawful.

In the context of voluntary exchange, to discriminate is to choose. Not all choices are equal. As Williams puts it, 'all selection necessarily and simultaneously requires non-selection. Choice requires discrimination'.[91] The view that it is morally suspect to distinguish between people or things is interpreted by Furedi as part of a broader anti-judgmentalism ethos, the idea that it is judgemental and simplistic to define, categorise or derive conceptual boundaries.[92] But some choices are more suited to specific goals than others, and some choices cost more than others. To discriminate is to choose the option best suited to one's goals, to decide

[91] *Race and Economics*, p. 113.

[92] Furedi, *Why Borders Matter*.

in favour of one option at the expense of another. Decades of legislative measures designed to advance equality have failed to meet their stated aims mainly due to a failure to acknowledge that irrational discrimination is not, by itself, problematic. An irrational buyer will pay over the odds for something he might purchase for better value elsewhere by reason only that he likes the look of the seller—he thinks she is pretty. Much commercial advertising takes advantage of consumers' irrational decision-making. This is no reason for legal interventions to nudge people to make more rational decisions. Much depends on personal taste, the context of the decision, the costs and benefits of discriminating between one choice and another and the social and economic implications of that choice. The prevailing discourse on equality therefore lacks a realistic account of how people make decisions and it is not surprising that, from that starting point, the equality measures continually fail to achieve their goals.

The law recognises that discrimination may be justifiable in various contexts, for example where the discriminatory effect is 'indirect' or where 'reasonable adjustments' have been made to ameliorate the discriminatory effect. There are many reasons why it might be rational to discriminate in some circumstances. For instance in the UK equality legislation permits an exception to the discrimination provisions in the context of a 'genuine occupational requirement' for a particular race.[93] This is however likely to be tightly construed, and has most practical significance in the context of sex and religious belief, typical examples being a care home hiring women to a live-in role providing personal care for women, or a religious foundation choosing to hire someone who shares their religious faith. The old examples offered in textbooks about requiring a white man to play King Henry are clearly no longer tenable as the BBC and the Royal Shakespeare Society regularly cast black actors in white roles (though not, it must be noted, white actors in black roles as that would breach the asymmetrical expectations of modern racial sensitivities). The exception nevertheless recognises that discrimination may be rational in certain cases, where it functions as a crude proxy for decision-makers in conditions of limited information: a police officer

[93] S. 83(11) and Schedule 9 Equality Act 2010.

who does not know whether every passer-by might be the miscreant he is looking for is likely to make stop-and-search decisions based on superficial characteristics to reduce his sample to a manageable size as this may be more rational than stopping everyone or letting everyone go.

One of the reasons why modern theories of anti-racism are suspicious of open markets is that free markets do not appear to be able to punish the racists. In theory racists should suffer from reputational harm as nobody would want to do business with them. It might be expected that they would be ostracised and shunned, that the market in which they operate would teach them a lesson by bankrupting them. A racist employer, for example, would eventually fold because no workers would want to remain in that employment. Reputational effects are borne out to some extent. As discussed earlier Higgs records examples of racist white farmers whose reputation for brutality preceded them, making it difficult for them to find labourers and leaving them in a precarious position in a labour-intensive industry. But it cannot be ruled out that some racist employers may not only survive in free markets, but in fact thrive. Whether this should be morally concerning in a cosmic sense is an interesting debate. It is an ancient philosophical question. Within the confines of an institution such as a school a case could perhaps be made for zero tolerance towards racism, although even in that context there is an important counter-argument about resilience as reflected in the old 'sticks and stones' playground saw, together with other ideas such as tolerance, forgiveness and the self-esteem that comes from rising above the taunts, being the bigger person.[94] But the case is altogether different in open markets where, in the absence of a monopoly, the solution lies in simply choosing to deal with someone else. In an open market everyone is free to side-step those who do not wish to trade with them and still enjoy ample opportunities to deal with those who do. A more pressing question is whether this would mean, in practice, fewer market opportunities for ethnic minorities to the extent of making their lives difficult or intolerable. In theory it is possible to change jobs and move house following a racist engagement, but it would be intolerable to spend a

[94] Simons, J. W. (2021, June 3). I'm not sitting next to the Jewish girl: Why I'm glad my daughter let an anti-Semitic remark at school go unpunished. *The Telegraph*. https://www.telegraph.co.uk/family/life/not-sitting-next-jewish-girl-glad-daughter-let-anti-semitic/.

lifetime constantly on the move in a bid to escape a tsunami of racist employers.

Fortunately, the heterogeneity of market participants permits ample scope to choose different transactions and enter or exit different deals, ensuring that there will never be a world in which most people, or too many people for life to be tolerable, discriminate against others. Even if those who wish to engage in irrational discrimination remain free to do so, those who disapprove of discrimination are able to choose to deal with non-discriminatory firms. An examination of market economies reveals that due to the 'spread in the distribution of human traits and preferences'[95] there are always sufficient people to allow even the most disadvantaged minority to flourish and thrive, either because most people do not have a taste for discrimination, or because those who would prefer to discriminate may not consider the cost of indulging their taste for discrimination to be worth paying in most circumstances. The scope for even the most disadvantaged minority to flourish and thrive can be seen in the experience of slaves in the American south who made progress, in the world as it then was.

There will never be a perfect world in which nobody ever discriminates against others, where every last racist has been successfully hunted down by the social justice warriors and destroyed. There will always be people who weigh the benefits and costs of discriminating in a particular context and decide that the benefits of choosing someone exactly like them would be worth more than the cost, such as the cost of conducting further investigations into the suitability of all applicants, or the risk of overlooking the perfect partner because they happened to be a different race. When everyone is free to choose, based on their own assessment of the costs and benefits, analysis of costs and benefits varies from one person to another and is context-dependent. There will always be those miscreants whose taste for racism is so high that they are prepared to suffer any cost to indulge that taste. But, as Sowell argues, the unlimited potential for human flourishing in the context of free enterprise renders the moral status of individual racists utterly irrelevant to the socio-economic progress of ethnic minority groups, a position well

[95] Epstein, *Equal Opportunity or More Opportunity*, p. 32.

substantiated by numerous economic studies spanning several decades.[96] The preoccupation with wealth distribution is better displaced by a fuller appreciation of the value of human productivity, resilience and ingenuity.

5.8 Knowledge and Costs of Decision-Making

All choices have attendant costs, and as outlined above discrimination may be a costly choice for those who prefer to discriminate. The question arises whether discriminators value their preferences to the point where they consider the price worth paying (e.g. the cost of foregoing better staff if they have an 'undesirable' identity characteristic or the reputational cost of being known to discriminate). On the whole, rational people set out (albeit imperfectly) to reduce the costs of their transactions. Thus regardless of the law, most people would not choose to discriminate regardless of the cost. Yet the law, in attempting to regulate decision-making, introduces costs of its own.

Decision-makers are constrained in making choices by a lack of full information. Informal norms therefore play a role in making decisions, where in the absence of fuller information and depending on one's appetite for risk it will often make sense to choose the course of conduct that one knows most about. In that context it is rational to suppose that the risks and costs of doing business within one's own social networks will be lower than doing business with strangers. A preference for one's own social networks does not imply malice or ill will to outsiders, and so should not invite moral sanction. Similarly an employer who does not know whether a job applicant will be industrious and hardworking, in circumstances where regulation makes trial and error costly (if he makes the wrong hiring choice employment protection legislation regulating dismissal ensures that he will not be able costlessly to fire the worker) is more likely to rely on preconceived prejudices in making hiring decisions. If he is going to be stuck with the new hire indefinitely, it is rational to choose the person, in conditions of limited information, that

[96] Higgs, *Competition and Coercion*; Williams, *Race & Economics*.

he seems most likely to get along with. Antidiscrimination law, by forbidding the sorts of hiring questions that might yield information valuable to the employer, not only fails to resolve the information deficit but exacerbates it. Further rigidities are introduced by laws, such as unfair dismissal laws, that inflate the costs of correcting decision-making errors.

Without legal regulation of private choices, anybody who wishes to prefer disadvantaged groups in order to 'help them' would remain free to introduce affirmative action measures in their own private transactions. One of the unexpected effects of prohibiting discrimination is that it is *more* difficult, and indeed unlawful, to prefer underprivileged candidates. Discrimination is forbidden without regard to motive, so even discrimination based on *good* motives is prohibited even in cases where, potentially, private actors might wish to do what they perceive as some good through positive discrimination or affirmative action measures. Where public funds are not involved people would be free to make preferential decisions should they wish. The decision whether or not to discriminate should be one for individual decision-making. The individual decision-maker is the person best placed to decide, in light of all the relevant facts. Part of the challenge in understanding the effects of discrimination lies in acknowledging uncertainty, factoring in the limits of our knowledge and what can reasonably be known with any degree of certainty.[97] But regulation is a weak and ineffective way of resolving the knowledge problem. Nobody knows an individual decision-maker's circumstances as well as the decision-maker, nor can an external edict ensure that all decision-makers are doing what is best for their circumstances because there is no way of knowing what would be best in all the circumstances in which people will make decisions.[98] Nobody has, or can

[97] 'the strongest case for prioritizing markets is that social coordination involves cognitively constrained agents who cannot be fully aware how their actions affect macro patterns. Where social wholes are more complex than the sum of their individual parts, people are necessarily ignorant of the "whole picture."' Pennington, Robust Political Economy and the Priority of Markets, p. 11.

[98] 'Man must be free to follow his conscience in moral matters if his actions are to be of any merit...he should be free to make full use of his knowledge and skill, that he must be allowed to be guided by his concern for the particular things of which he knows and for which he cares, if he is to make as great a contribution to the common purposes of society as he is capable of making': Hayek, F.A. (1958). Individualism: True and False, p. 14.

have, complete knowledge or foresight; at best we make decisions within the limits of bounded rationality, but it must be remembered that the knowledge problem applies to governments and other collective decision-making bodies in the same way as it applies to individuals. The costs of getting it wrong are higher when the mistake is made by legislation than when an individual makes the wrong decision. Consensual arrangements between individuals can be exited following a pre-agreed formula if they prove to be unwise, but where legislative mandates apply there are no easy correction mechanisms and no possibility for exit.[99] The more appropriate principle is experimentation and adaptation, trial and error and learning from what works. If people make the wrong choices they soon learn from their mistake from many different sources: being disadvantaged in the market relative to their non-discriminatory competitors, suffering reputational damage or losing out on good workers. This gives persuasive force to Epstein's caution against fashioning new employment rights that are 'heavily parasitic on the basic right to trade' by inhibiting the parties' freedom to enter into employment contracts on terms of their choice, and instead prescribing a set of terms that seem to be preferable:

> It is a vast mistake to assume that I – or anybody else – have a cache of legitimate information that allows me, or you, to set the preferences and control the choices of other individuals. Something is of value to an individual if it enhances his or her utility, which is subjectively determined.[100]

The impossibility of investigating the actual preferences of every individual in society (and a great many individuals would not be able to enlighten us on their own preferences even if it were possible to ask them) does not mean that it is futile to view society through the prism of individual preferences. It is neither possible nor necessary for each individual to know what motivates every other individual in a long chain of market interactions. Markets offer more effective solutions to the knowledge problem: the complexity of social problems and impossibility of

[99] Pennington, Robust Political Economy and the Priority of Markets, pp. 11, 12.
[100] Epstein, *Equal Opportunity or More Opportunity?*

capturing all variables. Multiple factors might explain the variance in different contexts. For example, it is impossible to 'know' whether affirmative action policies are the best policy or not in every situation. The decision, ultimately, is for each individual or firm, none of which has a monopoly on what is wise or best for everyone. Those who want to prefer dealing with those of a particular disadvantaged race, in order to compensate for what they perceive as historical wrongs, would be free to do so. Others would be free to follow a different path. Private ordering works more effectively than legislative edicts, as it enables 'discovery and communication of alternative terms of cooperation in conditions where no central agency or group can be aware of how to deliver fair terms of exchange'[101] thereby enhancing the overall fairness of free market exchange. Fairness in the context of limited knowledge is reflected through process not outcome. Where central coordination or prescription is effectively unworkable local or individual knowledge becomes paramount. Fair outcomes emerge where the law enables free expression of the 'individual liberty, spontaneity and experimentation' that are necessary to improve and advance knowledge.[102] Fairness in this context does not depend on equality or any other moral value, but on expanding the scope of individual freedom and capacity to make something of one's life regardless of one's race or any other characteristics of group identity.

[101] Pennington, Robust Political Economy and the Priority of Markets, p. 19.

[102] Tebble, *Epistemic Liberalism*, p. 9.

6
Conclusion

This book has sought to defend the priority of economic liberty in a just society, based on its essential role in enabling us to live meaningful lives to the fullest possible extent. As Tomasi observes,

> Economic liberties have intrinsic value: they carve out a sphere of protection that allows people to become responsible authors of their own lives. Economic liberties are instrumentally valuable too: the protection of such liberties helps generate a social world of variety and abundance.[1]

The book offers an ethical defence of economic freedom as an emanation of individual liberty in contexts of racial diversity. While proponents of social justice protest that they do not deny the importance of individual liberty, the true test of the importance we accord to liberty is the priority we confer upon it in our conceptualisation of justice. In order to highlight the threat posed to economic freedom by egalitarian liberalism

[1] Ibid., p. 29.

W. Njoya, *Economic Freedom and Social Justice*, Palgrave Studies in Classical Liberalism, https://doi.org/10.1007/978-3-030-84852-1_6

the book identifies some of the ways in which the regulatory preoccupation with racially delineated codes of conduct destroys economic freedom, individual liberty, the well-being of racial minorities and society as a whole. An idealistic and unthinking egalitarianism demands equal outcomes without regard to effort or merit. It claims equal entitlement to wealth and power without regard to productivity or skill. Claims to equal outcomes are based on collective interests and group identity, with no role envisioned for individual character traits such as industry, resilience, self-reliance. A short-term preference for immediate dramatic results for disadvantaged groups promises to advance universal equality for the underprivileged, while deeming the longer term implications for individual liberty and economic prosperity to be irrelevant. In a bid to mollify mob demands for their 'justice', special rights are conferred on one group at the expense of another, conveying a superficial aura of fairness but lacking awareness of or interest in the general welfare impact on society.[2] The book questioned the legitimacy of substantive equality as a key component of modern social justice, arguing that formal equality within the classical ideal of justice is an essential component of the rule of law.

Such a challenge to substantive equality is apt nowadays to be misconstrued as an attempt to dismiss or discount the importance of justice. This misconception arises from the belief that there is only one correct or acceptable way to understand the moral demands of justice, so that any critique of popular notions of social justice is thought to oppose the ideal of justice itself. The premise of the book is that open debate on these issues is essential. In an increasingly divided world Rawlsian liberals long ago ceased to engage in meaningful dialogue with classical liberals, encouraged no doubt by Rawls's declaration that it was not necessary to define justice or engage with the classical definitions of justice before going on to identify its appropriate substantive moral

[2] 'The great mass of people do not inquire what will happen the day after tomorrow or later on. They think of today and, at most, of the next day. They do not ask what must follow if all other groups too, in the pursuit of their special interests, were to display the same unconcern for the general welfare.' Mises, *Liberalism*, p. 137.

content.[3] By the 1980s Hirschman remarked on the tendency for conservatives and progressives not only to disagree with each other, but to fail utterly to understand each other's worldview. By the 1990s antidiscrimination law had made serious inroads into individual liberty, and by the dawn of 2000 it had become unacceptable to express views regarded by egalitarian activists as inconsistent with their moral codes.[4] The Rawlsian attempt to delineate a space within which all liberals could arrive at a consensus based on public reason turned out to be yet another avenue to entrench the supremacy of progressive over classical liberal ideals. But it is futile for the progressive simply to claim lordship over what counts as justice. Rawlsians may imperiously declare that classical liberal perspectives are unreasonable and irrelevant to public discourse, but we are free to disagree. Freedom permits everyone to agree to disagree, and to live peacefully with those who embrace a different moral vision of how to live the good life. This book offers an argument that supports peaceful coexistence in a world of philosophical and ideological diversity.

The claim that economic inequality is the most urgent social problem of our time and warrants the political prioritisation of redistributive goals is by no means unanimously accepted. Not everyone is persuaded by the socialist ideological worldview. Therein lies the crux of the matter. It would be easier to achieve social justice if we all shared a unanimous commitment to socialist ideology, but in reality people will always hold widely divergent political and philosophical beliefs. In that light we must presume that persuasion and debate are preferable to coercion, and accordingly question the legitimacy of using legislative mandates to implement redistributive goals. The book has argued that the popular enthusiasm for justice defined as legislatively engineered equality is rooted in the seductive moral emotionalism of social justice and the idea that governments should play the dominant role in keeping us safe from racial discrimination and other forms of emotional and psychic harm. The sensitivity and urgency of socio-economic vulnerability, coupled with a desire to redress historical oppression, is deemed to obviate critical

[3] Gordon, One Flew Over Equality.

[4] Bernstein, D. E., *You Can't Say That!*

inquiry into the causes of social problems or the effectiveness of progressive solutions. Indeed, the mere attempt to ascertain the empirical facts regarding causes of inequality, or efforts to approach the problem intellectually and methodically, tend to be derided as an immoral lack of concern for the plight of the disadvantaged and their sensitive historical legacies. Equality has in this context become established as the holy grail. Substantive equality is scarcely ever subjected to critical analysis, and is instead presumed to be self-evidently justified, its worthiness too compelling to warrant expending energy on how or whether its precepts are true, or the cost to be extracted from society in terms of diminishing freedom.

The book set out to highlight the importance of freedom in contexts of racial diversity, rather than to prescribe policy responses or new legislation that governments could introduce to make everything magically better. To introduce more layers of legislation to fix the problems caused by the existing layers of legislation is not the liberal way.[5] Liberalism, as a philosophy of freedom, offers only 'the substance and the arguments' in defence of truth and is thus not tailored towards identifying a prescriptive political agenda.[6] This is confusing for government officials who pay lip service to economic liberty while seeing no contradiction in declaring their determination to wage war against racism through an expansive scheme of costly legislative mandates. Governments are ever in search of what they can do to intervene, to help, to protect, to control, and for that purpose social justice initiatives with their equality measures, guidelines and targets seem, superficially, more promising than an appeal to the classical liberal values which this book has defended. In the context of racial equality classical liberalism offers little for governments to do other than to step back and make way for market participants to 'do for self'.[7] Self-responsibility has its hazards. Liberalism makes no promises of

[5] Leoni, *Freedom and the Law*.

[6] 'Rhetorical bombast, music and song resound, banners wave, flowers and colors serve as symbols, and the leaders seek to attach their followers to their own person. Liberalism has nothing to do with all this. It has no party flower and no party color, no party song and no party idols, no symbols and no slogans. It has the substance and the arguments. These must lead it to victory'. Mises, *Liberalism*, p. 151.

[7] See discussion in Thomas, C. (2008). *My Grandfather's Son: A Memoir*. Harper Perennial.

easy success and quick preferment, but instead demands individual sacrifices in particular the need to forgo short-term make-believe equality in favour of long term sustainable economic progress and personal gains in terms of self-esteem and self-worth.[8]

We have argued that equality legislation is founded upon egalitarian ideals which are subjective and wrong. The discussion identified various ways in which these ideals have spawned a form of 'equity' that is unethical, costly and harmful. As Richard Epstein argued in *Equal Opportunity or More Opportunity*, the legislation represents a mistake that can only be corrected by being altogether repealed: 'Anti-discrimination laws of the type now in force in Britain expose us dangerously to this problem—so much so that, in my view, the entire statutory apparatus should be scrapped'.[9] Epstein does not recommend that the legislation be scrapped because he is unconcerned by human suffering; on the contrary, he cautions that we ought not to be beguiled by the fantasy that legislative declarations of social justice will magically alleviate suffering: 'We should not be fooled by an abstract argument that we need such a statute for a just, kind, and compassionate society. All of us can be just, kind and compassionate without governmental instruction'.[10] The evidence of kindness and compassion is all around us, and if the egalitarians do not see it perhaps they do not wish to see it.

In his commentary on Epstein's analysis, Simon Deakin acknowledges that equality legislation 'has not consistently brought about the desired results' and that 'anti-discrimination legislation may not always be the best means of dealing with social exclusion' but nevertheless considers it to serve an important market-correcting or market-supporting function.[11] Many might suppose that this legislation may not be perfect but we ought to make the best of it as the voters have acquired a taste for equality schemes and would feel unprotected from market forces if

[8] '[Liberalism] promises special favours to no one. It demands from everyone sacrifices on behalf of the preservation of society. These sacrifices – or, more accurately, the renunciation of immediately attainable advantages – are, to be sure, merely provisional; they quickly pay for themselves in greater and more lasting gains. Nevertheless, for the time being, they are sacrifices.' Ibid., p. 139.

[9] Epstein, *Equal Opportunity or More Opportunity*, p. 1.

[10] Ibid., p. 8.

[11] Ibid., p. 42.

asked to give them up. Equality legislation has come to be regarded as a social safety net. Like any addiction, costly and harmful social welfare programmes can perhaps only be managed carefully without expecting their dependents to quit cold turkey. It may seem to be politically impossible for any modern liberal democracy to abandon their equity schemes now, as the promises have already been made. Such schemes provide an avenue which many elites value very highly as a platform for expressing their moral emotionalism. They help egalitarians to feel that they are good people who are doing what they can to expiate the guilt of their ancestors and earn their redemption from the Original Sin.[12] That may be so, but important legal and ethical questions and a vision for the path ahead require something more than a preoccupation with what will appeal to voters at the next election. Such questions call also for a sustained focus on our highest ideals and values, and to that end the book has sought to defend the ideals of economic freedom as an emanation of individual liberty. As Shelby Steele suggests, the time has come to offer a new vision of the good, one rooted in reality rather than woeful egalitarian narratives which yearn in vain for the moral innocence of paradise lost:

> Today there are signs of what I have called race fatigue. People are becoming openly cynical toward the left's moral muscling with racism. Add to this liberalism's monumental failure to come even close to realizing any of its beautiful idealisms, and the makings of a new conservative mandate become clearer. As idealism was the left's political edge, shouldn't realism now be the right's? Reality as the informing vision—and no more wrestling with innocence.[13]

The debate about the role of law in promoting racial equality is at heart a disagreement about ideals and values, not a dispute over the labels we attach to various policies such as 'justice' or 'equity'. This is not simply a debate over whether 'liberty' should trump 'equality' in an abstract sense, but a deeper and more concrete debate concerning what is meant by these terms in the first place and how we wish them to shape our world.

---

[12] See discussion in Caldwell, *The Age of Entitlement*.

[13] Steele, S. (2018). A Sick Hunger for Racism. *Hoover Digest*, 158, p. 160.

The time has come to venture beyond mere exhortations about equality, in order to determine how best to meet the demands of justice in contexts of ideological disputation. Simply attaching the label of 'social justice' to a claim or demand does not automatically constitute a sound basis for diminishing economic freedom. It is easy enough to declare that justice must be pursued at all costs—*fiat justitia, et pereat mundus*! But rousing slogans mask deeper political contestation concerning the meaning behind the mantras of social justice and the ideological justifications underpinning its legislative prescriptions. This book has shown that the classical ideal of justice based on formal equality before the law upholds liberty, where the machinations of egalitarian social justice dictators would destroy liberty and the individual pursuit of economic freedom and happiness. As Mises reminds us, the aim of justice in the classical tradition is to liberate, not to coerce:

> The utilitarian economist does not say: Fiat justitia, pereat mundus. He says: Fiat justitia, *ne* pereat mundus. He does not ask a man to renounce his well-being for the benefit of society. He advises him to recognize what his rightly understood interests are. In his eyes God's magnificence does not manifest itself in busy interference with sundry affairs of princes and politicians, but in endowing his creatures with reason and the urge toward the pursuit of happiness.[14]

[14] Let justice reign, so that the world will *not* perish: Mises, L. v. (1998). *Human Action: A Treatise on Economics* (p. 147). Martino Publishing (Original work published 1949).

Bibliography

Atkinson, A. B. (2015). *Inequality: What Can Be Done?* Harvard University Press.

Baker, J. A., & White, M. D. (Eds.). (2016). *Economics and the Virtues: Building a New Moral Foundation.* Oxford University Press.

Barnard, C., & Hepple, B. (2000). Substantive Equality. *Cambridge Law Journal, 59*(3), 562–585.

Bernstein, D. E. (2003). *You Can't Say That! The Growing Threat to Civil Liberties from Antidiscrimination Laws.* Cato Institute.

Bernstein, D. E. (2018). The Boundaries of Antidiscrimination Laws. In M. T. Henderson (Ed.), *The Cambridge Handbook of Classical Liberal Thought.* Cambridge University Press.

Caldwell, C. (2020). *The Age of Entitlement: America Since the Sixties.* Simon & Schuster.

Cleve, G. v. (2006). Somerset's Case and Its Antecedents in Imperial Perspective. *Law and History Review, 24*(3).

Commission on Race and Ethnic Disparities. (2021, March 31). *The Report.* https://assets.publishing.service.gov.uk/government/uploads/sys

W. Njoya, *Economic Freedom and Social Justice*, Palgrave Studies in Classical Liberalism, https://doi.org/10.1007/978-3-030-84852-1

tem/uploads/attachment_data/file/974507/20210331_-_CRED_Report_-_FINAL_-_Web_Accessible.pdf.

Corey, D. D. (2018). Against the Deformations of Liberalism. *Journal of American Affairs.*

Corey, D. D. (2020). 'Liberalism and the Modern Quest for Freedom'. In D. F. Hardwick & L. Marsh (Eds.), *Reclaiming Liberalism* (pp. 125–162). Palgrave Macmillan Studies in Classical Liberalism.

Deaton, A. (2013). *The Great Escape: Health, Wealth, and the Origins of Inequality*. Princeton University Press.

De la Mora, G. F. (1987). *Egalitarian Envy: The Political Foundations of Social Justice.* Paragon House.

Devine, D. J. (2021). *The Enduring Tension: Capitalism and the Moral Order*. Encounter Books.

DiQuattro, A. (1983). Rawls and Left Criticism. *Political Theory, 11*(1), 53.

Dworkin, R. M. (1977). *Taking Rights Seriously*. Duckworth.

Dworkin, R. M. (1981). What Is Equality? *Philosophy & Public Affairs, 10*(3), 185.

Epstein, R. A. (1984). In Defense of the Contract at Will. *University of Chicago Law Review, 51*, 947.

Epstein, R. A. (1992). *Forbidden Grounds: The Case Against Employment Discrimination Laws*. Harvard University Press.

Epstein, R. A. (2002). *Equal Opportunity or More Opportunity: The Good Thing About Discrimination.* Commentary by Simon Deakin. Civitas. http://www.civitas.org.uk/pdf/cs18.pdf.

Epstein, R. A. (2020). Meeting the Fundamental Objections to Classical Liberalism. In M. T. Henderson (Ed.), *The Cambridge Handbook of Classical Liberal Thought*. Cambridge University Press.

Equality and Human Rights Commission. (2019, October 23). *Tackling Racial Harassment: Universities Challenged*. https://www.equalityhumanrights.com/sites/default/files/tackling-racial-harassment-universities-challenged.pdf.

Finnis, J. (2007). *On Public Reason* (Notre Dame Legal Studies Paper No. 06–37; Oxford Legal Studies Research Paper No. 1/2007). http://ssrn.com/abstract=955815.

Finnis, J. (2011). *Human Rights and the Common Good: Collected Essays Vol III*. Oxford University Press.

Flew, A. (1986). Enforced Equality—Or Justice? *Journal of Libertarian Studies, 8*(1), 31.

Fowler, T. (2015). Markets, Choice and Agency. *Res Publica, 21*(4), 347.

Feldman, G., Farh, J.-L., & Wong, K. F. E. (2018). Agency Beliefs Over Time and Across Cultures: Free Will Beliefs Predict Higher Job Satisfaction. *Personality and Social Psychology Bulletin, 44*, 304.

Frankfurt, H. (1987). Equality as a Moral Ideal. *Ethics, 98*(1), 21.

Frankl, V. E. (2004). *Man's Search for Meaning: The Classic Tribute to Hope from the Holocaust*. Rider (Original work published 1946).

Fredman, S. (1997). Reversing Discrimination. *Law Quarterly Review, 113*, 575.

Fredman, S. (2016). Substantive Equality Revisited. *International Journal of Constitutional Law, 14*(3), 712–738.

Furedi, F. (2018). *How Fear Works: Culture of Fear in the Twenty-First Century*. Bloomsbury.

Furedi, F. (2020). *Why Borders Matter: Why Humanity Must Relearn the Art of Drawing Boundaries*. Routledge.

George, R. P., & Wolfe, C. (Eds.). (2000). *Natural Law and Public Reason*. Georgetown University Press.

Gordon, D. (2017a). *An Austro-Libertarian View Vol. I: Economics, Philosophy, Law.* Ludwig von Mises Institute.

Gordon, D. (2017b). *An Austro-Libertarian View: Essays by David Gordon. Vol. II: Political Theory*. Ludwig von Mises Institute.

Gordon, D. (2017c). *An Austro-Libertarian View: Essays by David Gordon. Vol. III: Current Affairs, Foreign Policy, American History, European History*. Ludwig von Mises Institute.

Hardwick, D. F., & Marsh, L. (Eds.). (2020). *Reclaiming Liberalism*. Palgrave Macmillan Studies in Classical Liberalism.

Hayek, F. A. (1958). *Individualism and Economic Order*. University of Chicago Press (Original work published 1948).

Hayek, F. A. (2013). *Law, Legislation and Liberty: A New Statement of the Liberal Principles of Justice and Political Economy.* Routledge (Original work published 1973).

Henderson, M. T. (Ed.). (2018). *The Cambridge Handbook of Classical Liberal Thought*. Cambridge University Press.

Herzog, L. (2013). *Inventing the Market: Smith, Hegel and Political Theory*. Oxford University Press.

Higgs, R. (1977). *Competition and Coercion: Blacks in the American Economy, 1865–1914*. Cambridge University Press.

Hirschman, A. O. (1991). *The Rhetoric of Reaction: Perversity, Futility, Jeopardy*. Harvard University Press.

Kay, J. (2011). *Obliquity: Why Our Goals Are Best Achieved Indirectly*. Profile Books.

Kukathas, C. (2003). *The Liberal Archipelago: A Theory of Diversity and Freedom*. Oxford University Press.

Leoni, B. (1961). *Freedom and the Law*. D. Van Nostrand Company.

Lucas, J. R. (1965). Against Equality. *Philosophy, 40*, 296.

Mieschbuehler, R. (2019). *The Minoritisation of Higher Education Students: An Examination of Contemporary Policies and Practice*. Routledge.

Mises, L. v. (1998). *Human Action: A Treatise on Economics* (B.B. Greaves, Ed.). The Ludwig von Mises Institute (Original work published 1949).

Mises, L. v. (2005). *Liberalism: The Classical Tradition* (B.B. Greaves, Ed.). Indianapolis: Liberty Fund (Original work published 1927).

Modood, T., Berthoud, R., Lakey, J., Nazroo, J., Smith, P., Virdee, S., & Beishon, S. (1997). *Ethnic Minorities in Britain: Diversity and Disadvantage* (Series: PSI report (843)). London: Policy Studies Institute.

Niemietz, K. (2019). *Socialism: The Failed Idea That Never Dies*. Institute for Economic Affairs.

Nozick, R. (1990). *The Examined Life: Philosophical Meditations*. Touchstone.

O'Shea, M. L. (1999). *A Cure Worse Than the Disease: Fighting Discrimination Through Government Control*. Hallberg.

Otteson, J. R. (2016). Adam Smith on Virtue, Prosperity and Justice. In J. A. Baker & M. D. White (Eds.), *Economics and the Virtues: Building a New Moral Foundation*. Oxford University Press.

Pennington, M. (2017a). Robust Political Economy and the Priority of Markets. *Social Philosophy and Policy, 34*(1), 1.

Pennington, M. (2017b). *Robust Political Economy: Classical Liberalism and the Future of Public Policy*. Edward Elgar.

Pennington, M. (2014). Realistic Idealism and Classical Liberalism: Evaluating Free Market Fairness. *Critical Review: A Journal of Politics and Society, 26*(3–4), 375.

Pinker, S. (2019). *Enlightenment Now: The Case for Reason, Science, Humanism, and Progress*. Penguin Books.

Rawls, J. (1999). *A Theory of Justice*. Belknap Press (Original work published 1971).

Ridley, M. (2011). *The Rational Optimist: How Prosperity Evolves*. Fourth Estate.

Riley J. L. (2014). *Please Stop Helping Us: How Liberals Make It Harder for Blacks to Succeed*. Encounter Books.

Riley, J. L. (2021). *Maverick: A Biography of Thomas Sowell*. Hachette Book Group.

Rothbard, M. N. (2000). *Egalitarianism as a Revolt Against Nature and Other Essays*. Ludwig von Mises Institute (Original work published 1974).

Sandel, M. J. (2020). *The Tyranny of Merit: What's Become of the Common Good?* Allen Lane.

Smith, A. (1993). *An Inquiry into the Nature & Causes of the Wealth of Nations: A Selected Edition* (Vol. 1, ch. 2, K. Sutherland, Ed.). Oxford University Press.

Sowell, T. (1999). *The Quest for Cosmic Justice.* Touchstone.

Sowell, T. (2013). *Intellectuals and Race*. Basic Books.

Steele, S. (2015). *Shame: How America's Past Sins Have Polarized Our Country*. Basic Books.

Steele, S. (2018). A Sick Hunger for Racism. *Hoover Digest*, 158.

Tebble, A. (2016). *Epistemic Liberalism: A Defence*. Routledge.

Thomas, C. (2008). *My Grandfather's Son: A Memoir.* Harper Perennial.

Tomasi, J. (2012). *Free Market Fairness*. Princeton University Press.

Tomasi, J. (2015). Market Democracy and Meaningful Work: A Reply to Critics. *Res Publica*, 443.

Williams, W. E. (2011). *Race and Economics: How Much Can Be Blamed on Discrimination?* Hoover Institution Press.

Index

W. Njoya, *Economic Freedom and Social Justice*, Palgrave Studies in Classical Liberalism, https://doi.org/10.1007/978-3-030-84852-1

GPSR Compliance
The European Union's (EU) General Product Safety Regulation (GPSR) is a set of rules that requires consumer products to be safe and our obligations to ensure this.

If you have any concerns about our products, you can contact us on

ProductSafety@springernature.com

In case Publisher is established outside the EU, the EU authorized representative is:

Springer Nature Customer Service Center GmbH
Europaplatz 3
69115 Heidelberg, Germany

www.ingramcontent.com/pod-product-compliance
Lightning Source LLC
Chambersburg PA
CBHW020231100226
39428CB00001B/2
9783030848514